MARKETS AND JUSTICE

NOMOS
XXXI

NOMOS

Harvard University Press

The Liberal Arts Press

Atherton Press

Aldine-Atherton Press

Lieber-Atherton Press

New York University Press

NOMOS XXXI

Yearbook of the American Society for Political and Legal Philosophy

MARKETS AND JUSTICE

Edited by

John W. Chapman, *University of Pittsburgh*

and

J. Roland Pennock, *Swarthmore College*

New York and London: New York University Press · 1989

Markets and Justice: Nomos XXXI
edited by John W. Chapman and J. Roland Pennock
Copyright © 1989 by New York University
Manufactured in the United States of America

Library of Congress
Library of Congress Cataloging-in-Publication Data

Markets and justice / edited by John W. Chapman and J. Roland Pennock.
    p.   cm. — (nomos : 31)
  Bibliography: p.
  Includes index.
  ISBN 0-8147-1421-8
  1. Capitalism—Moral and ethical aspects.   2. Distributive
justice.   I. Chapman, John William, 1923–   . II. Pennock, J.
Roland (James Roland), 1906–   . III. Series.
HB501.M33125 1989
330. 12′2—dc19   88-23164
                                                                 CIP

New York University Press books are printed on acid-
free paper, and their binding materials are chosen
for strength and durability.

CONTENTS

CONTRIBUTORS

JOSHUA COHEN
Philosophy and Political Science, Massachusetts Institute of Technology

GERALD F. GAUS
Political Science and Philosophy, University of Minnesota, Duluth

JOHN GRAY
Political Science, Jesus College, Oxford University

ROBERT E. LANE
Political Science, Yale University

ERIC MACK
Philosophy, Tulane University

JAN NARVESON
Philosophy, University of Waterloo

MARGARET JANE RADIN
Law, University of Southern California

ANDRZEJ RAPACZYNSKI
Law, Columbia University

JONATHAN RILEY
Political Science, Tulane University

BERNARD SAFFRAN
Economics, Swarthmore College

CASS R. SUNSTEIN
Law and Political Science, The University of Chicago

PREFACE

This volume began with papers presented at the thirty-first annual meeting of the Society held in December 1986 at the Sheraton-Boston Hotel in conjunction with the convention of the American Philosophical Association. We are grateful to T. M. Scanlon, Jr., of Harvard University for having organized our meeting.

Once again we thank Eleanor Greitzer, Assistant to the Editors, for her valued services. And our thanks go also to Despina P. Gimbel, Managing Editor of New York University Press, for her efficient assistance.

On a personal note. This is the twenty-second volume of NOMOS on which I have worked with Roland Pennock. And I deeply regret that it will be the last. Time seems to have gone by with the speed of an express train. Still I would like to think that we, with the help of many others, have pretty much accomplished what Carl Friedrich had in mind when he founded our Society, namely, to establish a continuing interdisciplinary forum in which to consider the problems thrown in our path by political and legal philosophy.

J. W. C.

INTRODUCTION

J. ROLAND PENNOCK AND
JOHN W. CHAPMAN

John Gray's chapter, which leads off part 1, is at once a defense of a certain version of contractarian theory and an argument that his theory supports reliance on a market capitalist economy as opposed to market socialism, which many today find morally and politically attractive. These two components of his essay are so intricately intertwined that it is difficult to treat them separately, and our remarks will do so only in part.

Gray welcomes the development of John Rawls's thought in a contextualist direction, which seeks to avoid entanglement with metaphysical issues. At the same time he thinks Rawls goes too far in adopting a radically pluralistic position on values, à la Sir Isaiah Berlin. (In view of the fact that Gray later denies the priority of liberty, it is not clear how he himself avoids the charge of value-pluralism.) Gray also accuses Rawls of failing to rid his theory entirely of metaphysics, because his reliance on a conception of the person, which depends in part on a theory of human nature, verges on the metaphysical.

Up to this point, Andrzej Rapaczynski, our legal commentator, largely agrees with Gray, but he wonders whether Gray appreciates how much he has undermined the generalizations achievable by the contractarian method. Although Gray argues that his version of contracting does yield some determinate propositions—for example, the impossibility of efficient central allocation of capital is presumably known to the contractors, and they act accordingly—both Rapaczynski and Joshua Cohen, our philosophical critic, take sharp issue with this conclusion. They hold that Gray's acceptance of Hayek's rebuttal of the Lange-Lerner conception of market socialism moves on too abstract a level to touch the real world. Hence he overlooks both the extent of market failures under capitalism and the possibility that state-socialist bankers, subject to bureaucratic and political oversight and influence, may be as efficient as fallible private bankers. Perhaps Gray would reply that it is unrealistic to underestimate the vulnerability of socialist bankers to both political and economic opportunism.

As for justice, Gray contends that his Hobbesian contractarianism, with its minimal equality and neutrality as to values, embodies essential liberal values that socialism denies. Socialism is unneutral in that it rules out any wage-labor system. And it is unjust because it forbids individuals the right to use their productive resources as they prefer, thus effectively running counter to the equality mandate. Gray's opponents, for their part, launch a two-pronged counterattack: (1) they say that neutrality is not essential to liberalism, calling attention to the prohibition of slavery by both capitalists and socialists; and (2) they assert that capitalist economies operate in unneutral fashion, not only by the ban on slavery, but also through the prohibition of practices such as the sale of votes. They argue further that it is proper, indeed just, for societies to take sides in favor of certain values over others, as they do when they subsidize uneconomic aspects of a culture, such as Navajo rug-making. Moreover, Cohen emphasizes that private property systems are biased against autonomy and community in favor of productive efficiency. More obviously, the notorious neglect of third-party interests and the public interest by unchecked market operations under capitalism calls for state intervention for the sake of valued states of affairs.

Both of Gray's critics, but Cohen in particular, protest his apparent lack of concern for substantive, rather than merely formal, neutrality and equality—the weakness in the marketplace of the underprivileged, not to mention failure to take into account the values of power, self-respect, and others that cannot be monetized. Presumably Gray would respond that both Cohen and Rapaczynski fail to appreciate the strength of a Hobbesian understanding of ourselves and our situation. One feels the presence of divergent conceptions of human nature.

As a final mark of Gray's abstractness and shortage of empirical reference, both Rapaczynski and Cohen note, either overtly or by implication, that he thinks market socialism would tend, in practice, to mutate inexorably into either capitalism or a command economy. Rapaczynski points to Sweden as a stable mixed economy. And societies do change direction, as under Ronald Reagan and Margaret Thatcher. Still, Gray could fall back on his citation to Janos Kornai's analysis of the natural bent of bureaucratic socialism in Hungary.

Jan Narveson has chosen to devote his essay to comments on both John Gray and Margaret Jane Radin. That essay itself we include in part 3. It seems appropriate, however, to examine its contents, as they relate to Gray, at this point.

While agreeing with Gray in part, Narveson questions his conclusion that a Hobbesian contract would be so egalitarian as to guarantee to each person an initial capital endowment (and therefore a productive system that would admit of and require it). Universal agreement on this point at the contract stage of negotiation seems highly implausible. (Narveson accepts David Gauthier's version of contractarianism, rather than Gray's.) Further, according to Narveson, it is not correct that Hobbes's account contains *nothing* that might guarantee the absolute priority of liberty. He says, "It is difficult to see how [Gray] can say both that the enforcement of any particular system or, among mutually agreeing persons, distribution, would be *unjust* if it were also true that liberty has *no special claim on our attention.*"

Moreover, Narveson affirms that Gray is mistaken in trying to build liberalism on the basis of an ideal of the person. For no such ideal could command universal assent. What has to be agreed to originally and can be universally is simply recognition of one's ownership of one's natural endowment, mutual respect, and contractual obligations. As Narveson put it, "The market is not a separate 'institution' in the free society. It simply *is* the free society."

Less radical forms of individualism than John Gray's inform the thinking of our authors in part 2, Gerald F. Gaus and Jonathan Riley. One senses that ultimately at stake is what to do about human inequality. The radical individualist's answer is "nothing." Let it work itself out, and that is what markets based on private property do. You can reach this prescription by way of Gray's Hobbesian contract. (But notice that Hobbes was not prepared to rely on private charity.) Or by way of Robert Nozick's natural rights. John Rawls, of course, offers a more "Christian" interpretation of justice in which the more able are obliged to help the less able. Gaus presents an outlook on economic justice that stands as a compromise somewhere between the "pagan" and the Christian attitudes.

According to Gaus, arrangements in the just society must serve the interests and values of all, whatever these may be. These arrangements must also respect our common morality, about the existence of which John Gray has doubts, as we have seen. Gaus says we experience ourselves as self-directing agents, and so we affirm an equal right to natural liberty. This affirmation may well be at the heart of classical liberalism. And we believe that people ought to get what they deserve. Gaus thinks that taken together these basic moral sentiments are sufficient to support a market economy based on private property, that is, capitalism. But these arrangements benefit the able far more than the less able among us. It is as though the market unduly magnifies the pay-off for scarce abilities of all kinds. (Recall that John McEnroe once pronounced the earnings of the top tennis players "obscene.") And so rightly we must compromise. Nobody gets all he wants, neither the gifted nor the least advantaged; all must gain. Therefore Gaus's contractual justification of capitalism incorporates a principle of fair compromise that dictates some redistribution in favor of the less able. How much? Apparently less than would be called for by Rawls's "maximin" principle of justice. Probably less than goes on in Sweden. In line with the "new" liberalism, Gaus seems to have in mind some kind of "basic minimum" conception of social justice as integral to capitalism.

Inspired by John Stuart Mill, Jonathan Riley is also concerned about the inequalities generated by capitalism as we know it. As an alternative he outlines a cooperative capitalist ideal based on strict application of the principle of desert. People deserve what they can earn in a long run competitive equilibrium and also whatever wealth they can accumulate on the basis of their earnings. Holdings above and beyond that are morally suspect. Property rights in land and natural resources cannot be grounded on desert. Still, it may be expedient for society to recognize these rights as important incentives. Gifts and inheritances may also be allowed as a matter of general expedience. Capitalist desert-based justice is to be qualified by a principle of need. The outcome of Riley's eclecticism, as he portrays it, is a kind of classless, egalitarian form of capitalism, somewhat akin to J. E. Meade's vision of a "property-owning democracy."

Neither Gaus nor Riley have much to say about the role of luck in the game of life. But Riley does assume that when people have equal access to education and job training the differences between them are pretty much a matter of voluntary choice. And so by way of conclusion he raises the possibility of a radical and acceptable redistribution of personal wealth in a generation or two. His ideal capitalism is clearly more egalitarian than the society Gaus has in mind, and vastly more egalitarian than John Gray's Hobbesians would be willing to accept. It may well be more egalitarian than ordinary people think justice requires.

Part 3 deals with questions as to what life in a market society does to people. The fear is that it will encourage people to treat themselves and others as commodities, to acquire what Eric Fromm once referred to as a "marketing orientation" to life. In her chapter "Justice and the Market Domain," Margaret Jane Radin seeks to allay this fear, which she shares, by way of what she calls "incomplete commodification."

Radin opens by attacking the liberal theory of a "wall" protecting certain restricted areas, such as the ban on the sale of votes, not on the ground that these matters should not be protected, but rather because this setting aside of domains for absolute protection implies that all else should be subject to the rule of laissez-faire. This she refers to as "universal commodification." This is straight Hobbism, the idea that everything, including persons, has its price.

The problem with this sharp delineation, she says, is that it raises barriers that do not exist, between sales and gifts, for instance. A transaction may be both at one and the same time. We should recognize and indeed foster the nonmarket aspects of commercial transactions. Consider housing. A house is much more than a house; it is a home. My home is part of my self. When, because of my poverty, I am threatened with its loss, state interference with standard property rights is justified. What the limits to intervention should be she does not attempt to prescribe. Indeed, when poverty is to blame it may be that maldistribution of wealth is at the root of the matter. She sees no immediate solution, but the implication is that many ameliorating regulations are warranted despite running counter to orthodox property rights. This approach to living, which she recommends, is an instance of what she calls "incomplete commodification." Incidentally, she challenges Michael Walzer's notion of "spheres of justice" on the ground that it, like the metaphor of the wall, leaves too much room for complete commodification.

Radin finds no "slippery slope" or "domino effect" entailed by incomplete commodification, which might lead to gradual erosion of all or most property rights. But she does think that the domino possibility justifies absolute prohibition of serious intrusions on personal dignity, such as the sale of bodily parts. True, she says, cases may arise where the indignity involved is less than the need. Here again society is faced with a problem that demands an overall solution by means of redistribution.

Finally, she holds that protection of life, health, self-development, and also community development should not be "completely monetized," and that "regulation that does not [theoretically] meet an efficiency test is in principle justified." Moreover, "it is at least wrong to commodify everything in rhetoric."

Hence for Radin the best defense against commodification is not to build walls. Rather, it is to recognize and sustain the personal aspect present in market transactions. Our humanistic attitudes point the way to greater social justice in the shape of distributive justice and respect for personhood and community. To foster these attitudes already and always present in our dealings is the way to save us from the moral disaster of commodification.

Eric Mack is much less fearful of rampant commodification. Indeed, his fear is that misplaced worry about commodification may lead to unwarranted restrictions on the scope of the market. He points out that so long as we distinguish between the intrinsic and the instrumental dimensions of our lives, as we naturally do, coming to treat each other as things is an unlikely prospect. Moreover, according to Mack, life in a market society liberates. It frees us from oppressive and intrusive relations precisely by depersonalizing and monetarizing aspects of our lives that should be so defined.

In his comments on Radin's essay, Mack deals principally with her attitude toward domino effects. The possibility of universal commodification is so clearly false, he argues, that one need not at all be concerned with it. He goes on to point out that not all "external" or instrumental motivations are bad, and not all "internal" ones, where something is sought for its own sake, are good, as for example, malice or lust for power. Market relations enable us to keep one another at arm's length where called for and so promote greater freedom and individuality—all to the good.

Robert E. Lane reviews the literature and the evidence that bear on the question of markets and character. Distinguished observers differ in their assessments, but Lane thinks it reasonable to doubt the charges levelled against market societies. Nor does the evidence from socialist, primitive, and peasant societies lend support to the market's critics; nor does it wholly refute them. Perhaps this is not surprising in view of the fact that all human choices are "priced," that is, have opportunity costs. Lane reminds us to keep an eye on systemic effects: economic efficiency, justice, personality development, and quality of life are all interconnected.

As to the theory that commodification of human relations, allegedly entailed by the market, destroys community, Lane finds that it simply does not fit the facts. He cites numerous studies in support of this assertion. One survey, for example, discovered that "a prosperous life" is ranked thirteenth out of eighteen "terminal values." And in this market society it has been found that number of friends is a better predictor of life satisfaction than is size of income. Other lines of inquiry yield similar results. More generally, Lane's analysis lends support to Margaret Radin's belief in the presence and value of incompletely commodified human relations.

Furthermore, according to Lane, many choices are just as selfish and degrading as market choices. Moreover, a "wall" between the market and other parts of society could never produce the desired result because of the interdependence and interaction that characterize our relations and values. Nevertheless, certain social subsystems can be given protection against other subsystems, as Michael Walzer's "spheres" might do, and as prohibitions of child labor in fact do. Radin's fostering of humanistic attitudes combined with selective "walling" should take the sting out of domino effects and universal commodification.

Jan Narveson reenters the conversation. He holds that Radin's conception of "commodity" is too broad. It should be confined to things that are normally for sale. This, of course, would rule out sale of oneself into slavery. To have a market, Narveson seems to say, implies that not everything is for sale. The "market value" of something I own is seldom what it is "worth" to me— otherwise I would sell it. It may be, he says, that parents *ought* not to sell a child even if they know they are poor parents and that they could sell the child to people who would be good for the child. But that is not necessarily a reason for not *permitting* the sale. If the child knew his parents would like to sell him, he would probably run away! But one must also consider the effect on the community. Narveson's conclusion is that a market defender *need* not object to stopping the sale of children any more than he need object to prohibition of the sale of automatic rifles.

As to "incomplete commodification," noting that for Radin it seems to apply to cases of great inequality, which she identifies with injustice, Narveson questions this identification. He doubts that regulations foster either personhood or community. On the other hand, Radin's humanistic valuation of having persons relate to each other is fostered by the market. "One suspects," he concludes, "that in Radin's proposal, we will find community often taking precedence over personhood."

In part 4 Cass R. Sunstein and Bernard Saffran take us to the legal and economic frontiers respectively of thinking about markets and justice. Sunstein's "basic goal is to set out a range of reasons for disrupting voluntary transactions, even if such transactions deserve prima facie respect." This he accomplishes in a lawyerlike manner that is both subtle and detailed while cautioning that much work remains to be done. Saffran provides a survey of the latest developments in economic theory and research, the upshot of which casts serious doubts on the possibility of achieving substantive or end-state conceptions of justice. Moreover, he finds that "A just economy may require a substantial reduction in output and efficiency." This is a conclusion that many will feel disturbing.

Sunstein presents a catalogue of considerations that justify intervention in markets, either real or potential. Some considerations have to do with justice, others with autonomy realistically conceived, and still others with welfare. And he mentions cases in which considerations overlap. His catalogue goes as follows: (1) collective action problems and externalities, for example, pollution; (2) preferences about preferences that are well grounded and widely shared; (3) adaptive preferences that are clearly harmful and can be altered for the good; (4) intrapersonal collective action problems that have to do with addiction, myopia, and the like; (5) absence of information, the possession of which would change behavior; and (6) protection of goods that should be inalienable. On the basis of his analysis, Sunstein concludes that "in a wide range of cases voluntary transactions should be disrupted. The market outcome is distinct from the outcome justice requires." Still, he reminds us that sometimes disruption may only make things worse. "The case for intervention . . . is only presumptive."

Bernard Saffran, our economist contributor, relates an essentially cautionary tale. Realistic thinking about economic justice must be informed by what Frank Knight used to refer to as "human nature as we know it." It seems appropriate, therefore, as Saffran brings to our attention, that recent work in economic theory has been preoccupied with analysis of incentive and informational effects. Strategic behavior is taken to be "a primary force in economic behavior." As Oliver Williamson, whose thinking displays a blend of Burke and Machiavelli, would say, people tend to be "opportunists." They are guilefully self-interested. They disguise, obfuscate, lie, withhold relevant information. These incentives may well defeat efforts to design "just" schemes of taxation. More generally, Saffran draws an important lesson: "Since our moral theories lead to implications so contrary to any likely behavior, they clearly omit important considerations and we should be sceptical about their cogency."

Important new empirical findings bear on questions of economic justice and productivity, and yet motivations remain somewhat murky. Evidently taxation and transfers do not adversely affect the supply of labor. Recently, when after-tax rates of return to savings increased, rates of saving decreased. According to Saffran, "This increasing scepticism about the strong effects of changing incentives on labor supply and savings behavior should encourage those who believe in the possibility of a more just distribution of income without greatly decreasing the potential for growth." Still, large intergenerational transfers of wealth are taking place. People want to do well by their children. Perhaps it would be unwise to go too far in limiting inheritance for the sake of greater equality of opportunity. Our world is riddled with trade-offs.

Saffran remarks that, "Historically, a major source of the demand for economic justice was not so much inequality as the fact that people were living in extreme poverty." It may be a risky generalization, but our impression is that economists generally tend to be more concerned about poverty than about equality, unlike some egalitarian theorists of justice. Saffran himself would seem to be a case in point. Typically the economist's perspective on justice appears to be both utilitarian and procedural, to maximize by way of structuring incentives, while providing a basic minimum for all. That brings us back to the classic liberal way of thinking about markets and justice, with the proviso that much remains to be done before we fully understand ourselves.

PART I

CONTRACTUALISM AND CAPITALISM

1

CONTRACTARIAN METHOD, PRIVATE PROPERTY, AND THE MARKET ECONOMY

JOHN GRAY

How does contractarian political philosophy stand as to the justice of private property and the market economy? In the work of John Rawls, the contractarian method avowedly tells us nothing about the justice of these institutions. Rawls says:

> It is necessary . . . to recognize that market institutions are common to both private-property and socialist regimes, and to distinguish between the allocative and distributive function of prices. Since under socialism the means of production and natural resources are publicly owned, the distributive function is greatly restricted, whereas a private-property system uses prices in varying degrees for both purposes. Which of these systems and the many intermediate forms most fully answers to the requirements of justice cannot, I think, be determined in advance. There is presumably no general answer to this question, since it depends in large part upon the traditions, institutions and social forces of each country, and its particular historical circumstances. The theory of justice does not include these matters.[1]

Research for this chapter was conducted during a period of residence as Distinguished Research Fellow at the Social Philosophy and Policy Center, Bowling Green State University. I am indebted to the Center and its Directors for the support they have given to my research on these questions.

Here Rawls makes two major claims. First, that private-property and socialist regimes are both bound to adopt market pricing as a centrally important allocative institution. For this reason, it cannot be the presence or absence of markets that decides whether an economic system be classified as capitalist or socialist. Nor, again, can it be the case that it is an assessment of the market in terms of efficiency and justice that settles the normative issue between capitalism and socialism. Here Rawls departs radically from a traditional understanding of the debate between exponents of capitalist and socialist economic systems. Marxism condemns market institutions as inherently exploitative and chaotic. In Austrian traditions the Marxian project of suppressing or transcending market institutions is condemned as leading to calculational chaos and a system in which labor and capital alike are subject to political exploitation.[2] Rawls's first claim, then, is that since market institutions figure prominently in both socialist and private property regimes, the issue between them cannot be resolved by a judgment on the merits of market institutions.

Rawls's second claim is that justice is neutral as to the choice between capitalist and socialist regimes. Whereas elements of the theory of justice may, indeed, inform our assessment of rival economic systems, it cannot dictate which is to be adopted. The subject matter of justice, for Rawls, is not the choice of economic system, but rather the social distribution of primary goods.

I aim to challenge both of these claims. As against Rawls, I wish to reassert the traditional understanding of the issue between capitalist and socialist regimes. I will submit that an assessment of the merits of market institutions—an assessment as much in terms of their justice as of their efficiency—is central to the appraisal of alternative economic systems. I will do this, in part, by criticizing the type of market socialism that I take to be implicit in Rawls's claim that market allocation mechanisms are present in both capitalist and socialist systems, arguing that market socialism is a hybrid that is morally indefensible and practically unstable. My principal argument is that, because market socialism lacks a market for capital, it is vulnerable to most of the moral and practical criticisms that have been levelled against command economies. In the real world, market socialist institutions have an inherent propensity to mutate into market capitalism or else to degenerate into a socialist command economy. It is, for this reason, an illusion to conceive of market socialism as a viable *tertium quid* between capitalism and socialism.

My second argument against Rawls is more fundamental. I shall argue that justice cannot be silent or neutral as to the choice of economic system. For us, the contractarian method yields a definite result, namely that justice enjoins an economic system encompassing both private property and market freedoms. I argue this, despite the fact that contractarian method cannot in general yield results with the sort of determinacy that Rawls expects.

Beside defending these substantive claims, I hope to advance understanding of the scope and limits of the contractarian method itself. As we know, Rawls's own conception of that appears to have shifted in his recent work. I will try to specify which of the conceptions of contractarian method adumbrated in his writings is most consistent with the spirit of his latest work. Further, I will compare and contrast the various conceptions of the contract method to be found in Rawls's work with others, such as those of David Gauthier and James Buchanan. Most radically, however, my larger goal in the sections of the chapter concerned with the methodological content of the various contractarian approaches is to say something about the scope and limits of political philosophy itself. Here I will aim to counterpoint Rawls's view, in which political philosophy may have a constructive role while yet distancing itself from fundamental questions, with two other views—the view, found in Wittgenstein, Oakeshott and Rorty, that philosophy may illuminate but cannot otherwise change practice, and the view, which I hold myself, that philosophy may be subversive of practice without thereby founding one set of practices or grounding any single form of life. Though I cannot here give anything like a satisfactory defence of this last position in philosophical method, a number of arguments in its support are suggested by the immanent criticism I shall develop of the later work of Rawls. My argument has, on the whole, the form of an immanent criticism of Rawls's later work. At the same time, I shall suggest that results closely converging with those issuing from an immanent criticism of the later Rawls may be derived from an external perspective on it that treats the propositions of a Hobbesian contractarian moral and political theory as being substantially true. The result of my inquiry, accordingly, is the claim that an immanent criticism of Rawls's later theorizing supports conclusions that we have other reasons to accept.

I. THE CHARACTER OF CONTRACTARIAN METHOD

It is common knowledge that, in the period since the publication of *A Theory of Justice,* Rawls's conception of philosophical method has changed. At the same time, there is very little agreement as to how radical this shift has been. In my own view, to entertain radical methodological rupture in Rawls's thought is exaggerated and misleading. For example, his constructivism in moral theory, strongly emphasized in the later writings, is present in the moral epistemology of reflective equilibrium in *A Theory of Justice.* Here, as elsewhere in his thought, we have development rather than discontinuity. There is not much basis in Rawls's work for a "two Rawlses" thesis on the lines advanced in respect of Marx or Mill.[3] Neither can important discontinuities in Rawls's work be denied.

A striking feature of *A Theory of Justice* is the Kantian universality of application attributed by him to the theory and, thereby, to the principles that the theory of justice yields. On any natural interpretation, Rawls in *A Theory of Justice* is concerned to defend and justify principles whose range of application extends to all mankind. The basis from which the principles of justice are derived in Rawls's book is a conception of rational choice by autonomous agents in a hypothetical circumstance of fair equality. It is clear that the conception is intended by Rawls to express the requirements of human moral personality and that it is not conceived by him merely as a distillate of a particular cultural tradition. The shift in Rawls's philosophical method occurs at several levels. It is apparent, in the first case, in his account of the *goals* of the theory of justice. Rawls tells us that "since justice as fairness is intended as a political conception of justice for a democratic society, it tries to draw solely on intuitive ideas that are embedded in the political institutions of a constitutional democratic regime and the public traditions of their interpretation. Justice as fairness is a political conception in part because it starts from within a certain political tradition."⁴ Later Rawls refers to justice as fairness as "a reasonably systematic and practical conception of justice for a constitutional democracy."⁵ The goal of the theory of justice, then, is restricted to that of providing a systematic set of practicable principles of justice for societies whose historical traditions are those of constitutional democracy. Further, the *basis* of the theory of justice is in the political tradition of those societies. This is to say that the essential elements of justice as fairness are now understood as distillations of those specific traditions. Thus the primary goods, for example, are not specified primarily by any set of anthropological or sociological conjectures: they are normative constructions, derivations from a conception of the person that is itself a practical notion. So, "the account of what I have called 'primary goods' is revised so that it clearly depends on a particular conception of persons and their high-order interests; hence this account is not a purely psychological, sociological or historical thesis. . . . There is throughout . . . a more explicit emphasis on the role of a conception of the person as well as the idea that the justification of a conception of justice is a practical social task rather than an epistemological or metaphysical problem."⁶

Two fundamentally important theses are advanced here. First, the thesis that the task of a theory of justice, as presumably of political philosophy as a whole, is a practical task—that of constructing principles of social cooperation. But second, the key notions of justice and fairness are themselves understood as practical constructions from elements of the historical traditions of constitutional democracies. It must be evident that the Kantian ideal of universality has been relinquished and, likewise and as a consequence, the conception of political philosophy as a form of inquiry whose *telos* is the discovery or formulation of principles or conceptions applicable to all human societies has likewise been abandoned. This is not to say that Rawls's methodological shift is a turn to relativism or, still less, that it expresses the thesis that philosophical questions are unanswerable or misconceived. For, despite his avowed debts to Dewey, Rawls is not advancing any sort of relativism or pragmatism in philosophy, so that the practical interpretation of justice as fairness that Rawls advances in no way associates his view of philosophy with that of Rorty, for example. Rawls's methodological shift is, at bottom, a shift to a position in which political philosophy is separated from other areas of philosophy in such a way that its progress does not wait on progress on central questions in, say, epistemology, metaphysics, or the philosophy of mind. It is this project of disseveration, and not any doctrine of relativism, that animates Rawls's most recent work. Political philosophy is, if not metaphysically neutral, then at least metaphysically uncommitted. As Rawls puts it:

> As a device of representation the original position is likely to seem somewhat abstract and hence open to misunderstanding. The description of the parties may seem to presuppose some metaphysical conception of the person, for example, that the essential nature of persons is independent of and prior to their contingent attributes, including their final ends and attachments and, indeed, their character as a whole. But this is an illusion caused by not seeing the original position as a device of representation. The veil of ignorance . . . has no metaphysical implications concerning the nature of the self; it does not imply that the self is ontologically prior to the facts about persons that the parties are excluded from knowing. We can, as it were, enter this position any time by reasoning for principles of justice in accordance with the enumerated restrictions. When, in this way, we simulate being in this position, our reasoning no more commits us to a metaphysical doctrine about the nature of the self than our playing a game like Monopoly commits us to thinking that we are landlords engaged in a desperate rivalry, winner take all.[7]

The contrast between Rawls's position and that of, say, Rorty, should now be clear. It is not that Rawls, in antiphilosophical spirit, is claiming that fundamental metaphysical questions are rationally undecidable: he is leaving open the possibility of their resolution. Nor is he claiming, in relativistic fashion, that philosophy cannot help operating within the postulates of a particular culture, epoch, or worldview. Instead, his argument is that, since the task of political philosophy is a practical task—that of securing agreement on basic principles of social cooperation— it can and ought to proceed independently of controversial commitments in other areas of philosophical inquiry. It does so, when its key conceptions—conceptions of the primary goods and of the person, for example—are conceived as being themselves practical notions, constructions of the understanding from elements in our moral and political tradition. Again:

> the aim of justice as fairness as a political conception is practical, and not metaphysical or epistemological. That is, it presents itself not as a conception of justice that is true, but one that can serve as a basis of informed and willing political agreement between citizens viewed as free and equal persons. . . . To secure this agreement we try, so far as we can, to avoid disputed philosophical, as well as disputed moral and religious, questions. We do this, not because these questions are unimportant or regarded with indifference, but because we think them too important and recognize that there is no way to resolve them politically. Thus, justice as fairness deliberately stays on the surface, philosophically speaking.[8]

The motivation for the method of avoidance of philosophical controversy in the theory of justice is, then, a practical motive, and not a philosophical one. It is a motive rooted in the history of Western societies at least since the Reformation. Rawls says, "Philosophy as the search for truth about an independent metaphysical and moral order cannot, I believe, provide a workable and shared basis for a political conception of justice in a democratic society."[9] Rawls's methodological position, then, is not the antiphilosophical one, perhaps found in Rorty, which views philosophical questions as unanswerable or wrongly posed (and not as merely practically intractable and politically irresolvable). It is instead to be contrasted with the antiphilosophical view, because it comprehends no doctrine about philosophy. It is a thesis of the independence of political philosophy from the rest of philosophy. Political philosophy, at any rate, is an effort at finding a basis of agreement and not a search for truth. One may even say, not without a hint of paradox, that political philosophy encapsulates a contractarian view of truth.

Another way of framing the distinctively practical character of justice as fairness is by contrasting it with other liberal theories. That Rawls's is a liberal theory is evident in any manner of ways, but at the simplest it is liberal in that it is a response to *the liberal problem*—the problem of finding fair terms of peaceful coexistence among persons with different conceptions of the good. Rawls's liberalism differs from that of Kant or Mill, for example, precisely because of its insulation from metaphysical commitments and comprehensive moral doctrines. Unlike Kant's or Mill's, Rawls's liberalism does not rest upon (though it aims to encompass) moral ideals of individuality and autonomy, with their strong metaphysical presuppositions. The detachment of justice as fairness from such doctrines and presuppositions is, once again, motivated by practical considerations rooted in our history. Political philosophy must take as its point of departure the brute historical fact of rival moral outlooks and philosophical viewpoints in our society. This fact disqualifies from serious consideration any political position, including that adopted in many liberal theories, that tries to argue away these intractable differences and which postulates agreement or convergence where none exists.[10]

Rawls's variant of contractarian method has clear advantages over others. It seems superior to Gauthier's version, which (despite its many important achievements in developing the contractarian project) is burdened by a conception of practical reasoning as maximization whose rationale is obscure, and which sets itself the heroic task of giving morality itself a contractarian reconstruction. Rawls's position in contractarian method is preferable because it acknowledges explicitly the status of the key notions of his theory as practical and normative constructions. I will refer in the last section to the relations between such constructions and the empirical or anthropological propositions that they stand upon or presuppose. At this stage, I wish to argue only that the method of construction of the key terms in contract theory appears to have significant advantages over a method in which they are treated in quasi-naturalistic (but hardly realistic)[11] fashion. Further, Rawls's method has a real advantage over Gauthier's inasmuch as its goal is the contractarian reconstruction, not of morality, but of *political justice*. It seems inherently improbable that a contractarian analysis can be given of the whole of moral life, and the conception of philosophical inquiry as having a practical character—as consisting in a search for agreement—has its clearest application in political, not moral, philosophy.

The question remains: notwithstanding its advantages over other contractarian methods, can the purely practical character of Rawls's version be sustained? Having distinguished Rawls's theory from a general antiphilosophical doctrine, and having pointed to its advantages over other variants of contractarianism, we may nevertheless suggest at least two ways in which the purely practical character of his theory may be compromised. In the first place, despite his intentions, Rawls's method of avoidance may itself invoke substantive philosophical doctrines and, for that reason, prove self-defeating. Consider, in this connection, his statement of "the requirements of a workable conception of political justice": "Such a conception," he tells us, "must allow for a diversity of doctrines and the plurality of conflicting, and indeed incommensurable, conceptions of the good affirmed by the members of existing democratic societies." [12] This statement goes beyond a sheer report of the brute historical fact of intractable evaluative disagreement to affirm the rational incommensurability of the values expressed in the various moral outlooks that the democratic societies comprehend. It affirms a thesis of value-pluralism akin to that defended by Sir Isaiah Berlin. It is a straightforwardly philosophical thesis, and the method of avoidance will have a self-defeating effect if it depends upon (or presupposes) it. Such an assertion of value-incommensurability appears to involve just the sort of definite position in moral epistemology that Rawls seeks to circumvent when he tells us that "in what I have called 'Kantian constructivism,' we try to avoid the problem of truth and the controversy between realism and subjectivism about the status of moral and political values." [13]

Again, Rawls's conception of the person is a practical and political, that is to say, a normative conception. He contrasts it, in his lectures on Kantian constructivism, with a theory of human nature: "the conception of a well-ordered society. Like any other ideal, it must be possible for people to honor it sufficiently closely and hence the feasible ideals of the person are limited by the capacities of human nature and the requirements of social life. To this extent such an ideal presupposes a theory of human nature, and social theory generally, but the task of a moral doctrine is to specify an appropriate conception of the person that general facts about human nature allow."[14] Here the relation between the conception of the person and the theory of human nature is one of compatibility. But it has not been shown that the theory of human nature is itself metaphysically uncommitted. Recent controversy in sociobiology, perhaps,[15] suggests that competition among theories of human nature is not merely a competition among rival empirical conjectures, but also among incompatible metaphysical and epistemological views. Insofar, then, as the conception of the person must be compatible with a theory of human nature which may itself incorporate substantive metaphysical elements and presuppose positions in other areas of philosophy, adopting the conception of the person will entail adopting or endorsing substantive positions in philosophical inquiry. If this is so, the method of avoidance will fail.

My aim here is not to settle decisively whether the method of avoidance is ultimately viable. I will in the last section consider how the Rawlsian method of avoidance compares with other recent positions in philosophical method. So far, I have tried only to characterize Rawls's method justly, and to voice a few suspicions as to its viability. I have done so as a prelude to the first main substantive part of my argument, in which I consider the bearing of Rawls's later methodological position on the content of his theory. Throughout I assume the substantial correctness of the historicist or contextualizing move in Rawls's later work. I am presupposing, but not arguing for, the view that the move away from a political philosophy with universalist pretensions is a desirable, or at any rate an inevitable move. To this extent my criticism of Rawls is an immanent one.[16] I will in the last section consider whether a method in political philosophy that explicitly acknowledges the culture-specificity of its postulates may nonetheless make some universal claims. At this stage I wish to proceed by asking: How does Rawls's methodological shift to a strategy of avoidance affect the political substance of justice as fairness?

II. Post-Kantian Methodology and the Substance of Justice

Recall that the methodological shift in Rawls's later work is a shift from Kantian universality to Deweyan and perhaps Hegelian historicity. It is a shift to culture-specificity inasmuch as the subject matter of justice as fairness is a distillation of the civic cultures and political traditions of Western constitutional democracies. The theory is contextualized in another sense inasmuch as its application is restricted not only to a given cultural tradition, but also to a definite moment within it. The moment in which the theory applies to the Western cultural tradition is specified by reference to such crucial events as the Reformation, and the consequent establishment of toleration in religion and personal morality, and by reference to the emergence of the institutions of constitutional democracy.[17] In general, the theory is contextualized in its application to Western cultural traditions by reference to that moment in the history of our culture, since which we have witnessed the proliferation of incommensurable value-perspectives and worldviews. Indeed, one may even say that, abstracted from this moment in the development of our tradition, the central problem of the theory of justice—the *liberal problem* of establishing fair principles of social cooperation among persons having incompatible and incommensurable conceptions of the good—does not exist.

We can see how this contextualization affects the political substance of the theory of justice by considering two attributes of Rawls's conception of justice—that the principles it yields be fully determinate, and that they be fixed. As Rawls presents his project in his book, he demands of the problem of choice in the original position that it be solved by uniquely determinate principles that, once chosen, are fixed forever. Consider his account of the basic liberties. The theory of the basic liberties was developed by Rawls partly in response to questions about the determinacy of "the greater liberty" raised in criticism of his book by H. L. A. Hart.[18] Such questions, which I have considered at length in the context of an assessment of the coherence of Rawlsian (and other) liberalism,[19] focus on the fact that comparative or on-balance judgments about liberty appear to presuppose rankings of the worth, value, or importance of the different liberties that are being aggregated. These rankings, however, themselves appear to encompass controversial judgments about the worthwhileness of different forms of life of precisely the sort that Rawls—like other "neutralist"[20] liberals, such as Ackerman and Dworkin—seeks to extrude from the theory of justice. In other words, for Dworkin, as for other liberals in a

Kantian neutralist tradition, principles of justice must not discriminate among different conceptions of the good, if they are
to figure as candidates for the solution of the liberal problem.
The difficulty for such neutralist liberalism is considerable, then,
if comparative judgments about liberty—judgments of the sort
needed for the coherence and applicability of a Greatest Equal
Liberty Principle—turn out to hinge upon controversial evaluations of the contribution made by exercise of the various liberties to the promotion of specific conceptions of the good.

The problem has a reverse side. If, in order to avoid dependency on controversial judgments, we eliminate them from assessments of on-balance liberty, we face *a problem of determinacy*
in a stark form. We will have no way, in many important hard
cases, to make judgments about the greatest liberty. For liberties
are not physical behaviors, and cannot be individuated except
by reference to conventional, and in part normative, standards.
Without controversial standards of the choiceworthiness of different options and lives, we cannot even count liberties, still less
weigh them. Principles like the Greatest Equal Liberty Principle
fail then for the reason that they lack determinate content. They
escape being dependent on controversial judgments about the
good only at the cost of being empty.

It is as a solution to this difficulty that Rawls has developed
the theory of the basic liberties, which aims to circumvent the
necessity for on-balance assessments. I am less concerned at this
point with the adequacy of Rawls's solution than I am with his
view of the necessary condition of such a solution—that it yield
a uniquely determinate set of basic liberties that, once specified,
is fixed forever. This requirement makes sense, perhaps, in a
theory committed—as *A Theory of Justice* was—to Kantian universality in respect of the principles of justice. If the theory of
justice is culture-blind, founded on the requirements of generic
human rationality and moral personality, it is natural to suppose
that the principles of justice will be one and the same for all
human beings.[21] When justice is contextualized and restricted
in its application to a particular moment in the development of
a special cultural tradition, the rationale for the requirements
of fixity and determinacy disappears. Take now the requirement of fixity. This makes sense within the terms of a Kantian
account of the powers of practical reasoning, in which it is

supposed that autonomous reasoners can arrive at maxims for all rational agents. When this Kantian view is abandoned, or subjected to drastic qualification on Hegelian or Deweyan lines, there seems no basis for demanding, or expecting, fixity in regard to the basic liberties. How could a variant of the contractarian method that has as its subject matter the distilled deliverances of a changeable historical tradition yield principles that, once arrived at, are timeless? It would seem more natural to suppose that the set of basic liberties changes as the tradition that is its basis changes. In other words, it is hard to see how something as pre-eminently mutable as a political tradition could support fixity in the list of basic liberties.

I have elsewhere[22] argued in criticism of Rawls's account of the basic liberties that it hypostatizes elements of the Western individualist tradition—in particular, elements having to do with political equality and democratic participation—that are recent and, arguably, peripheral features of it. I argued that the political liberties are to be included in the set of basic liberties if, and only if, the account of the Western individualist tradition is confined to the history of the past century, in which the classical liberal demand for constitutionalism and equal liberty before the law has been supplemented, and in some measure supplanted, by revisionary liberal demands for democratic equality.[23] In the same paper, I argued for the inclusion of economic liberties (that is to say, liberties in the private ownership of the means of production) in the set of basic liberties. I do not want here to argue for a substantively different list of basic liberties, since I will address the question of the place of economic liberties in justice in the next section. My point is instead the methodological one that, given the historicist turn of Rawls's later thought, the class of basic liberties will vary at different moments in the development of the Western political tradition, so that, as technology develops, social and economic conditions alter, and the moral and intellectual life of our culture changes, the contractarian method will yield a variable set of basic liberties. This will be so, even if we accept that within a contract theory such as Rawls's the choice of principles in the original position is bound always to have a certain *finality*. It will have a character of finality whenever we enter the original position and deliberate therein. What is objectionable in Rawls's method is not the finality of its results, but rather his failure to recognize that *different* results will emerge from the method as it is applied at different movements in our historical tradition. Rawls fails, in short, to justify the move from finality to fixity in the deliverances of the method. There is a contrast here between Rawls's requirement of fixity in the basic liberties, for example, and the less conservative perspective of other contemporary liberal thinkers, such as Hayek, who argues explicitly that the basic liberties change as social and economic conditions change, and are, in fact, never exhaustively denumerable.

Consider, next, Rawls's other criterion of adequacy for a solution to the problem of choice in contractarian method, that it yield a highly, if not uniquely determinate set of principles. If we have reason to think that the method should yield different results as it applies to different moments in our cultural and political tradition, why should we suppose that it should *at any time* yield a uniquely determinate set of results? There are several reasons for supposing otherwise. It could do so, only if there prevailed in our culture a deep convergence on fundamental political ideals, from which a unique set of principles could be derived. It seems plain that, even if deep consensus on certain questions in our political tradition exists, it does not cover all questions that may become vital issues in public controversy. Some questions of this sort may well be rationally undecidable in Rawls's variant of the contract approach: the issue of abortion liberty may be one. In short, we have no strong reason to suppose a deep convergence of moral traditions within our civic culture on all important questions having to do with the basic liberties and the distribution of the primary goods.

This first reason for refraining from imposing a test of full determinacy on the results of the contractarian method is acknowledged by Rawls himself in his recognition[24] that Kantian constructivism differs from other standpoints in moral theory in that it does not suppose all moral questions to be answerable. My point is slightly different: Once the subject matter of contractarian choice has been contextualized, we lack reason for supposing that the political tradition that is its basis will contain resources sufficient to settle all important questions relevant to the principles of justice. A second reason is that the requirement of unique determinacy neglects the real possibility that several principles might *tie* as acceptable solutions to the problem of contractarian choice. One way of putting this is to say the principles of justice may be underdetermined by the contractarian method once that has been historicized in the fashion of the later Rawls. Not one set, but several sets of principles, might present themselves as credible candidates for solutions to the problem of contractarian choice, and the method would then be itself neutral between them. Public choice within the range of credible principles would then proceed by reference to local circumstances, political bargaining, and practical political reasoning.

Given the methodological shift in Rawls's later work, the Kantian requirements of determinacy and fixity in respect of the principles of justice are indefensible and indeed unreasonable. What remains, then, of the contract method? And what might it still have to say on central questions such as the justice of private property and market exchange? The contract method may yield definite results at a particular moment in the development of our political tradition, despite all that I have argued, inasmuch as it may serve as a filter for principles, by which some are decisively rejected. Here I would wish to endorse Scanlon's judgment,[25] that the contract method is best framed in terms of deriving principles no one could reasonably reject, rather than in the terms of principles all must reasonably accept. The natural tendency of Rawls's later work is in the direction of abandoning the agenda of determinacy and fixity for the results of the method that he inherits from his book. It is to adopt a humbler role for the contractarian method, in which it has a less radically constructive leverage on political practice. The contract method may eliminate certain solutions of problems of liberty and distribution, but it will not plausibly issue in a definite solution for any of them.

It will be a disappointing upshot of the contract method if it had little to say on the fundamental questions of economic justice. As against this possibility, I want to argue the contract method does yield a definite result in the area of economic justice in that it endorses the institutions of private property and market exchange. It does so, however, by disqualifying their socialist alternatives as credible answers to the problem of contractarian choice. The institutional framework thereby endorsed by the contract method will not be specified in all of its important features. It will be a framework, nevertheless, in which the central institutions of capitalist economic organization are clearly present.

III. THE JUSTICE OF PRIVATE PROPERTY AND MARKET EXCHANGE

We may begin our exploration by noting the dependency of contractarian method upon the results of social theory. Central among the results accepted by Rawls[26] for the purpose of his theory is the indispensability of market mechanisms for the efficient allocation of resources in complex modern economies. It is important to be clear what is and what is not being asserted here. It is not claimed that there cannot be economies in which market institutions play a small role in the allocation of resources. The economies of primitive or traditional cultures, where technology is static and preferences are slow to change, where a general medium of exchange is barely developed and prices are largely governed by convention, may be instanced at once. Again, even in modern complex economies, there are countless areas of social life that are not regulated by market mechanisms. Aside from communes, monasteries, charitable institutions, and bureaucracies, there is the example of the family or domestic household, within which market exchange is untypical.[27] Again, all modern governments are involved in the supply of more or less public goods, whose special attributes exclude their production on the market. Even where it is dominant, market allocation of resources is never, and perhaps can never be, all-pervasive. Nevertheless, it is a well-established result of economic theory, amply supported by empirical evidence from socialist command economies, that in the absence of market pricing of most factors of production we may expect widespread waste, malinvestment, and discoordination of economic activity.

The logic of the argument for market institutions is, however, incompletely developed by Rawls, and has implications that undermine his thesis that market allocation and socialist property institutions may coexist in market socialism. It is worth recalling that the most intellectually powerful case against central economic planning, now widely accepted[28] both in mainstream economics and in Marxist political economy, is that developed by Mises and Hayek in their controversies with the socialist economists of the thirties. In its most fundamental aspects,[29] the Mises-Hayek argument against the possibility of rational economic calculation under socialism is an epistemological argument. It maintains that the knowledge that the public authority needs for successful economic planning simply is not, and cannot be available to it. In part, this is because much of that knowledge is local knowledge, knowledge of specific and often fleeting circumstances, which would be prohibitively costly to collect and in all likelihood dated once gathered. But more fundamentally, much of this knowledge is not only local knowledge but tacit knowledge—knowledge embodied in skills and dispositions, stored in customs and practices and expressed in use. If, as is likely,[30] part at least of this practical knowledge is inarticulable in theoretical or propositional form, there will be insuperable difficulties in the way of any central authority collecting or gathering it and using it for planning purposes.

The epistemological case against central economic planning invokes the fact of the dispersal of knowledge in society, its largely practical character, and its consequent irretrievability by central authority. The epistemological case for market institutions is as discovery procedures for recovering and utilizing the dispersed knowledge scattered throughout society. Without attempting to centralize such dispersed knowledge, market institutions make it available to society in the medium of price information, which expresses and coordinates local practical knowledge of the structure of preferences and relative resource scarcities. Inasmuch as it allows for general social use of knowledge that would otherwise have remained local and dispersed, the market process generates information that would not otherwise have existed of the preferences and resources of unknown persons. The market not only makes best use of dispersed knowledge, it also generates new knowledge, of which economic agents can then make use for their own purposes. The idea of market institutions as epistemic devices, mechanisms for the generation and transmission of information that would otherwise be available only locally, or not at all, is the central theme of the Austrian economists, that until recently was lost in an Orwellian memory-hole because of its vicissitudes in the history of economic ideas.[31] It has now been recovered, partly because of the failings of dominant macroeconomic paradigms and partly because of a growing knowledge of the disastrous consequences of attempts at central economic planning in command economies. But, except among Marxists, who remain the most historically literate among political economists, the Austrian argument that suppression of market institutions inexorably produces calculational chaos remains unfamiliar to mainstream economists, especially in the United States.

How does the calculation argument (as the Austrian argument has come to be called) bear upon the prospect for market socialism of the sort envisaged by Rawls? As the Austrian argument is stated in Hayek's decisive papers of the Thirties,[32] it is successful against the Lange-Lerner model of socialism in which a central planning authority simulates market processes by shadow prices. Its relevance to the very different market socialism of worker-managed enterprises (which I take to be Rawls's conception of it) should be no less clear. In this model, most factors of production, including labor but excluding capital, are subject to market pricing. The wage relation is abolished in that all workers are owner-managers of socialist enterprises that compete with each other for markets, but workers may not alienate their share in their enterprise, and investment capital is obtained from a public investment bank. Whereas market socialism on this model achieves a considerable measure of decentralization of economic decision-making, it remains authentically socialist (but thoroughly un-Marxian)[33] in virtue of the communal ownership and consequent individual inalienability of socialist enterprises and because productive capital is obtainable only from state investment banks. These aspects of market socialism merely illustrate its constitutive institutional features—that the hiring of labor by capital and the investment of capital in enterprises for the profit of others apart from those who work in them are forbidden. Capitalists and proletarians are, in this model, abolished and replaced by a single class of worker-managers of enterprises that remain themselves communally owned.

Market socialism on this model (an imperfect variant of which has been attempted in Yugoslavia)[34] has many incidental disadvantages. The fusion of job-holding with access to profits from capital, which is central to the system, makes enterprises reluctant to take on new worker-cooperators, who tend to dilute the share of profit from capital available to each existing worker. Newcomers to the economy, such as immigrants or new generations, are likely to find it difficult to obtain employment in the worker-managed sector, and high levels of unemployment are likely to result. There will be a strong tendency for enterprises to be risk-averse in their research and development policies and a resultant low level of technological innovations in the economy. Ordinary economic assumptions, when applied to the model, produce a picture of self-managed firms behaving very much like family partnerships in private-property regimes, tending to be conservative in admitting newcomers, and to function by slowly depleting the capital stock of the enterprise. These theoretical results are amply confirmed by the Yugoslav experience and should raise doubts about the desirability of market socialism from the perspectives of efficiency and equity.

It is not upon these incidental defects of market socialism that I wish to focus here. I wish rather to highlight fundamental problems in the operation of the mechanisms for allocating capital under market socialist institutions. I have noted already a constitutive feature of market socialism, that (private ownership of productive capital being prohibited) all investment capital other than that laid aside by existing enterprises will be allocated by state investment banks. The question arises, then, How, and by what criteria, is this investment of capital to be made? It is clear, in the first place, that enterprises can be established, and for that matter wound up, only by a decision of a state investment bank. The bank will for this reason have a decisive effect on the pattern of economic activity in the society. Its allocative decisions will need to be taken with the utmost care. The fundamental problems of the system appear to be two. There is the technical or theoretical problem of deciding upon a rule, or set of rules, for determining the rate of return on capital lent by the state bank, and there is the political or institutional problem of keeping to such rules, if they can be formulated. The first of these problems is commonly neglected by those noneconomists and economists reared in a mathematical idiom of general equilibrium analysis, who suppose there to be a simple formula somewhere available whereby investment decisions can be made almost mechanically. I do not think I exaggerate when I say that this supposition is entirely delusive. It neglects the subjective character of economic costs, the conventional and variable forms of accounting systems, and the purely entrepreneurial aspects of many investment decisions.[35] Though I cannot here show this to be so, I shall take it that the hope that a state investment bank could avoid arbitrariness in its decisions by reliance on a fixed rule is vain.

Against my argument, it may be objected that arbitrariness is not the only alternative to a fixed rule. The state investment bank could be guided in its decisions by political and normative principles—principles having to do with the distribution of resources between regions and industries, with cross-generational justice and so forth. This rejoinder has the merit of acknowledging that investment policy in a market socialist economy would in practice be motivated chiefly by political considerations. It suggests that, even if a fixed rule for investment decisions is not forthcoming, this need not concern us overmuch, since such a rule is neither necessary nor appropriate. The institutional problem with reliance on normative standards for the allocation of investment capital is, however, a fundamental one. We have no reason whatever to suppose that a political institution equipped with massive discretionary powers (which is what a state investment bank would have to be) would be able to keep to and implement the normative standards by which its decisions were supposedly guided. All our knowledge of bureaucracies suggests that the permanent officials of the state bank would be conservative and risk-averse in the extreme and would shy away from investment strategies involving substantial speculative risks even if these were dictated by principles of justice.

Again, the normative principles supposed to guide the decisions of the investment bank would sometimes conflict with each other, and would often be vague in their practical implications. Whenever room for discretion existed, we would confidently expect decisions to be taken by reference to the kind of interests identified in governmental institutions in the literature of the Virginia Public Choice School.[36] For example, large existing enterprises with political clout would be favored over small and struggling ones—and certainly over enterprises projected but not yet in a position to lobby for capital. In these circumstances, malinvestments would be unlikely to be eliminated, but instead would be concealed by further inputs of capital. The picture derivable from theoretical considerations of the sort developed by the Public Choice School is that of a vast auction for public capital, in which successful bids would be made primarily by entrenched enterprises having political skills and connections and (a crucial point) with the ability to control the flow of information to the central allocative institutions. (Nor is there any good reason to suppose that institutions providing for the democratic accountability of the state investment banks would improve the situation. Given the historical record of the ineptitude and corruption of economic policy in democratic regimes, market socialism might well be rendered less efficient and less equitable by the adoption of democratic procedures for the allocation of investment capital.) Market socialist institutions would not in this central area of the allocation of investment capital differ materially from command economies, where all the evidence we have supports and corroborates the theoretical expectations of the Public Choice School.

Against this last point, it may be objected that market socialist institutions could be decentralized further than is suggested in my model of them. In particular, it might be urged, there could be a plurality of state investment banks, competing with each other in the supply of capital just as the worker-cooperatives do in the supply of products. What is to be said of such a proposal? On the positive side, it is at least possible that such a system of competing state investment banks would do for the allocation of capital what the system of shadow pricing is supposed to do in the Lange-Lerner model for the allocation of resources other than capital. It would effectively simulate the mechanism for the elimination of errors in capital-allocation that exists under a system of private ownership, and to this extent it would represent a marked improvement on other models of market socialism. Against this proposal, on the other hand, there is the claim (which I make against all species of market socialism) that it occupies an ultimately uninhabitable no man's land between full liberal ownership and the socialist command economy. Consider the system of competing state investment banks. Where would they acquire their initial lending capital, and how would they be wound up in the event of insolvency? It seems plain that central planning of resource allocation has not been avoided but simply pushed one stage further back. Like the worker-cooperatives themselves, the state investment banks will be dependent for their creation and liquidation on central political authority. It seems plain that, given the similarities in incentive structure, all the problems in resource allocation theorized by the Public Choice School in bureaucratic institutions would persist in a market socialist system characterized by competing investment banks.

It would be possible to circumvent these problems, perhaps, by conferring on the several investment banks substantial property rights in their initial capital endowment and then allowing them to invest it at will, at their own risk, in the various worker-cooperatives. To do this, however, would be to abandon normative criteria for investment and allow investment decisions to be made (as under capitalist institutions) by criteria of expected profitability. Allowing for market allocation of capital in this way amounts to a reinvention of one of the central institutions of capitalist economic systems. It is hard to see how such a move could avoid bringing about an unravelling of the market socialist system itself. Once the incentive structure of the state banks is altered so as to be oriented toward maximum profits, Public Choice theory will predict (other things being equal) that profit-seeking lenders would attempt to uncover sources of profit in areas of the economy as yet subject to regulation and would act in many instances as agents of deregulation. Whatever the outcome of such developments, they introduce a profound instability into market socialism as a system and generate deep doubts as to its long-term viability.[37]

The theoretical basis of the Public Choice School is in the proposition that human action in the political dimension is guided by much the same interests and motivations that govern economic behavior. This assumption of constancy of motivation will be fiercely contested by normative theorists, despite the fact that it is amply confirmed by political experience. I will not attempt to defend it here, but will account it part of that social theory that the covenanters in Rawls's original position are allowed to know. Once this has been done, and the results of the "calculation debate" are similarly included within the knowledge of the covenanters, it is clear that contractarian method cannot be neutral, or silent, in regard to the choice of an economic system. For the upshot of the Austrian calculation debate, reinforced by considerations from the Virginia Public Choice School, is that calculational chaos—waste, malinvestment, and discoordination in the economy—can be avoided, or at any rate minimized, only if decision-making is decentralized to the level of the individual through the institution of private or several property. Then, and only then, in a regime in which individuals have the legal power to alienate their resources from any collective body to which they have been provisionally entrusted, can the local knowledge that is dispersed throughout society be put to use to secure a reasonable degree [38] of economic coordination. The policy upshot of the calculation argument, insofar as the institutional design of the economic system is concerned, is thus full liberal ownership of the means of production. It is not, indeed, that malinvestment, or waste, will not occur under a regime of full liberal ownership, since the imperfect coordination of economic life is an inevitable consequence of limitations in human knowledge, but rather that a decentralized system will promote coordination, and eliminate errors in decision-making, better than a centralized system could. This last point is reinforced by the insights of the Public Choice School into the incentive structure of governmental institutions and the consequent lack of any error-elimination mechanism for mistaken allocations of resources. Knowing these results of social and economic theory, the deliberators in the original positions will opt for a regime of private property in the means of production and market allocation of all factors, including capital. They will do so because such a regime will make best use of available resources and is likely to yield greatest prosperity. Indeed, Rawls's covenanters will be compelled to adopt a private property regime if, as is suggested by my argument, the Difference Principle minimum achievable under capitalist institutions is higher than that achievable under market socialism.

My argument has been that the Austrian account of the epistemic role of market pricing, in conjunction with Virginian insights into the mechanisms of government failure, constrain the operations of the contract method to the point of yielding an endorsement of a private property regime. My argument to this conclusion might be accepted, and it could nevertheless be denied that a private property regime emerges from contractarian choice *as a matter of justice*. After all, it might be objected, the

principal burden of my argument has been only that opting for
private property in the means of production is collectively prudent: I have said nothing, or little, to show that opting for
socialist institutions is *unjust*. To this extent, I have not defeated
Rawls's thesis of the neutrality of the theory of justice in respect
of the choice of economic systems. So far as my argument has
gone, a different reading of the results of social and economic
theory could support an endorsement of socialist institutions.
The argument for the non-neutrality of the contract method in
respect of economic systems, if there is one, must then appeal
to considerations other than those I have invoked so far.

IV. THE JUSTICE OF PRIVATE PROPERTY AND MARKET EXCHANGE: A CONTRACTARIAN DERIVATION

The conception of the person deployed in the later version of
Rawls's contractarian project is a political construction. It is not
supposed to be the best conception of human nature, or even
an empirical generalization of persons as we find them, but
instead a device intended to model the circumstance of persons
as political actors in the historical context with which Rawls is
concerned. This context is one in which society contains diverse
and perhaps incommensurable value-perspectives and worldviews. For this reason neither the theory of justice as a whole,
nor the particular conception of the person that it encapsulates,
expresses any comprehensive moral doctrine. But this much is
only half the story. For, whereas our culture encompasses incommensurable outlooks and practices, it also exhibits *overlapping consensus*—a tacit convergence on basic values having to do
with the moral claims and powers of individuals. This consensus, though it incorporates no specific conception of the good,
informs the contract method so as to prevent its upshot being
simply a Hobbesian modus vivendi.[39] Rawls's conception is deep
and subtle. Undergirding our experience of moral diversity and
conflict, our culture contains a subterranean layer of convergence on how persons are to be conceived as moral beings.

This conception is a remarkable achievement. It aims to capture, and in considerable measure does so, the modern Western
experience of moral conflict among individuals who share an
underlying conception of themselves. Rawls's representation of

our experience seems to me to be sound in many of its most fundamental aspects. It acknowledges that we are, none of us, radically situated subjects—this is to say, moral agents whose identity is constituted by membership of a single moral community. It is true of most of us that we belong to a complex diversity of moral communities, so that our sense of our identities is itself complex and even multiple, a microcosm of the conflicting traditions in the wider culture to which we belong. Rawls's conception is faithful to our moral life in its *individualism* —in its frank recognition and acceptance of the experience of individuality as a central and constitutive element in our culture. Because of its fidelity to the protracted historical experience that gave rise to our contemporary sense of self, Rawls's conception is resistant to the criticisms of it developed forcefully by Michael Sandel.[40] Because of its insight into the strength and depth of the experience of individuality, Rawls's conception refutes absurd claims about the demolition of modern moral life by triumphant individualism.[41] It captures the common experience that our society does harbor value-perspectives and views of the world that are incommensurable and, despite this, that we do appear to be animated by a shared sense of ourselves as individuals.

It is in the delicate balance between moral divergence and shared values that the chief difficulty of Rawls's conception lies. It is far from clear that an investigation of our cultural tradition in its contemporary manifestations would yield much in the way of a shared conception of self. It seems highly questionable to suppose that any overlapping consensus can be discerned in the welter of forms of life among which we move. Our culture contains born-again Christians as well as many for whom religious belief is barely intelligible, those who cleave to science and some who hold to magic. Indeed, it is not at all uncommon to find conflicting commitments of this sort in a single person, spread out over a lifetime. It is unclear that there is any common denominator among the rich variety of worldviews our culture contains. For this reason, I cannot see that overlapping consensus has any definite content—unless it be only the minimal sense of self, or individuality, that is preserved across conflicting commitments and forms of life. Certainly, the moral content of the overlapping consensus will be minimal—and there is no reason to suppose that it will be liberal. This is to say that, precisely in virtue of a constitutive feature of the cultural tradition that Rawls is theorizing, he is disqualified from erecting on the basis of a supposed overlapping consensus any liberal civic ideal. Our culture contains forms of life that embody liberal self-conceptions of persons as free and equal agents, and forms of life that do not. Because even nonliberal forms of life are in our culture voluntarily assumed commitments from which exit is possible and commonplace, we cannot avoid trying to construct a conception of the person from which attributes derived from any specific form of life are excluded. This prevents us from giving the conception of the person the liberal content that it has in Rawls, and which it needs if it is to support his liberal political ideal.

How, then, is the conception of the person to be constructed? We are faced with the necessity of constructing a political conception of the person in a form appropriate to the circumstances of a culture where members share centrally the experience of conflict and coexistence among incommensurable values and forms of life. I suggest that the appropriate conception of the person for our historical circumstance is closer to that which Hobbes presented at a time of profound religious conflict. In Hobbes's model the person is equipped with desires and goals and with the disposition to prevail over others in contexts of material and moral scarcity. He is not a creature altogether devoid of moral attributes, since he has the capacity to make and keep promises, but he is not defined by any ideal. In Hobbes's own account, the person's ruling motives are those of prudence. We need not follow Hobbes slavishly in this, since much recent work (above all that of Parfit) has succeeded in calling in question the claim of reason on prudence. Let us say, instead, that we think of the person as being *autonomous*—as having beliefs and desires, goals and projects. This person, possessing this autonomy of Humean rather than Kantian kind, will have reason to be prudent, if and only if prudence is dictated by his goals. Nor need we, in adopting this modified version of Hobbes's conception of the person, accept his account of human psychology, which can be improved upon.[42]

If we want a formula for the conception of the person, we may turn from Hobbes to Spinoza, and equip our construction with the attribute of *conatus*—the disposition to assert power and freedom in the world.[43] If we do this in Rawlian spirit, however, we will not suppose that we are capturing a metaphysical truth about persons. We will understand ourselves, instead, to be grasping our own condition.

I make no pretence at fleshing out in any persuasive detail the conception of the person that I believe should be adopted as an alternative to Rawls's. My aim is to mark a number of features that any such conception must possess if it is to be adequate as a political construction adapted to the circumstances of pluralism in forms of life that is our common experience. If the conception of the person we adopt has the Hobbesian (and Spinozistic) features I have indicated, we can discern three characteristics that will have direct bearing on our problem of the justice of private property and markets. The conception of the person will, in the first instance, be *individualistic*. It must be so, not because of any metaphysical doctrine about personhood, nor in virtue of any moral doctrine of the value of individuality, but because we need political principles that abstract from particular attachments to specific moral communities. We need these principles because our historical circumstance is not one of moral communities with fixed and impermeable boundaries, but one of constant migration across communal boundaries. It is because we seek to mirror this historical reality that, in contractarian spirit, we deny to the hypothetical person knowledge of the moral community to which he belongs. We conceive the person as an unsituated or unencumbered individual, defined not by communal attachments but by autonomous choices.

Proceeding in this contractarian spirit, we can see that this conception of the person embodies a form of *minimal egalitarianism*. Since they are denied knowledge of their place in specific moral communities, persons cannot apply particular conceptions of the good so as to rank different forms of life. From the perspective of contractarian choice, all forms of life are equally worth living. The hypothetical persons in the circumstance of contractarian choice will themselves have equal worth in the absence of any criteria that could establish otherwise. The construction of the person in the original position, as of the original position as a whole, then embodies a *neutralism* in respect of the claims of particular moral communities and their associated conceptions of the good. The principles of justice that emerge from the contract will have to be *neutral* in respect of the opposed forms of life that the society contains.[44] That is the rationale for denying the contractors knowledge of them.

How do these characteristics of individualism, equality, and neutrality bear on the justice of private property and market exchange? Let us take neutrality first. In its application to the choice of economic systems, this requires that no ideal of productive enterprise be favored over any other. Our society contains many such ideals, after all: the socialist ideal of cooperative productive activity directed to the direct satisfaction of human needs, religious ideals in which secular are subordinated to spiritual concerns, ideals of self-realization through individual entrepreneurship and productivity[45] and so on. Certainly no consensus exists. Any economic system that imposes on all a productive ideal that not all share must be condemned as unjust from the standpoint of contractarian method. Within a private-property regime, but not within a socialist, individuals may join workers' cooperatives or communes: they may achieve a partial or (as with the Amish) a near-total withdrawal from the surrounding capitalist economy.

The argument in favor of a private-property regime from the principle of neutrality is, in virtue of this permanent possibility of withdrawal from capitalist institutions, perhaps not best characterized as an argument for capitalism. For the virtue of a private-property system is that it, unlike any socialist regime, permits a diversity of productive enterprises. Recall that even under market socialist institutions at least one form of productive enterprise—that involving wage labor—is prohibited: workers are denied the legal power to alienate their shares in the cooperatives and to set up enterprises of their own, even if these embody an ideal of productive association that they prize. In a private-property regime, by contrast, *no one* may elect to live within capitalist institutions. What Robert Nozick says of his own meta-utopian framework is true of every system of private property: "In *this* . . . system it could turn out that though they are permitted, there are no actually functioning 'capitalist' institutions; or that some communities have them and others don't or some communities have some of them, or what you will."[46]

It is in virtue of its capacity to permit many different forms of enterprise that the private-property regime is endorsed by the principle of neutrality and a socialist economic system condemned as unjust. It is worth nothing here in parenthesis that the principle of neutrality, whereas it favors a private property system, does *not* enjoin a minimum state (*contra* Nozick) or presuppose a Lockean theory of property rights.

The same conclusions may be reached by way of the egalitarian component in the construction of the person. Any particular ideal of productive association could be enforced on others who do not share it, only if the latter are denied moral equality with the advocates of the favored ideal. If the contractors have equal moral standing, *any* ideal of productive association is as good as any other from the standpoint of justice. The economic system that is favored, then, from the standpoint of equality in the original position, is that which permits individuals to use their resources to express their own ideal, whatever this may be. It is evident that, because of the constitutive features of a private-property system—its decentralization of decision-making and the ability individuals have to deploy their resources without recourse to any procedure of collective choice—that that system, and that alone, allows for such self-expression. A regime of private property, because it alone allows for diversity of productive ideals, is dictated by the principle of moral equality that the original position embodies in its Hobbesian (as, in a different form, in its Kantian and Rawlsian) constructions.

The three characteristics of the person in the original position I have identified are not altogether distinct and independent of one another. Consider neutrality and equality. It seems plain that the former is an implication of the latter, and not an independent principle. It is important that this be so, since otherwise a principle of neutrality might make unacceptable demands on the economic system. If neutrality were a primordial principle, it might demand *nondiscrimination* among ideals of productive enterprise, where this might be interpreted as meaning that each and every ideal has as good a chance of being realized as any other. That such a principle of neutrality as nondiscrimination among productive ideals is impossible of realization is too obvious to require explication. By contrast, the neutrality that is demanded by moral equality requires only that the legal and institutional framework of society does not favor any one ideal over any other: It is a neutrality of intent, not of outcome. This has the important consequence that neutrality cannot be a fundamental principle in liberalism, even in its Rawlsian variety.[47] Further, in envisaging a single-status domain of persons, the individualist and the minimalist-egalitarian components of the Hobbesian contractarian construction are also clearly interdependent.

The advantage from the standpoint of justice of private property over socialist institutions is that it permits individuals to opt out of market exchange relations if their productive ideal so dictates. A question arises as to the endowments individuals posseses with which they may so contract out of market exchange. Here two points are crucially relevant. First, because the person is in the Hobbesian construction conceived as autonomous and devoid of communal attachments, no policy of pure redistribution can emerge. But, second, because the Hobbesian construction does not contain proprietary rights, nothing is exempt from redistribution. From the standpoint of Hobbism, all assets pass from civil society back into a circumstance of no-ownership (not collective ownership)[48] when initial endowments are to be allocated. Because of its egalitarian element, again, it is improbable that the Hobbesian contract could yield an outcome in which some have no assets at all. Rather, it is reasonable to suppose that the Hobbesian contract would assign to each an initial capital endowment to dispose of.

My aim here is not to try to theorize the structure and outcome of an Hobbesian contract. I have described the persons in contractarian deliberation as autonomous agents, with desires and goals, but I have not aimed to determine whether the principles of practical reasoning they are equipped with are those of maximizing *homo economicus* or other, less stringent and more realistic principles. I have not attempted to judge whether the veil of ignorance that conceals from the contractors knowledge of themselves is to be designed in the strong form that Rawls stipulates. (For what it is worth, I believe the natural implication of the Hobbesian variant of the contract project to be that convenantors are denied knowledge of the final position they occupy in society, but not of their abilities, tastes, moral conceptions, and so forth.)[49] Nor have I explored the difficult question of the "baseline" of the contract. It seems to me that

James Buchanan's variant of Hobbesian contractarianism, in which the method aims to specify Pareto-optimal departures from a baseline specified by the status quo distribution of holdings,[50] forms a neglected strand in political philosophy that is well worth developing. Buchanan's approach avoids the difficulties which abound in Gauthier's attempt to stipulate Lockean bargaining constraints so as to guarantee a Smithian system of natural liberty and it expresses the important insight that, contrary to common intuition, redistribution need not be a zerosum game. But Buchanan's proposal regarding the baseline and criteria for Hobbesian redistribution is plainly not the only one worth exploring. The contract method consists in identifying the principles for distribution, filtering out some of those principles and leaving the choice among the remainder to practical political deliberation. It seems clear that, on this view of contractarian method, the distributive principle adopted might vary from Buchanan's Paretian liberalism through principles specifying an equal level of initial holdings, and so forth. My own judgment favors the former option, but I do not claim that it can be derived as a demonstrative result of the application of contractarian method. At the same time, I would wish to claim that any fully worked out version of the Hobbesian contract will filter out some principles, among which the Rawlsian maximin principle may be singled out.[51]

My argument is that, whatever principle is adopted, Hobbesian contractarianism will regard property rights as conventional and the allocation of initial holdings as a fundamental dictate of justice. In its applications to economic life, I claim, justice demands the assignment of rights to holdings in private property. Further, I see no reason for supposing that this demand does not exhaust the content of economic justice. Indeed, once holdings are assigned as justice dictates, it is unjust to attempt to maintain any pattern in the distribution of income, or to thwart freedom of exchange. For the same reason, it is an injustice once holdings are assigned to impose upon their holders any ideal of productive enterprise. Justice is satisfied by the allocation of initial endowments, and is violated when persons are denied freedom to exchange their endowments or to withdraw from market exchange in the service of an ideal of productive association that they prize.

How does this Hobbesian theory of contractarian justice differ from Rawls's? It shares with Rawls's account elements of a liberal political morality—its individualism, neutralism, and moral egalitarianism. Again like Rawls's theory, but especially the later Rawls's, it is a variant of contractarian method that is explicitly contextualized and historically situated in its application. In this it differs from most varieties of liberalism, including almost all forms of classical liberalism. The Hobbesian theory of justice differs also from liberal theories of all sorts in a respect I have not so far discussed—namely, it contains nothing that guarantees the priority of liberty over other goods. This is not just the thesis that no determinate list of basic liberties may be expected to emerge from the contract. It is the more radical point that the basis liberties themselves will not in the Hobbesian account be immune from trade-off with other values such as peace and security. It is in this fact that, even when it issues (as it does in Buchanan's work) in endorsement of constitutional limited government, the Hobbesian contract differs most profoundly from liberalism, classical as well as revisionary, in denying to liberty an absolute priority among political goods and interests. This is a result that flows inexorably from the chief alteration that the Hobbesian view makes in Rawls's theory—its modification of his conception of the person so as to empty it of any distinctively liberal ideal. The motive for this evacuation of the person's liberal moral content is, in its turn, that very incommensurability in value-perspectives that generates the liberal problem. If this reasoning is sound, it has the consequence that, once the liberal problem is framed in this fashion, it becomes insoluble in liberal terms.

Concluding Observations on Contractarian Theory and Philosophical Method

In Rawls's later work, reflective equilibrium expresses intimations of our political tradition. This political tradition—the tradition of the Western constitutional democracies—emerged from the Wars of Religion and the subsequent establishment of religious toleration. In the modern world, our political tradition harbors deep conflicts that mirror the diversity of incommensurable values that our culture displays. Rawls's project is to diminish the incoherence of our political tradition and, by so doing, to solve the liberal problem by specifying principles of political justice that permit fair coexistence of the rival forms of life that our culture contains. He aims to uncover a convergence that undergirds the conflicts—between libertarians and egalitarians, for example—that our political culture exhibits. He seeks to achieve this by a strategy of avoidance that extends the principle of toleration to philosophy itself. The substance of the contract method is given, not by metaphysical commitments, or by comprehensive moral doctrines, but by an overlapping consensus that undergirds our culture. The result of the application of the method to this consensus is the various principles that are the prescriptive content of the theory of justice.

In accord with the strategy of avoiding fundamental controversies, Rawls holds the principles of justice are neutral on questions of economic organization. They are neutral between private property and collective ownership. I have criticized his argument, firstly, by arguing against Rawls's attempted divorce of private-property institutions from market allocation of resources. The same criterion of efficiency that dictates market pricing of other factors of production dictates market allocation of capital—but this entails private ownership. My second argument against Rawls's thesis is the fundamental one. It is that, because it entails imposing a productive ideal choice of collective ownership is precluded by justice. My argument is contractarian, having important elements in common with Rawls's and differing principally in its construction of the person who is the subject of contractarian choice. Even where it differs from Rawls, my argument thus has the form of an immanent criticism, since it contends that the very circumstance of value-pluralism that frames Rawls's problem disqualifies him from giving to the conception of the person a specific normative content, that of a liberal political ideal. When, as in our own case, a culture contains both liberal and nonliberal forms of life, we lack an overlapping consensus that might sustain such an ideal. For this reason, I have submitted that the person is better conceived in Hobbesian and Spinozistic fashion as being motivated by autonomous choices and lacking in communal attachments or social ideals. Such a construction preserves some elements of liberal political morality, but not all. It endorses what Oakeshott has illuminatingly called *civil association*,[52] but it does not always or necessarily support liberal ideals of the priority of liberty. The modified version of the contract method that I have defended sponsors a juridical and political order that embodies no ideal of the person and so no ideal of productive enterprise. Such an order is best conceived as promoting no enterprise of any sort, but instead as simply securing the conditions in which persons may, however they conceive themselves, engage in their several and different projects.

The contractarian method that I have developed differs from Rawls's, then, in giving a definite answer to a question on which he aspires to be neutral or silent. Nevertheless, it differs most radically from Rawls's in that it does not issue in definite propositions about liberty and distribution. It is an *indeterminate contractarianism* that leaves the choice of such principles largely to political practice. It filters out some principles as being ineligible because incongruent with the central elements of the contract —the conception of the person and the circumstance of uncertainty about his position in society—and it has something of substance to say about the procedures whereby principles to do with liberty and distribution may be chosen. A full version of the Hobbesian theory—which I have certainly not tried to give here—would address and answer questions about the circumstance of contractarian deliberation and it would thereby constrain the choice of principles; but it would not identify them. The choice of such principles would be a matter of political life itself, for bargaining, compromise, and ordinary political reasoning. Indeterminate contractarianism acknowledges that political life is always radically underdetermined by theory, and it abandons the idea that the adoption of political principles can ever be solely or primarily a matter of rational choice. It thereby abandons the central modern project, which is to confer a privileged status on liberalism.

Whereas it has been derived by means of an immanent criticism of Rawls's later work, the sort of Hobbesian contractarianism I have sketched exhibits many points of sharp contrast with the contract approach sponsored by Rawls. It does not seek to privilege liberty over other political goods, and it does not aim to issue in any specific principle of economic justice. Again, whereas it yields a definite result on the justice of economic systems, it is silent on the merits of constitutional democracy.

The Hobbesian contract sketched here, unlike Rawls's Kantian variant and, for that matter, Gauthier's Hobbesian-Smithian variant, is not necessarily a liberal political doctrine, though it may in some circumstances have applications that are recognizably liberal. This divergence in political substance between Rawls's contract approach and the Hobbesian approach supports a deeper methodological difference and identifies a point at which immanent criticism is followed by external critique. For, by contrast with the method practiced by Rawls and Gauthier, the Hobbesian approach does not seek (by a restrictive design of the original position or stipulations on bargaining rights) to derive specific principles by an application of the method. Rather, the method itself is applied to the salient contexts, and its results accepted as having a claim on reason. In the form in which it is here advanced, the contract method can represent itself as a genuine discovery procedure in political philosophy.

In the Hobbesian vision, then, the relations between method and results that hold in the theories of Rawls and Gauthier are virtually reversed. This reveals another point of divergence between Rawls's thinking and that which I defend here. In Rawls's work, the theory of justice depends above all on the conception of the person, which is a practical construction, and not part of any empirical theory in anthropology or psychology. For the purposes of my project of immanent criticism, I have not dissented from this treatment of the idea of the person, nor to the contextualization of the rest of the theory of justice. I have claimed that my project of immanent criticism shows a Hobbesian conception of the person to be a more appropriate construction than Rawls's for the purposes of contractarian theory. At this stage, however, it is worth remarking that another strategy of argument is open to development that yields results closely akin to those emerging from the immanent criticism, but having radically divergent implications for philosophical method. This is the strategy, powerfully defended by Kavka in his recent study of Hobbesian moral and political theory,[53] in which the central propositions of Hobbesian theory are taken as being substantially true. In this theory we have a rich account of human nature and the human circumstance that, because it is represented as being universally true, may be applied to any number of historical milieus and cultural traditions. The results of the theory will be variable, and in most cases only partly determinate, across the various cultures and historical contexts in which it is applied. The conception of persons as autonomous agents, with desires and goals that they pursue in contexts of material and moral scarcity, which in the immanent criticisms of Rawls's account was treated as a practical construction, will here be treated as a central element in an explanatory theory of human nature having universal scope. In its applications, however, it will rarely yield universal principles, since the content of the principles yielded by applications of the method will depend on the relevant milieus and circumstances, with their distinctive self-conceptions. In our case, in which there is diversity of incommensurable self-conceptions, the Hobbesian account of human nature may perhaps be applied most directly in a contract model in which the covenanters are allowed knowledge of their self-conceptions, but not of their positions in society. My claim is that, if we apply the Hobbesian apparatus to our circumstance in this direct fashion, we arrive at the result obtained from an immanent criticism of Rawls's theory—namely, an endorsement of the institutions of private property and market exchange.

The conception of political philosophy that emerges from these last considerations differs from Rawls's in several ways. Inasmuch as the Hobbesian account of human nature will enter into the contract apparatus at the level of the original position, the Hobbesian contractarian method as defended here will be far less radically contextualized than Rawls's. Insofar as its results are also much less determinate in most areas, it will also have far less constructive leverage on political practice than Rawls's method is intended to achieve. The Hobbesian approach will filter out some principles for the assignment of holdings and the allocation of liberties, and in the case of the choice of economic systems it will have a definite result. Otherwise, political philosophy in the contractarian idiom returns us to political practice, where the decisive choices are to be made. Because the Hobbesian approach generates a vital perspective on our current political life, it does not leave everything as it is, but nor does it pretend to be able to govern practice.

In generating a critical perspective on our current doings, the Hobbesian strategy distinguishes itself from the theory of philosophical method intimated in the writings of Wittgenstein and

Oakeshott. To be sure, political philosophy in the Oakeshottean and Wittgensteinian idioms will not always be conservative in its effect, since in illuminating neglected aspects of our practices, it may open up possibilities—ways of thinking and valuing—that are genuinely novel. Again, in showing up as elements of local practice postulates, such as those of liberalism, which have claimed for themselves a spurious universality, philosophy as Wittgenstein and Oakeshott conceive of it cannot avoid altering that practice. Even in their account of it, philosophical inquiry cannot be insulated from practical life.[54] Nor can it have the constructive leverage on practice that it seeks in Rawls's conception of it.

By contrast with both of these ways of thinking, the Hobbesian perspective intimates a position of philosophical method in which political philosophy may be genuinely critical and indeed subversive of practice. It achieves this critical, but not constructive, leverage on practice inasmuch as Hobbesian theory itself confutes or deflates central elements in our political tradition. In undermining the idea of a natural right to property, for example, Hobbesian theory opens up a space of criticism of existing holdings, so to speak, it delegitimates current distributions. Again by dissolving the idea that there might be a fixed set of basic liberties, immune to revision or trade-off, Hobbesian theory compels adoption of a critical perspective on current conceptions of liberty. The effect of philosophical inquiry on this Hobbesian conception of it is likely to be far from conservative, since it may set in motion a course of change—if not in practical life, then at least in our theorizing of it—whose outcome cannot be foretold. When this happens, however, it happens as an unpredictable by-product of philosophical inquiry, and not as its goal.

In the Hobbesian contractarian standpoint I have tried to open up by way of an immanent criticism of Rawls's later thought, political philosophy lacks the constructive leverage on political practice that it seeks in Rawls's work. It does not merely illuminate practice, since is suggests a critical perspective on the historic distribution of liberties and capital holdings. Yet, because of the indeterminacy of its results when applied to any specific circumstance, the Hobbesian project in contractarian philosophy may be thought to be wanting. Except perhaps insofar as certain principles of distribution are disqualified by the filter mechanisms of the contract device, the Hobbesian approach may appear to be empty of prescriptive content. This thought may be amplified to frame a criticism of contractarian method in all its variants. Where the contract method envisages a hypothetical circumstance of deliberation and agreement, as it does in Rawls and Gauthier, it is unclear how its results (whatever their degree of determinacy) can have a bearing on practice. More specifically, it is unclear how conclusions in ideal theory about what it would be rational for imaginary agents in a hypothetical circumstance to adopt as principles of social cooperation can tell us about the reasons for action agents have in the nonideal world in which we have to live. In its most radical and general form, this criticism of contract method submits that hypothetical contract theories do not, and cannot, bridge the "is-ought" gap.[55] Nor does recourse to a variant of contractarianism that postulates an actual, if tacit, agreement as the source of reasons for action go any distance to answering the criticism. In that model (as developed by Harman,[56] among others) the tacit agreement is postulated as an element in an a priori descriptive moral sociology, conceived in empirical terms that have no action-guiding force. On both the hypothetical-consent and the actual-agreement models, then, it seems that the contract method in all of its varieties is destitute of prescriptive content. How powerful is this fundamental criticism of contractarian methodology in political philosophy?

The criticism is a powerful one that stands in need of a contractarian response, if only because nothing in it turns on taking literally the metaphor of contract itself. In its hypothetical-consent version, contract theory is a species of rational choice theory, which in the Hobbesian perspective I have elaborated aims to achieve partial determinacy in its solutions of problems of choice. Even when the heuristic fiction of bargaining and agreement in a hypothetical initial position is dropped, the criticism still stands that the results of rational choice theory in an ideal circumstance have no clear implications for agents in the real world. Above all, such results fail utterly to establish the rationality of compliance in the real world with constraints on conduct whose rationality has been demonstrated in ideal theory. I see no way of answering this criticism, with all of its fatal consequences for the prospects of Gauthier's (if not Rawls's) project.

If the argument I have outlined is sound, then Hobbesian theory (as a species of state-of-nature, hypothetical-contract ideal theory) has no definite prescriptive content for action in the real world. It cannot enjoin action on real-world agents, still less motivate them to act in specific ways. It nevertheless has implications of a normative kind. Insofar as it can show that some principles and institutions definitely would not be chosen in a hypothetical state of nature, Hobbesian theory condemns as unjust such institutions in the real world. If, as is plausibly the case, Hobbesian theory can show that the institutions of slavery, absolutism,[57] or of a socialist command economy could not be chosen by rational contractors in a state of nature, then these institutions are morally delegitimated in the real world. Ceteris paribus, their abolition is then licensed as permissible in terms of justice (though perhaps not mandated) by Hobbesian theory. In its ideal-theoretical component, then, the Hobbesian approach has normative fallout even if it is not straightforwardly prescriptive in its content.

What of the contribution made to real-world political deliberation by the Hobbesian approach? That it cannot be directly prescriptive follows from our argument to the indeterminacy of its results. Contractarian method may nevertheless inform political deliberation in the real world by way of the insights it contains into distribution and constitutional changes which benefit all, or nearly all. It does so, most particularly, in the mode in which it has been developed in Buchanan's work, in which a thin veil of ignorance is combined with a status-quo baseline.[58] For Buchanan, we approach the problems of political practice equipped with the normative conceptions of Hobbesian state-of-nature theory, and we seek to raise ourselves from our current distributional conflicts by forging a new constitutional contract. Contractarian theory does not aim to set the terms of such a contract, which (aside from those which are filtered out by the normative elements in Hobbesian theory) must be forged in practice. Nor, again, does contractarian theory suppose that the negotiation of a new social contract is always possible. It recognizes the reality of *the political state of nature* in which recurrent prisoner's dilemmas throw up overwhelming disincentives to cooperation. Recurrent prisoner's dilemmas are found in many contemporary totalitarian states, and help to explain the massive stability of such states. It recognizes, in other words, that there are in the real world political dilemmas for which no rational solutions can be found. Where social cooperation for mutual benefit is feasible, however, contract theory may inform and illuminate our efforts to find and hold to principles that enhance the benefits and prolong the life span of cooperative solutions to social conflicts. Whereas it is rarely, if ever, directly prescriptive in its content, contractarian theory may possess an *indirect normativity* in which it contributes to our practical struggles as it refines our understanding of the world in which we find ourselves. Its *telos* may, in the end, be explanatory rather than practical in character, but in assisting us to understand practical life it cannot help changing it.

The methodological shift in the thought of the later Rawls is from the hallucinatory perspective of Kantian universality to a conception of philosophy as the definition of the conditions of social cooperation. This is a welcome change. It brings with it recognition that the central elements of thought and practice in civil societies—such as the experience of individuality—are not eternal verities, but transitory historical achievements, whose future philosophy cannot underwrite.

My aim has been to take one further step on the path on which Rawls's thought has set us. I have argued that contractarian theory can no more give us a criterion of political choice for our contemporary dilemmas of liberty and distribution than it can deliver universal prescriptive principles of political justice. In its Hobbesian variant, contractarian theory is less radically contextualized than it is in the later Rawls, but it is also less determined in most of its results. Indeed, the upshot of contractarian theory, as I have presented it, is to return us to practice, to seek in its vicissitudes the conditions of a precarious modus vivendi.[59] The substance of my argument has been in the thesis that we are most likely to achieve such an accommodation if we accept the institutions of private property and market exchange. I have claimed for the reasoning in support of this conclusion that it has a contractarian form and character.[60]

NOTES

1. John Rawls, *A Theory of Justice* (Oxford: Oxford University Press, 1972), 273. Rawls also asserts (271): "It is evident . . . that there is no essential tie between the use of free markets and private ownership of the instruments of production."

2. I have tried to summarize the Austrian argument to this conclusion in *Hayek on Liberty*, 2d ed. (New York: Basil Blackwell, 1986), 34–40; and in "Marxian Freedom, Individual Liberty and the End of Alienation," *Social Philosophy and Policy: Marxism and Liberalism* 3 (Spring 1986): 174–80.

3. The "two Mills" thesis is discussed and criticized by J. C. Rees in "The Thesis of the 'Two Mills,'" *Political Studies* 25 (1977): 368–82. I have argued for a thesis of the unity of Mill's work in *Mill on Liberty: A Defence* (London: International Library of Philosophy, Routledge and Kegan Paul, 1983). I argue against a "two Marxes" thesis in a forthcoming critique of Marx's system of ideas.

4. John Rawls, "Justice as Fairness: Political not Metaphysical," *Philosophy and Public Affairs* 14 (Summer 1985): 225. Rawls clarifies his view on p. 228, as follows: "We collect such settled convictions as the belief in religious toleration and the rejection of slavery and try to organize the basic ideas and principles implicit in these convictions into a coherent conception of justice. We can regard these convictions as provisional fixed points which any conception of justice must account for if it is to be reasonable for us. *We look, then, to our public political culture itself, including its main institutions and the historical traditions of their interpretation, as the shared fund of implicitly recognized basic ideas and principles* [emphasis added]. The hope is that these ideas and principles can be formulated clearly enough to be combined into a conception of political justice congenial to our most firmly held convictions, We express this by saying that a political conception of justice, to be acceptable, must be in accordance with our considered convictions, at all levels of generality, on due reflection (or in what I have called 'reflective equilibrium')."

5. Rawls, "Justice as Fairness," 226.

6. Ibid., 224 n. 2.

7. Ibid., 238–39.

8. Ibid., 230.

9. Ibid.

10. Rawls's is not the only contemporary liberal theory to take as its departure point a notion of value incommensurability. For Isaish Berlin's statement of such a theory, see my "On Negative and Positive Liberty," *Political Studies* 28 (Dec. 1980): 507–26, collected in *Conceptions of Liberty in Political Philosophy*, ed. John Gray and Z. A. Pelczynski (London: Athlone Press; New York: St. Martin's Press, 1984).

11. See D. Gauthier, *Morals by Agreement* (Oxford: Oxford University Press, 1986), 353–55, for a brief discussion of the moral and historical particularity of the conception of the individual that he employs somewhat naturalistically elsewhere in the book.

12. Rawls, "Justice as Fairness," 225.

13. Ibid., 230.

14. John Rawls, "Kantian Constructivism in Moral Theory," *Journal of Philosophy* 77 (Sept. 1980): 534.

15. I have in mind, of course, controversy surrounding the work especially of E. O. Wilson. Wilson gives an excellent statement of his views in his *On Human Nature* (New York: Bantam Books, 1978).

16. I argued for the culture-dependency of Rawls's earlier version of contract method in my "Social Contract, Community and Ideology," in *Democracy, Consensus and Social Contract,* ed. P. Birnbaum, J. Lively, and G. Parry, Sage Modern Politics Series, (Beverly Hills: Sage Publications, 1978), 2: 225–43.

17. Rawls, "Justice as Fairness," 225: "The social and historical conditions of such a state (a modern democratic state) have their origins in the Wars of Religion following the Reformation and the subsequent development of the principle of toleration, and in the growth of constitutional government and the institutions of large industrial market economies."

18. Hart stated his criticism of Rawls in his "Rawls on Liberty and Its Priority," in *Reading Rawls,* ed. N. Daniels (Oxford: Basil Backwell, 1975), 230–52. Rawls replied to Hart's criticism in his "The Basic Liberties and Their Priority," in *Tanner Lecture on Human Values* (Salt Lake City: University of Utah Press, 1981).

19. See my "Liberalism and the Choice of Liberties," in *The Restraint of Liberty: Bowling Green Studies in Applied Philosophy,* ed. John Gray, D. Callen, and T. Attig (Bowling Green, Ohio: Department of Philosophy, Bowling Green State University, 1985), 7: 1–25.

20. For an important discussion of neutralist liberalism, see Joseph Raz, *The Morality of Freedom* (Oxford: Clarendon Press, 1986), chap. 5.

21. For a subtle exploration of the themes of universality vs. localism in the theory of justice, see Sir Stuart Hampshire, *Morality and Conflict* (Oxford: Basil Blackwell, 1983), chap. 6, especially 154–55: "not only may a way of life fail to satisfy the purposes, and to permit the virtues, which it purports to satisfy and to permit, and be internally incoherent; but it may also lead to the destruction of life and to a greater misery and degradation and to gross injustice, as Nazism did. These are always and everywhere considerations that count for evil in striking the balance between good and evil. There are obvious limits set by common human needs to the conditions under which human beings flourish and human

societies flourish. History records many ways of life which have crossed these limits."

22. See note 19 above.

23. I have argued against the revisionary liberal commitment to democratic equality as a fundamental principle of liberalism in my *Liberalism* (Minneapolis: University of Minnesota Press, 1986), especially in chaps. 4 and 8.

24. See Rawls, "Kantian Constructivism," 563.

25. See T. M. Scanlon, "Contractualism and Utilitarianism," in *Utilitarianism and Beyond*, ed. A. Sen and B. Williams (Cambridge: Cambridge University Press, 1982), 103–128.

26. See Rawls, *Theory of Justice*, sec. 42.

27. I do not mean to imply that family life cannot be subject to an illuminating economic analysis. Such an analysis has been attempted, and in some measure achieved, in the work of Gary Becker.

28. The indispensability of market allocation of most factors of production seems to be assumed by the ablest of contemporary analytical Marxists, Jon Elster, in his monumental *Making Sense of Marx* (Cambridge: Cambridge University Press, 1985).

29. For a careful history of the economic calculation debate, see D. Lavoie, *Rivalry and Central Planning: The Socialist Calculation Debate Reconsidered* (Cambridge: Cambridge University Press, 1985).

30. For an argument that much social knowledge is tacit knowledge and only partly articulable, see my *Hayek on Liberty*, 13–16, 21–26.

31. See Lavoie in note 29, above, chap. 1, for an account of the inadequacy of the standard version of this debate.

32. I refer to the papers collected in Hayek's *Individualism and Economic Order* (London: Routledge and Kegan Paul, 1976), especially chapters 2, 4, 7–9.

33. I suggest the un-Marxian character of market socialism in my "Marxian Freedom, Individual Liberty and the End of Alienation," 177–80.

34. See on this James Dorn, "Market, True and False: The Case of Yugoslavia," *Journal of Libertarian Studies* 3 (Fall 1978): 243–68.

35. I have discussed briefly the entrepreneurial aspects of economic decision-making in my *Hayek on Liberty*, 37 ff. For a useful discussion of investment decision-making that takes into full account the Austrian insight into dispersed social knowledge, see Brian J. Loasby, "The Economics of Dispersed and Incomplete Information," in *Method, Process and Austrian Economics*, ed. I. Kirzner (Lexington: D. C. Heath, 1982), 111–30.

36. For an excellent general introduction to public choice theory see James Buchanan and Gordon Tullock, *The Calculus of Consent* (Ann Ar-

bor: University of Michigan Press, 1962). See also James Buchanan and
Geoffrey Brennan, *The Reason of Rules: Constitutional Political Economy*
(Cambridge: Cambridge University Press, 1985), chap. 4.

37. For a brilliant theoretical investigation of the inherent instability
and internal contradictions of market socialism in most, probably all, of
its variants, by an intellectual leader of the Hungarian reform movement, see J. Kornai, "The Hungarian Reform Process," *Journal of Economic Literature* 24 (Dec. 1986): 1687–1737, especially 1726–27: "Lange's
model is based on erroneous assumptions regarding the 'planners.' The
people at his Central Planning Board are reincarnations of Plato's philosophers, embodiments of unity, unselfishness and wisdom. They are
satisfied with doing nothing else but strictly enforcing the 'Rule.'. . . Such
an unworldly bureaucracy never existed in the past and will never exist
in the future. Political bureaucracies have inner conflicts reflecting the
divisions of society and the diverse pressures of various social groups.
They pursue their own individual and group interests, including the
interests of the specialized agency to which they belong. Power creates
an irresistible temptation to make use of it. A bureaucrat must be interventionist because that is his role in society; it is dictated by his situation.
What is now happening in Hungary with respect to detailed microregu-
lation is not an accident. It is rather the predictable, self-evident result
of the mere existence of a huge and powerful bureaucracy. An inherent
tendency to recentralization prevails."

38. It is recognized in both the Austrian and the Virginian schools
of political economy that macroeconomic discoordination may occur
endogenously in the market process. See Gordon Tullock, *The Economics of Wealth and Poverty* (Brighton: Wheatsheaf Books, 1986),
chap. 15.

39. For his insistence that the outcome of the contract is not a Hobbesian modus vivendi, see Rawls, "Justice as Fairness," 247.

40. See Michael Sandel, *Liberalism and the Limits of Justice* (Cambridge:
Cambridge University Press, 1982).

41. I refer to Alasdair MacIntyre's *After Virtue* (London: Duckworth,
1981).

42. On the strength and weakness of Hobbes's psychological theory,
see Elias Canetti, *The Human Province* (London: Picador, 1986), 115–16:
"He [Hobbes] explains everything through selfishness, and while knowing the crowd (he often mentions it), he really has nothing to say about
it. My task, however, is to show how complex selfishness is; to show how
what it controls does not belong to it, it comes from other areas of human
nature, the ones to which Hobbes is blind." See also Canetti's fascinating
study in Hobbesian political psychology, *Crowds and Power* (New York:
Viking Press, 1962).

43. For an illuminating account of Spinoza's political philosophy, see Douglas den Uyl, *Power, State and Freedom* (Assen: Van Gorcum, 1983).

44. I do not suppose that neutrality can be other than a matter of degree in these contexts.

45. The writings of the novelist-philosopher Ayn Rand contain a presentation of an ideal of self-realization through entrepreneurial work.

46. Robert Nozick, *Anarchy, State, and Utopia* (Oxford: Basil Blackwell, 1974), 321.

47. For an interesting argument that neutrality cannot be a fundamental principle of liberalism, but only an implication of a liberal ideal of autonomy, see Larry Alexander and Maimon Schwarzschild, "Liberalism, Neutrality and Equality of Welfare vs. Equality of Resources," *Philosophy and Public Affairs* 16 (Winter 1987): 85–110.

48. I mean to distinguish the Hobbesian conception of no-ownership from the idea of collective ownership. For a useful discussion of collective ownership, see G. A. Cohen, "Self-Ownership, World-Ownership and Equality: Part II," *Social Philosophy and Policy* 3 (Spring 1986): 77–96.

49. Allowing the convenanters knowledge of their abilities, histories, and conceptions of the good, etc., though not their social position, goes far to answering Bernard Williams's objection that contract theory (in the Rawlsian variant most specifically) works with so attenuated a conception of the person as to be entirely indeterminate in its results. See Bernard Williams, *Ethics and the Limits of Philosophy* (London: Fortuna, 1985), 103: "At the end, there is nothing to bring to that question [what the underlying ethical theory might contain] except, once more, the conceptions of what any rational agent as such must reject, and this conception is very indeterminate." Williams's more general argument runs parallel to mine, in that he argues of ethical life (what I argue of political life) that it is only partially theorizable.

50. On this see James Buchanan, *Limits of Liberty: Between Anarchy and Leviathan* (Chicago: University of Chicago Press, 1975), chaps. 1–5.

51. For the argument that maximin could not be chosen by Hobbesian contractors, see the important book by Gregory P. Kavka, *Hobbesian Moral and Political Theory* (Princeton: Princeton University Press, 1986), 196–98.

52. See on this Michael Oakeshott, *On Human Conduct* (Oxford: Clarendon Press, 1975), chap. 2.

53. Kavka, *Hobbesian Moral and Political Theory*, 196–98.

54. I owe much to conversations with Richard Flathman on this point.

55. See on this Jeffrey Paul's important paper, "Substantive Social Contracts and the Legitimate Basis of Political Authority," *The Monist* 66 (Oct. 1983): 513–28.

56. See Gilbert Harman, "Justice and Moral Bargaining," *Social Philosophy and Policy* 1 (Autumn 1983): 114–31.

57. For the argument that Hobbesian theory (contrary to Hobbes's own theorizing) does not mandate political absolutism, see G. Kavka, *Hobbesian Moral and Political Theory*, chap. 5, sec. 5.

58. I owe my understanding of these aspects of Buchanan's work, most particularly, to his paper "The Gauthier Enterprise," to be published in a forthcoming issue of *Social Philosophy and Policy*.

59. Or, as Oakeshott puts it in *Rationalism in Politics* (New York: Methuen, 1962), 127: "In political activity, then, men sail a boundless and bottomless sea; there is neither harbour for shelter nor floor for anchorage, neither starting-place nor appointed destination. The enterprise is to keep afloat on an even keel; the sea is both friend and enemy; and the seamanship consists in using the resources of a traditional manner of behavior in order to make a friend of every hostile occasion."

60. I am indebted to John Rawls for conversation on the subjects of this essay. For their extensive written comments, I am indebted to James Buchanan, Joshua Cohen, Christopher Morris, and Andrej Rapaczynski. I am grateful for comment and criticism to Norman Barry, Gerry Cohen, Stephen Darwell, Ronald Dworkin, John Finnis, Robert Gay, Donald Hay, Jan Narveson, Roland Kley, Steven Lukes, Fred Miller, Robert Sugden, Norman Schofield, Albert Weale and Andrew Williams. Discussions with David Gauthier, Gilbert Harman and Jeffrey Paul have also been important in developing the ideas presented here. Many detailed editorial and stylistic suggestions by John Chapman have helped me to make my meaning clear. For its argument, including its interpretation of Rawls's work, I alone am responsible.

2

THE VAGARIES OF CONSENT: A RESPONSE TO JOHN GRAY

ANDRZEJ RAPACZYNSKI

I understand Gray to be making three points:
1. That political theory in general (and the contractarian method, in particular) is to be understood as a practical inquiry, embedded in the context of particular historical situations and independent of the finding of solutions to the eternal problems of philosophy;
2. That an efficient market economy necessarily entails the institution of private property and is incompatible with socialism;
3. That a market economy (and hence private property) is necessary for a just society—where by "just" is meant derived with the help of the contractarian method—even though such things as the primacy of liberty are not among the prerequisites of a just society.

I have no quarrel with Gray's first claim, concerning the contextual nature of political philosophy. If anything I could make the point more stark and bring out more distinctly its consequences for the method of contractarianism. Thus, while I think Gray is on the right track when he says that a contextualization of the contractarian method makes the results that the method

I would like to thank Rebecca Berlow for her comments on the first draft of this chapter. I also profited from a discussion with John Gray and Joshua Cohen at the annual meeting of the American Society for Political and Legal Philosophy held in Boston in December 1986, and from written comments by J. Roland Pennock.

yields much less determinate, I am not sure whether he realizes how far-reaching a limitation on the utility of contractarianism this entails. Quite obviously, contextualization means that contractarianism, like any other method of political philosophy, does not produce a priori, historical results, valid for all societies and all circumstances. Gray also argues that even when the method is contextualized to the conditions of "constitutional democracies," it still underdetermines the answers to most important political questions (although he believes it suffices to decide in favor of a free-market economy), so that only an actual, rather than hypothetical, political discussion can result in a set of particular norms that give a concrete shape to a political community. But then what *does* the method allow us to accomplish?

It is, of course, an important element of the strategy of moral and political argument to be able to say that one's opponent's views are tainted with self-interest and that justice does not admit of such a taint. It is also a very appealing view that the boundary between coercion and legitimacy involves some notion of consent. Both of these intuitions are deeply embedded in the idea of contractarianism and both are entailed by the Rawlsian "original position." But the broader the scope of the particularistic interest from which we must abstract in considering the issues of justice and the stricter the notion of consent that is seen as entailed by our concept of legitimacy, the less likely it is that anything of interest will follow. This seems true not only with respect to the possibility of discovering any "eternal" truths of political theory, but also with respect to any context-embedded conversations as well. From a certain point on, on the one hand, there is simply not enough to go on and, on the other hand, the conversation is more and more unlikely as a real event. An increase in the level of abstraction very quickly leads not only to a multiplicity of possible solutions, but also to a situation in which the choice of the rules governing the acceptability of any given outcome is itself underdetermined. As consent becomes more and more hypothetical, what one is supposed to consent to becomes either more suspect or more inane.

Not only is the type of rational consensus concerning the basic ideas of justice envisaged by the contractarian method unlikely, but it is also arguably unnecessary. What the contractarian idiom suggests (and this is true not only of Rawls, but also of

Gray's admittedly in part nonliberal contractarian project) is that neutrality with respect to different lifestyles or conceptions of the good is a morally based requirement of political theory. But the idea of neutrality so conceived (as an inherent value, regardless of the actually existing diversity of the conceptions of the good) is quite controversial and probably unnecessary to underwrite the very liberal political theory with which it is usually associated. Liberalism, it seems to me, is not dogmatically committed to neutrality for its own sake, but rather rests on the (quite commonsensical) idea that, in structuring political institutions, we must not base them on those principles about which there is significant controversy, capable of undermining the stability of the social and political regime. Where there is no controversy, on the other hand, there is also no need for further neutrality. (The consensus that defines the absence of controversy is also to be understood as a practical matter—as not enough dissent to create trouble—rather than as that to which every rational agent must agree under any circumstances.) Thus, many matters of justice that are of great moment to us (such as the rules that prohibit a government from invidiously discriminating on the basis of race, extracting confessions by torture, punishing people for being sick, or allowing some citizens to starve) will (in our society, but not in some others) be resolved to most people's satisfaction long before the suspension of our particularistic interests reaches the level of the Rawlsian (or even Gray's) "veil of ignorance." On the other hand, many other issues (such as whether reverse discrimination is appropriate or whether abortion should or should not be allowed) will probably not be resolved for us even if we try to abstract from our particular situation in life (while they may be relatively uncontroversial in other societies). The kernel of truth in the contractarian intuition seems to be that social consensus is a crucial element of legitimacy and that an agreement to disagree is more valuable than a forced orthodoxy. But what the somewhat dogmatic contractarian idea is inherently prone not to appreciate is that the level at which the norms of justice are properly recognized and validated is most likely to differ from one issue to another, and that it is a fundamental element of the art of not only political but also moral discourse to know the appropriate level at which a particular debate is to be conducted. Against this background (which only extends further Gray's own departures from Rawls), I am somewhat puzzled by Gray's claim that private ownership of the means of production and market economy are seen by him as dictated by the most abstract principles of justice, to be arrived at behind the veil of ignorance. Depending on context, the idea of market economy may appear quite uncontroversial or be subject of hopelessly heated debates. But it strikes me as bizarre that one would think the contractarian metaphor useful in deciding about its merits or demerits. As a matter of fact, the great appeal of the idea of the market has always been as an *alternative* to the contractarian approach: the results of a market are supposed to come about spontaneously and to require no conventional agreement. It is because market transactions are thought to be *consensual* that markets are (rightly or wrongly) said to be not only efficient, but also just. To pile up a hypothetical consent designed to legitimize the market in a contractarian fashion on top of the actual consent involved in the market situation is unnecessary for those who believe in the justice of markets and useless for those who don't.

Not surprisingly, therefore, even though I am otherwise quite committed to the idea of a free market, I find Gray's "contractarian" arguments in favor of market economy unconvincing. I will come back to this in a moment. In the meantime, however, I want to address Gray's second point, namely, that markets cannot function in socialist systems. If he means that markets will never function well in what are today called "socialist" states of the Eastern bloc, i.e., in countries in which the ruling elites maintain themselves in power through an elaborate spoils system in which positions of economic power are distributed as rewards for political obedience and support, then I of course agree with Gray, but his claim is uninteresting. If, on the other hand, he means to include every socialist regime within his argument then I think we should inquire a bit deeper into what is meant by "socialism" here.

What Rawls meant by saying that socialist regimes may avail themselves of market mechanisms was that a market system of pricing does not determine a system of wealth distribution a society must adopt. In this sense, Rawls could very well have been talking about such countries as Sweden (or more advanced "socialist" countries of this kind) in which, as we know, markets function quite well, but in which personal incomes are severely circumscribed by a system of redistribution through taxation and provision of social services. To be sure, some system of economic incentives must be preserved in such regimes (and in fact nominally private ownership of most enterprises is also maintained), but it does not have to be anything like the distribution of income that would be produced by a free market.

This is clearly not what Gray means by "socialism." But what he does mean is a bit hard to discover. A (the?) distinguishing feature of socialism for him seems to be the absence of the wage system. In some sense (in which Marx, for example, understood it), the abolition of the wage system is tautologically incompatible with a full sovereignty of market mechanisms; not just because the market is viewed as leading to an unjust distribution of wealth, but also because the very idea of market pricing is viewed as unacceptable. Even a system of market pricing of the kind advocated by Lange[1] is a system in which planners attempt to adjust production to social demand understood as an aggregate of individual preferences—this much seems to be essential to every market system. As long as this is the case, it does not very much matter who makes the actual decision whether to produce widgets or whatchamacallits, since production is supposed to track social demand and the right decision will be the same, whoever makes it. In this context, abolition of the wage system (and the corresponding creation of a system of workers' control) may very well mean that productive choices (and the underlying judgments of social desirability) are not to be left to haphazardly formed individual preferences, but rather are themselves to become collective decisions. If this is so, in turn, that is, if the opposition between socialism and capitalism is based on their opposing views of the relation between individuals and the collectivity, then markets and socialism are clearly incompatible.

Sometimes Gray seems to rely on this kind of conception of socialism, since he often appears to assume that every socialist economy must involve an element of central ideological planning. Insofar as he makes such an assumption, Gray is again making an essentially trivial point: planning and free market cannot at once govern the same aspects of economic production. But at other times, Gray seems to be operating with yet another

conception of socialism. Unlike the (Marxist) view just presented, Gray assumes the individualist position as his starting
point, and seems to view the abolition of the wage system as
merely a change in factory ownership, so that factories become
worker-owned partnerships.[2] I don't want to be taken for a
proponent of such a system—it doesn't seem to me better than
other systems of property, since I don't see why the fact of
employment is any more a just source of ownership than the
fact of management, investment of life savings, inheritance, and
scores of other factors. I also agree with Gray that it leads to a
lot of inefficiencies and generational injustices. But I still fail to
perceive why a system of this kind cannot have an efficiently
functioning market for capital. For some reason, Gray seems to
believe that capital is different from other goods, so that the
same solution as in the case of factories (ownership by the
employees of a bank) does not seem to be sufficient for him
here: I take it that the ownership of capital must be collective in
some broader sense. So let's assume state ownership indeed. But
as Gray himself acknowledges, state ownership of banks is not
incompatible with decentralization and running them on a competitive basis. Having granted the point, however, Gray tries to
take it back without providing any new arguments, and simply
falls back on the idea that a truly free market for banking must
somehow "unravel" the rest of the socialist economy. The logic
of all this escapes me. After all, banks do not function in anything like an unregulated manner in most capitalist economies,
and in some of them they are indeed nationalized. Nor do they
function with anything resembling flawless efficiency, as indicated by their disastrous lending practices in developing countries in the 1970s or the need for state bailouts in the 1980s.
Undoubtedly, socialist banking systems run on a market model
would have their own problems and require periodic intervention as well. The ineptitude of government officials, be they of
socialist or capitalist states, is quite well known, so there is no
doubt that such intervention is often likely to do as much harm
as good. But other than Gray's own ipse dixit, I see no a priori
argument why a socialist state must be at a systematic disadvantage here, as compared with other politico-economic regimes.

Be that as it may, Gray's point that a socialist state could not
avail itself of efficiently functioning market mechanisms for

allocating its productive resources is, by itself, of secondary importance. More basic is his contractarian argument for the *justice*, as opposed to mere efficiency, of markets. I said already that the argument strikes me as fatuous. For those who believe that market transactions are essentially consensual, so that in the absence of externalities, they always lead to states that are Pareto-superior to the states that precede them, the contractarian argument seems quite unnecessary. Clearly, if we have *actual* uncoerced consent of all the parties affected, we have no need of any hypothetical one. Those, on the other hand, who are not persuaded that the consent of a market participant is always (or most often) free (even given some reasonably "just" initial distribution of resources) or that we can ever conceive of a market which entails no serious external effects on nonparticipants (especially if the worsening of one's relative position in society is deemed to be relevant) will be utterly unpersuaded by any contractarian embellishment of the old argument from consent. After all, the contractarian consent is merely parasitic on the actual one here, for if you believe that a worker's consent to a wage relation is merely Pickwickian and does not change the fact of his brutal exploitation, you will never believe that it would be rational for most people to agree to the institution of a market system without knowing that they would not end up among the exploited.

Gray's own argument involves exactly this fallacy of *petitio principii*. First, his contractarian method assumes a conception of human person that seems to be at least as controversial as the idea of the free market that it is supposed to support. To be sure, Gray's exposition of his theory of human personality is so schematic and undeveloped that it is hard to see what it really entails. But judging from his reference to Hobbes and Spinoza, Gray seems to view man as an essentially self-sufficient entity, not "radically situated" but rather autonomous and independent in forming his own individual life plan, a calculating maximizer for whom social interaction is a matter of choice rather than necessity. I doubt very much that the idea of political individualism needs a grounding in such a strange construct as the Hobbesian natural man (even if for Gray he is no longer "natural" but rather a projection of our own historically contingent selves), but if it does then woe to political individualism, since the idea seems so far removed from any reality recognized by anthropologists, psychologists, or even philosophers that it is likely to be much more controversial than any other idea (including that of the free market) that is to be derived from it.

Second, Gray is even more puzzling when he says that the social contract among individuals endowed with those characteristics of autonomy with which Gray's theory endows them would not contain the idea of liberty but would involve an establishment of a free market. The explanation seems to be that liberty, for the man Gray contemplates, would be just one value among others, and the contracting parties would not want to preclude the possibility that they might want to trade it for such things as increased security, peace, or greater prosperity. Now, maybe I am missing something, but I fail to see why the same argument would not hold with equal force about the free market: in some situations, most rationally maximizing people might come to the conclusion that a centrally regulated economy would lead to so much more power, security, prosperity, liberty, or whatever else they happen to value that they would gladly trade for them their preference for an unrestricted choice among a number of ways in which they could conduct their "productive enterprises." If anything, such a trade-off seems to be more, and not less, likely than the trade-off of one's basic protections against political tyranny for material prosperity. (That I disagree here with Gray also goes to show, once again, how controversial is his conception of the person upon which the whole edifice of his contractarianism so precariously rests.)

Third, Gray's argument about the neutrality of the free market with respect to various ideals of productive life seems to me grievously flawed. Gray claims that markets are neutral with respect to opposed ideals of productive life because they allow those who prefer individual private ownership to run their enterprises on that basis, whereas those who prefer communes or cooperatives can have those. I take it, however, that the justice of the market derives not only from the freedom of choice possessed by the various owners of "productive enterprises," but also from that possessed by the people who are employed in them. Thus, if it were to turn out that the workers employed in capitalist enterprises are in fact not really free to choose their occupation and if, in addition, it were to turn out that they are seriously exploited (in some sense of "exploitation" that would be reasonably uncontroversial), then Gray's hypothesis of the neutrality of the market with respect to various ideals of productive life would be shown to be groundless. Now, it should be clear that this is precisely what many socialists (and other critics of capitalism) have claimed all along, and I do not see any arguments that Gray has to offer against them (other than assuming them out of existence). To be sure, I do not want to sound as if I set great store by the standard Marxist theses, such as that workers are systematically afflicted with false consciousness or that individual preferences under conditions of market competition are effects of exploitative and brutalizing conditions of life under capitalism. It seems to me clear, however, that if you don't believe in any of these theories, you will never need Gray's contractarian argument, and if you do, Gray is mistaken if he thinks his contractarian method will do anything to convince you.

But even without such fundamental disagreements with the very notion of consent underlying Gray's account of market transactions, it is difficult to take seriously his claim that the market is really neutral with respect to different ideals of productive life. To begin with, some forms of "productive life" may simply be less efficient than others, and it is not immediately clear why they should not be subsidized. It might be said, of course, that the consumer of a product should be given a right to buy it at the lowest available price and that it would be wrong to force him to pay more in order to maintain someone else's productive preferences. But this simply amounts to saying that justice does, after all, track the concept of efficiency, rather than requiring a system in which different modes of productive life can genuinely coexist. This idea is not just controversial; it is quite probably false. It seems to me more than likely that persons in the original position would believe that the cultural diversity connected with various traditional ways of life is sufficiently valuable to require them to subsidize, say, the inefficient fishing methods of the Alaskan Eskimos, the weaving methods of the Navajo Indians, etc., none of which could be done without abandoning a dogmatic commitment to the free market. In fact, in accordance with my previous remarks, it seems to me that most people in America today are prepared to agree to these propositions even without leaving their present personae in favor of the vapid contractors in the "original position."

I will not, however, insist on a subsidy for inefficient modes of production, but will look instead at the alleged neutrality of the market from a somewhat different angle. Many modern proponents of the free market (Gray among them) seem to believe that market failures are a rather marginal phenomenon. I suppose, however, that most people opposed to capitalism (especially those who claim that exploitation of some social groups or classes is a foundation of the capitalist system) would be in one way or another committed to the argument that the free market ultimately fails to produce a level of aggregate welfare comparable to some other systems and that this failure dooms it on efficiency grounds as much as it makes it otherwise unacceptable. The reasons for that failure are often not stated in economic terms, but translated into the language of economics, they amount to the inability of the market to provide important public goods and the ability of the capitalists to impose external costs on the rest of society.

The latter kind of argument is most likely to be made by the most economically minded opponents of the market. Marxist socialists, who might say that the capitalist economy involves a creation of a significant "army" of the unemployed and that the capitalist who benefits most from the operation of the market can in this way "externalize" some of the costs of his operation (both by being able to pay his workers less than the full value produced by their labor and by making the rest of society share in bearing the burden of providing for the destitute and the unemployed). This makes the goods produced by a capitalist enterprise less expensive than the goods produced by a socialist one, which would be committed to ensuring that the workers enjoy the full fruits of their labor. Thus, even on the assumption that all the workers would rather work for socialist enterprises (and thus are not victims of false consciousness), the viability of the socialist enterprises would still require that the *consumers* of goods produced by them be prepared to pay for the fact that these goods are produced with the help of nonexploitative means. But even if we assume this as well, it would still make no sense for an individual consumer to pay more for goods produced by socialist enterprises, unless there were some means of coordinating the actions of all the similarly minded consumers as a group and of overcoming the free-rider problem that will otherwise pose insuperable obstacles for their collective aims. A comparison with the problem of child labor comes to mind here, since goods produced by exploited workers may be as much cheaper as goods produced by underpaid children. Not only is constant reliance on people's moral virtue (which in no society is in overabundant supply) required in order to limit the demand for goods produced by exploited labor, but also no individual's sacrifice (in the form of the higher price paid for "clean" products) significantly contributes to the overall goal of the elimination of the evil in question, and thus all have an incentive not to adhere to their ideological preferences, even if they would otherwise be willing to pay the higher price for having the evil eliminated. Thus, in the same way as child labor could only be abolished by legislation operating uniformly over the whole relevant market, the elimination of capitalist exploitation may require a similar collective decision.

That some special enclaves of ideological consumers, such as the Amish, have been able to persist in their withdrawal from the market despite all these disadvantages does not change very much here, for the price paid by these consumers (in terms of their life standard as well as submission to a system of communal controls necessary to counteract the otherwise irresistible incentive to free-ride) may simply be too high for an average person. Consider, in fact, someone committed to the Amish way of life. This person would most likely say that the environment in which an average American lives is spiritually impoverishing and that only by integrating his productive activities into an all-embracing, religiously inspired, communal way of life can man's dignity be restored. Translated into the language of economics, the objection of the Amish can be reformulated as follows: The operation of the capitalist economy requires the availability of a mobile labor force that, in turn, destroys the bonds of tradition. These bonds are of great value to an individual, but they are a quintessential "public good" and their preservation is possible only if very high coordination costs are borne by the community and a large number of people are made to resist the impersonal operation of the market. As it happens, the Amish, perhaps because of the low value they put on material prosperity, are

willing to pay the price of creating a separate autarchic society
that can protect their members from the temptations of the
market. But other groups, for whom a radical lowering of the
life standards necessary to preserve the social bonds differen-
tiating them from the capitalist world is not as easily acceptable,
have no chance of protecting themselves from extinction.[3]

Finally, even Gray himself seems not to take very seriously his
claim that the market is just because it allows for various forms
of productive life to coexist. After all, before coming to his
neutrality argument, Gray devotes a whole section of his chapter to the argument that market economy requires private ownership of capital and that any other form of capital allocation
must lead to crippling inefficiencies. Since the market is certainly not neutral with respect to efficiency, far from allowing
the noncapitalist forms of production to survive, it will merci-
lessly eliminate them. Gray may (and does) say, of course, that
efficiency is not itself a morally relevant characteristic, and thus
he may also maintain that the market does not discriminate on
moral grounds. But this does not make the moral neutrality of
the market any different in principle from that of the revolutionary struggle for survival (in which the good may be good
but the strongest never fail to win) or that of the market for
money (in which the most debased coins are bound to push out
the more honest ones).

All this is not to say that Gray is wrong that markets are just,
or at least more just than other systems of distribution. It might
also be that the successes of the market economy are now so
obvious that its proponents do not really have to defend it. But
if they do, they will have to address such issues as the voluntari-
ness of market transactions involving underprivileged members
of society, the problem of false consciousness, and, above all,
the pervasiveness of market failures in modern economies. Gray's
method of avoidance, on the other hand, is *too* successful: it
misses the issues that are truly decisive.

NOTES

1. Oscar Lange, "On the Theory of Socialism," in *On The Economic
Theory of Socialism*, ed., Benjamin E. Lippincott (Minneapolis: University
of Minnesota Press, 1938), 57–104.

2. That someone like Rawls essentially adopts the point of view of individualism is quite understandable, given that the main target of his attack was utilitarianism. But the very idea that one can successfully argue against *socialism* by simply assuming the point of view of individualism strikes me as odd.

3. Gray could perhaps reply at this point that if capitalist enterprises indeed involve serious external costs, the state could tax them to cover the value of any such externalities, thus equalizing the chances of capitalist and noncapitalist entreprises. In theory this would be possible, of course. In practice, however, the externalities involved here would be extremely hard to measure, and their very existence is denied by most admirers of the market economy. The differences between those who argue on both sides of the issue go to the very foundations of economic science, such as the basic theory of value for example, and their resolution is precisely what is at stake in the dispute between the proponents and the opponents of market economy. Without implying anything about who is ultimately right, I only want to argue that the resolution of this dispute cannot come through a simple device of the contractarian methodology.

3

CONTRACTUALISM AND
PROPERTY SYSTEMS

JOSHUA COHEN

John Gray's chapter, "Contractarian Method, Private Property, and the Market Economy," contains these principal theses:

1. For reasons of *efficiency*, private property in the means of production is mandated by Rawls's two principles of justice.[1]

2. Private property in the means of production is required as a matter of *justice*. This is so because Hobbesian contractarianism—which provides the most plausible account of justice[2]—requires neutrality among "productive ideals," and only a system with private ownership of capital is appropriately neutral.[3]

3. Apart from requiring markets and the private ownership of capital, a Hobbesian contract theory is largely indeterminate. It does not, for example, mandate political democracy, or the protection of liberties of thought and expression, and is consistent with a wide range of distributional principles, though emphatically not with the Rawlsian maximin principle.

In responding to Gray, I will focus primarily on the first two theses. Before turning to that response, I should emphasize one important limitation to it. In my not very idiosyncratic view, the central arguments for socialism are arguments about democracy —about the limits on democracy imposed by the private ownership of capital, and the possibilities of expanding democracy that might follow on the abolition of the private ownership of

I would like to thank Joel Rogers and John Chapman for helpful suggestions on earlier drafts of this paper.

capital.[4] Correspondingly, the main arguments against socialism aim to show that it is not an implication of or even a plausible extension of democratic commitments. As his third thesis indicates, however, Gray is not committed to democracy. He counts "political equality and democratic participation" among the "recent and, arguably, peripheral features" of "the Western individualist tradition." He does not discuss the implications of democratic commitment for the organization of the economy. Since I confine myself here to responding to the considerations that Gray does advance, I will not pursue those implications either. But the consequence of this restriction is that I will not be discussing the issues that are, I think, at the heart of debates about socialism.

I. Market Socialism: Background

In *A Theory of Justice* Rawls claims that his two principles of justice can be satisfied by either capitalist democracies or democratic, market socialist systems. Gray rejects Rawls's claim about market socialism, and proposes Thesis 1 in its place. I find the reasons offered in defense of Thesis 1 wholly unpersuasive. As background to explaining why I find them so, I will begin with a few remarks about a democratic form of market socialism. Like Gray's remarks on this subject, my discussion inevitably combines large elements of stipulation and speculation, not least because no such forms exist. But some account is needed as a supplement to Gray's, which is both excessively abstract and highly tendentious.

Since Thesis 1 addresses an issue *internal* to Rawls's theory, the appropriate characterization of market socialism must be attentive to both of Rawls's principles of justice. Specifically, we assume a set of background political arrangements that provides protection for basic political and civil liberties, that secures a fair value for the political liberties, and that provides fair equality of opportunity. Thus we assume, inter alia, the rule of law, competing political parties, public finance of education, inheritance taxes, and the full employment and dispersal of resources.[5]

Embedding a market socialist economy in this scheme requires a system of enterprises satisfying the following conditions:

1. The enterprises are *worker-managed.* Final authority is in the hands of workers, who may choose to delegate the exercise of that authority to managers. All and only the workers in the enterprise have voting rights concerning the operations of the firm—including what to produce, how much income to invest and how much to distribute as wages, what the distribution of earnings should be, whether to expand the scale of operations, how to organize the work itself, etc.

2. The enterprises are *publicly owned,* and leased to worker cooperatives. While enterprises can trade assets with other enterprises, the workers in the enterprise are barred from selling its assets to supplement their incomes.

3. Apart from taxes and interest payments on loans from the state, no one outside the firm has any claim on enterprise income. The only source of external finance for enterprises are state banks and development funds, and the aggregate level of finance is a political decision made by constitutionally designated, elected officials.[6]

Several elements of this sketch will figure in the discussion later on, and so I want briefly to highlight them.

First, that an enterprise is worker-controlled implies very little about its internal organization beyond the fact that it is to be determined by workers.[7] The size of the enterprise, the degree to which authority is delegated to managers, the extent of cooperation in the organization of work itself, the distribution of enterprise earnings, etc., could all in principle vary considerably across worker-controlled enterprises.

Second, the political system is not comprised solely of a bureaucracy that provides finance to firms. It also includes political parties, a legislature, courts, etc. So there is no justification for treating the state bank in a market socialist democracy as a monopolist with no limits on its power to set economic policy.

Finally, there are many alternatives between the arrangements I have just described and a system of "full liberal ownership" in which all capital is privately owned. There are, for example, endless varieties of a "mixed system" in which firms that are publicly owned and worker-managed exist alongside capitalist firms, as well as systems in which enterprises are cooperatively owned.[8] Indicating the difficulties with particular forms of market socialism, then, should not be confused with providing a case in favor of full liberal ownership.

II. EFFICIENCY AND MARKET SOCIALISM

With this background, I turn to Thesis I. I will begin by restating it in a way that locates more precisely the proposed challenge to Rawls's view: Given a market socialist system, it is reasonable to expect that an alternative arrangement based on private property in the means of production would improve the well-being of the least well-off.[9] Gray offers several considerations in support of this thesis, and here I will respond to two, a minor and a major consideration.

The minor argument is that worker-managed firms do not generate as much employment as capitalist firms do, because the former aim to maximize "profit" per worker while the latter aim to maximize aggregate profits.[10] As a consequence, an economy composed of worker-run firms is likely to feature higher levels of unemployment than a system with private ownership, and thus work to the disadvantage of those who are less well-off. But even if we assume that Gray has the right view about worker-run firms, nothing follows about the level of employment in a market socialist economy. That level is a function of at least two factors—the employment policies of firms and the number of firms. Employment for the less well-off could be expanded by easing the entry of new firms, for example by making finance available on favorable conditions.[11]

Gray's major argument concerns the determination of interest rates in an economy with no capital market: I will refer to this as the "Vienna-Virginia argument." According to the Vienna-Virginia argument: (V1) in the absence of a capital market in which shares in firms are traded and in which finance is raised from non-state lenders, the state bank will lack the information required for fixing the rate of interest in a way that promises an efficient allocation of investment; and (V2) even if the bureaucrat-bankers had the information, they could not be trusted to fix interest rates in an allocatively efficient way. Taking the two points together, (V3) we can expect greater "waste, malinvestment, and discoordination" than in a private property scheme. Gray acknowledges that "the imperfect coordination of economic life is an inevitable consequence of limitations in human knowledge." Still "a decentralized system will promote coordination, and eliminate errors in decision-making, better than a centralized system could." Drawing on (V3), Gray holds that Rawls's difference principle requires private ownership of the means of production, since the efficiency gains that result from such a scheme can be expected to improve the condition of the least well-off.

This argument has at least four problems.

First, let us assume with Gray that the shift in property system reduces "waste, malinvestment, and discoordination," and increases per capita GNP. It does not follow that the least well-off could reasonably expect their condition to improve, or that they could expect the new arrangement to protect fair equality of opportunity, or the fair value of political liberty. In particular, the less well-off might expect that the shift in property systems would increase the inequality of pre-tax/transfer distribution of income and wealth, and that the state would not be able to mitigate the consequences of that increased inequality. Thus the increase in per capita GNP might be associated with a worsening of the material circumstances of the less well-off. And even if increased inequality were materially beneficial to them, they might expect that the greater material inequality would undermine fair equality of opportunity and fair value of political liberties. Gray's remarks about the efficiency gains following on "full liberal ownership" fail even to acknowledge familiar sources of scepticism about the equitable distribution of those gains.

Second, income and wealth are not the only primary goods whose distribution is regulated by the difference principle; powers and positions of authority are covered as well.[12] In moving from the market socialist system with worker-run firms to the capitalist system, the less well-off might well lose power and positions of authority (in the firm), even if they gained in income and wealth. The difference principle properly understood does not, therefore, mandate the capitalist arrangement, even if there is uniform material improvement, and no other loss of liberties or opportunity. The switch would be inefficient in respect of the non-material components of the difference principle, and this might serve as sufficient reason for rejecting it.

Third, interest rates are deeper economic waters than I feel comfortable in. But it is not clear to me why (V1) is true, that is, why the absence of capital markets deprives policy-makers of the information required for setting reasonable rates of interest. In particular, it is not clear why the state bank would be in an essentially worse position than monetary authorities, budget-makers, or policy planners in capitalist systems. They would have some information concerning growth rates, capacity utilization, and past responsiveness to changes in interest rates. Citizen preferences would be revealed—however imperfectly—through representative institutions. If the government sold bonds to raise revenue, it would have information about time preferences. Of course, all of this information is very imperfect. But then so is the information transmitted by capital markets, and so is the information available to central banks and budgetary planners in capitalist democracies. Perhaps Gray thinks that, because of these imperfections, central banks in capitalist democracies should operate on fixed rules, or that there ought to be constitutionally balanced budgets. I will return to this speculation below.

Fourth, Gray's defense of (V2)—that bureaucrat bankers cannot be trusted to do what is correct, even if they know it—is weakened by the lack of institutional structure in Gray's account. Gray treats the state bank as, in effect, a monopolist in setting economic policy.[13] But as I indicated earlier in the discussion of market socialism, there is simply no justification for this assumption. Bureaus operate in complex institutional environments. In the case of a state bank in a democratic market socialist system, the institutional environment would include political parties and legislative committees. In the absence of an analysis of this institutional setting, including the information available to the different actors and the oversight powers of legislative committees, nothing specific can be said about the actions of such a bank. Furthermore, anything that might be said in general terms about the untrustworthiness of banker-bureaucrats can equally well be said about state officials in capitalist democracies.

In responding to Gray's Vienna-Virginia argument, I have suggested that there are important parallels with respect to information and trustworthiness between officials in capitalist democracies and in (hypothetical) democratic, market socialist systems. Gray would not, I think, wish to deny these parallels. He would, I think, allow that everything I have said about them is correct, and that this just serves to underscore the common sources of "waste, malinvestment, and discoordination" shared by socialist systems and interventionist, welfare states.[14] But if he did allow this, then he would be conceding that his efficiency argument has nothing in particular to do with socialism. He could with as much justification have argued that Rawls's difference principle requires a "non-interventionist" state with no stabilization, transfer, and distributional functions. But if he did, then he would owe us an account of the mechanisms for ensuring distributional equity. In the absence of such an account—and there certainly is none in either Vienna or Virginia—we are back in the business of assessing alternative politicized economies, and nothing that Gray says begins to address the question of which of these is best suited to the Rawlsian theory.

III. JUSTICE AND PRIVATE PROPERTY

I turn now to Thesis 2, that considerations of justice mandate private property in the means of production. Gray supports this by arguing that a just system must be neutral among different "productive ideals," and that such neutrality is achieved by a private property system but not by a market socialist system.[15] In response, I will first challenge the claim about the neutrality of private property systems, then qualify the claim that market socialism is non-neutral, and finally suggest that insofar as market socialism is non-neutral among productive ideals, this is not an important objection to it.

In support of the claim that systems with private property are neutral among productive ideals, Gray appeals to the fact that, roughly, individuals in these systems can form "worker's cooperatives or communes" if they want. Since private ownership "permit[s] individuals to use their resources to express their own ideal (whatever this may be)," it is neutral. This is weak support. Private property systems now all prohibit production based on slavery. In this respect at least they are not neutral among productive ideals, even if we follow Gray and confine ourselves to a formal conception of neutrality that "requires only that the legal and institutional framework of society does not favor any one ideal over any other." But for the purpose of evaluating the justice of basic institutions, neutrality ought not to be interpreted in formal terms. If we do not, then a variety of ways emerge in which private property systems appear to be biased against more cooperative ideals of productive association:[16]

1. Resource constraint. Forming enterprises requires resources. Productive ideals, like all ideals of the spirit, must be made flesh. Those who want to form cooperatives and are resource-poor may lack the resources to advance their associational ideal.

2. Collective action constraint. For reasons that are familiar from the theory of collective action, it is easier for single individuals or small groups to start firms than it is for larger groups, particularly when the larger groups are resource-poor. As a result, it may be easier to start a firm and hire labor than to form a cooperative.

3. Financial constraint. While access to finance can overcome initial resource disadvantages, cooperatives that are unwilling to sell voting shares to non-members are very likely to be at a competitive disadvantage. In particular, because of their unwillingness, they may need to borrow at especially high interest rates, or to pay unusually large dividends on nonvoting shares. And this imposes special burdens on their operations, making it difficult to compete with capitalist firms.[17]

4. Managerial constraint. It might be that, as a consequence of the historical absence of cooperatives, people who would prefer to work in them lack the managerial skills required for running them, those who have the managerial skills would prefer not to work in them, and private property systems do not help to overcome this disadvantage.[18]

Determining the importance of these and other potential sources of bias in private property systems, of course, requires empirical investigation, and the assessment of alternative explanations of the relative scarcity of more cooperative forms of work organization. Williamson, for example, argues that more hierarchical forms of productive organization exist because they are more efficient, in particular because they economize on transactions costs.[19] But the bearing of Williamson's important efficiency argument on the present argument is marginal, for two principal reasons. First, if capitalist hierarchy is the most efficient form of productive organization, it does not follow that a system of private property is neutral in the relevant sense. Instead, private property systems might be non-neutral precisely in that they exhibit an unwarranted bias in favor of productive efficiency, and against such competing values as autonomy or community. Second, Williamson classifies both capitalist firms in which capitalists themselves hire labor (the "Authority Relation," in his terms) and democratically organized, cooperatively owned firms ("Peer Group" organizations) as hierarchical. He argues that both forms of hierarchy are considerably more efficient than non-hierarchical, cooperatively owned firms in which there is no worker specialization (the Communal Every-Man-for-Himself form). But the efficiency advantages of the Authority Relation over Peer Groups are much less clear, even on Williamson's own argument.[20] In view of this, it is at least premature to opt for the organizational efficiency explanation.

Returning to the main issue, then, it is reasonable to doubt on the claim that the existence of private property is by itself *sufficient* for neutrality. Now, some of forms of non-neutrality I have indicated might be mitigated in a system with private property, by, for example, a more equal distribution of resources; others (e.g., problem (3) concerning finance) might require more complex measures. But all cast doubt on the force of Gray's assertion that private property brings neutrality in its train.

What about market socialism? In what way is it non-neutral? It is true that in such a system "one form of productive enterprise—that involving wage labor—is prohibited." But then, as I noted earlier, a similar point could be made about private property systems: One form of productive enterprise—that involving slave labor—is prohibited. So in respect of formal neutrality, the systems are on a par. To pursue the question of substantive neutrality, I want to refer to an earlier point about market socialism—that the details of enterprise organization are not fixed by the fact it is worker-controlled. As a consequence, a wide range of productive ideals—small/large, centralized/decentralized, cooperative/atomistic—may appear and flourish within this order. In principle at least a diversity of associational ideals are consistent with market socialism. In respect of substantive neutrality, then, the case is unclear, and not at all advanced by Gray's analysis.

That private property and market socialism regimes are each non-neutral suggests what may seem a natural solution to the problem of neutrality. There ought to be a "mixed system" with two sectors: the first composed of worker-managed, publicly owned firms, the second of capitalist firms that hire labor. The state would then aim to advance the goal of neutrality among productive ideals by seeking to preserve a balance between the two sectors. Preserving a balance would likely involve measures designed to address the several problems of bias enumerated earlier. There would, for example, need to be measures designed to maintain a fair distribution of wealth, to facilitate enterprise formation among groups of interested individuals, and to subsidize interest repayments for cooperative firms to ensure that they are not at a competitive disadvantage.[21]

But suppose that a mixed system is unstable, or that the state is unable to do what is necessary to preserve it, or that people in the cooperative sector hold the view that the private sector is unfairly imposing on them longer working hours and more intense labor than is consistent with preserving democratic enterprises. Would it be objectionable to eliminate the private sector? I do not see why, and certainly do not think that considerations of neutrality ought to guide the judgment, in part for resaons that I have already suggested. We now outlaw slavery. This is non-neutral among productive ideals, but unobjectionable. Democratic states all impose associational ideals by outlawing vote selling, and not requiring citizens to buy their rights. If these measures are non-neutral among associational ideals, then once again non-neutrality is unobjectionable. The U.S. Constitution contains a "republican form of government" clause, thus rendering the constitution non-neutral on the ideal of political self-government. If, then, in the name of advancing a recognized and firmly rooted ideal—that is, the ideal of democratic association—a market socialist system ruled out the "productive ideal" of wage labor, then it is not at all clear why that would be more troubling than any of the restrictions just canvassed.

In this last set of remarks, I have appealed to the ideal of a democratic association. In response to that appeal, Gray might argue that I have missed the point of the remarks about the contractual method that comprise a large part of his essay. According to Gray, the pluralism of values that marks our condition renders Hobbesian contractualism the appropriate theory of justice for contemporary circumstances. But Hobbesian contractualism treats democratic association as simply one among several forms of sovereign authority—and, in Hobbes's own view, as the last among equals. So we should not regard democratic order as a matter of fundamental principle, and should not appeal to this ideal in assessing forms of economic organization.

But an alternative conclusion seems more plausible. If it is true that Hobbesian contractualism construes democracy as simply one political option, then we have good reason for thinking that Hobbesian contractualism is an inadequate interpretation of "our historical circumstance." In particular, we have good evidence that Hobbesian contractualism does not provide an adequate rendering of the notion of equal citizenship—itself the product of the more than three hundred years of social and political struggle, institutional development, and cultural transformation since Hobbes wrote his *Leviathan*—and that it is this feature of Hobbesian contractualism that lies at the roots of the agnosticism about a democratic state. Once we find Hobbesian contractualism an unsatisfactory point of departure for political argument, however, we will land back in the intrademocratic disputes that I referred to earlier concerning the forms of property that are suited to a democratic order—and I promised to stay away from them in responding to Gray.

NOTES

1. Gray makes several additional descriptive claims about market socialism—e.g., that it is not stable, and for this reason is not "ultimately" a genuine alternative to a "command economy" or a private ownership regime. Much that he says in his analysis of the alleged inefficiency problem does not engage the details of Rawls's principles. I have focused on Thesis 1 because it is the only point that is both argued in the chapter and consistent with its stated aim of providing "immanent criticisms" of Rawl's view.

2. Gray cites James Buchanan's work—e.g., *The Limits of Liberty*—as an example of a contractarian theory of justice in the Hobbesian tradition. This rests, I believe, on confusion. Focused on Pareto-improvements from an initial state of anarchistic equilibrium, *The Limits of Liberty* is not about *just* distributions, but simply about the importance of *some*

initial distribution of rights for the functioning of markets and political institutions. On Buchanan's view, the notion of fairness is central to an account of just distributions. See James Buchanan, *The Limits of Liberty: Between Anarchy and Leviathan* (Chicago: University of Chicago Press, 1975). For discussion of the common misinterpretation of *Limits of Liberty,* see James Buchanan, "Rules for a Fair Game: Contractarian Notes on Distributive Justice," in *Liberty, Market, and the State: Political Economy in the 1980s,* ed. James Buchanan (New York: New York University Press, 1985), chap. 12.

3. In his account of the justice of private property, Gray actually offers two arguments, one from neutrality, another from the "minimal egalitarianism" of the Hobbesian view. But the notions of neutrality and equality deployed by Gray are virtually interchangeable, and the arguments from neutrality and equality are, as far as I can tell, virtually indistinguishable. I see no substantive loss from focusing on neutrality alone.

4. On socialism and democracy, see, among many others, V. I. Lenin, *State and Revolution,* in *Selected Works in Three Volumes,* by Lenin, vol. 2 (Moscow: Progress Publishers, 1970); Rosa Luxemburg, *Reform or Revolution* (New York; Pathfinder, 1970); Karl Kautsky, *The Dictatorship of the Proletariat* (Ann Arbor: University of Michigan Press, 1964); Michael Walzer, *Radical Principles: Reflections of an Unreconstructed Democrat* (New York: Basic Books, 1980), chaps. 15, 17; Joshua Cohen and Joel Rogers, *On Democracy* (New York: Penguin, 1983); Robert A. Dahl, *A Preface to Economic Democracy* (Berkeley: University of California Press, 1985); Samuel Bowles and Herbert Gintis, *Democracy and Capitalism: Property, Community, and the Contradictions of Modern Social Thought* (New York: Basic Books, 1986).

5. For a full discussion, see John Rawls, *A Theory of Justice* (Cambridge: Harvard University Press, 1971), chaps. 32–38, 41–43.

6. That is, in addition to a restriction on voting rights to firm members, we also stipulate that there is no market in nonvoting shares, and that there are no private financial intermediaries who loan money to firms and who earn interest on such loans.

7. Here I follow the discussion in Louis Putterman, "On Some Recent Explanations of Why Capital Hires Labor," *Economic Inquiry* 22 (1984): 171–72.

8. For discussion of mixed systems, see Richard Krouse and Michael MacPherson, "A 'Mixed'-Property Regime: Equality and Liberty in a Market Economy," *Ethics* 97 (Oct. 1986): 119–38. For recent discussion of cooperative ownership, see David Ellerman, "On the Labor Theory of Property," unpublished, 1983; Dahl, *Preface to Economic Democracy,* pp. 140–52. Others have argued for a system of worker-run firms with a market for nonvoting shares. See, for example, Michael Barzelay and Lee R. Thomas, "Is Capitalism Necessary: A Critique of the Neoclassical

Economics of Organization," *Journal of Economic Behavior and Organization* 7 (Sept. 1986): 225–33.

9. Gray's actual formulation is this: "Indeed, the covenanters will be compelled to adopt a private property regime if, as is suggested by my argument, the Difference Principle minimum *achievable* under capitalist institutions is higher than that *achievable* under market socialism" (emphasis added). But this is too weak for Gray's purposes, and so I have taken the liberty of reformulating the thesis. The issue is not the "achievable" minimum under different institutions, but the minimum that the least well-off could reasonably expect to achieve. Suppose that the achievable minimum under capitalist institutions is higher because those institutions maximize wealth. It is still possible that those who are less well-off would not expect, in the normal operation of capitalist institutions, to reap the benefits of the increased wealth.

10. For discussion and criticism of this theory of labor-managed firms, see Frank H. Stephen, "The Economic Theory of the Labor Managed Firm," in *The Performance of Labor-Managed Firms*, ed. Frank H. Stephen (New York: St. Martin's Press, 1982), chap. 1; Branko Horvat, *The Political Economy of Socialism: A Marxist Social Theory* (New York: Sharpe, 1982), chap. 12.

11. And also through state employment policies. See Dahl, *Preface to Economic Democracy*, 122 (and references).

12. See Rawls, *Theory of Justice*, 97.

13. For criticism of analyses of bureaus as policy monopolists, see Gary Miller and Terry Moe, "Bureaucrats, Legislators, and the Size of Government," *American Political Science Review* 77 (1983): 297–323; Terry Moe, "The New Economics of Organization," *American Journal of Political Science* 28 (1984): 765–72. In his discussion of competing investment banks, Gray appears to acknowledge this point. But inspection of his argument about the dependence of the banks on central political authority shows otherwise.

14. I do not mean to be conceding the thesis about waste, etc., and do not think that we will get anywhere on this question by comparing the performance of idealized systems with perfect capital markets with unidealized alternatives.

15. I am skeptical that neutrality is an important virtue of social systems, and not at all certain that it plays a central role in liberal political conceptions. For the purpose of addressing Gray's argument, however, I have put these considerations to the side.

16. For further discussion of the points that follow, see Bowles and Gintis, *Democracy and Capitalism*, 79–87; John Roemer, "Property-Relations and Surplus Value in Marxian Exploitation," *Philosophy and Public Affairs* 11 (1982): 306–9; David Miller, "Market Neutrality and the Fail-

ure of Cooperatives," *British Journal of Political Science* 11 (1981): 309–29; David Gordon, "Miller on Market Neutrality, Cooperatives, and Libertarianism," *British Journal of Political Science* 13 (1983): 325–28; Louis Putterman, "Some Behavioral Perspectives on the Dominance of Hierarchical over Democratic Forms of Enterprise," *Journal of Economic Behavior and Organization* 3 (1982): 139–60; Putterman, "On Some Recent Explanations of Why Capital Hires Labor"; Richard Krause and Michael McPherson, "A 'Mixed'-Property Regime: Equality and Liberty in a Market Economy," *Ethics* 97 (Oct. 1986): 119–38; Jon Elster, "Comments on Krause and MacPherson," *Ethics* 97 (Oct. 1986): 146–53; Horvat, *The Political Economy of Socialism*, 455–56; Barzelay and Thomas, "Is Capitalism Necessary."

17. For more detailed discussion of the financial constraint, see Bowles and Gintis, *Democracy and Capitalism*, 85–86; Putterman, "On Some Recent Explanations," 184–86; and Oliver E. Williamson, *The Economic Institutions of Capitalism: Firms, Markets, Relational Contracting* (New York: Free Press, 1985), 266–67.

18. For discussion of the managerial constraint, see Putterman, "Some Behavioral Perspectives," 157–58.

19. See Williamson, *The Economic Institutions of Capitalism*, chap. 9.

20. Williamson derives the overall efficiency ranking of different forms of organization by first providing dichotomous scores for the forms on eleven dimensions, and then summing the scores. Using this method, the Authority Relation is scored at 9, Peer Groups at 8, while Communal Every-Man-For-Himself receives a 4. This procedure obviously involves considerable simplification, and not much can be concluded from the aggregate scores. For example, peer groups perform better than capitalist hierarchy on the dimension of eliciting innovations from workers, while capitalist hierarchy is superior on the dimension of assigning people to suitable tasks. If we believe that the capacity of systems to elicit innovations from workers is more important to their efficiency than their capacity to assign people to suitable tasks—a judgment that plays no role in a scheme of unweighted summations of dichotomous scores—then the peer group form might turn out at least as efficient as capitalist hierarchy. Furthermore, some of the scoring on individual dimensions seems unmotivated. Thus, Williamson supposes that peer group and capitalist hierarchies share common problems of eliciting intensive work. It is not clear why this is so as a general matter. He also supposes that peer groups and hierarchical capitalist firms are both able to respond to shocks. But it is not at all clear why peer groups are not more responsive. For discussion of "shock responsiveness" see Charles Perrow, "Economic Theories of Organization," *Theory and Society* 15 (1986): 11–45.

21. See Krause and McPherson, "A 'Mixed-Property' Regime," 132–33.

PART II

CAPITALISM AND JUSTICE

4

A CONTRACTUAL JUSTIFICATION OF REDISTRIBUTIVE CAPITALISM

GERALD F. GAUS

1. CONTRACTUALISM, PROPERTY, AND THE STATE OF NATURE

Contractualist political theory reveals two competing accounts of the relation between property, the state of nature and the social contract. Locke and contemporary Lockeans such as Robert Nozick maintain that exclusionary property rights characterize the state of nature, and the main end of government is to secure them. "The great and *chief end* . . . of Men's uniting into Commonwealths, and putting themselves under government, *is the Preservation of their Property.*"[1] Although some recent interpreters would have us believe that Locke did not uphold private property rights in the state of nature and saw private property in civil society as conventional or based on consent,[2] I think this is to miss the real contribution of Locke to the natural law tradition; in contrast to the earlier theories of Grotius and Pufendorf, Locke justifies exclusionary property rights without any appeal to consent or compact.[3] In Lockean theory property rights are morally prior to the social contract that justifies government. Indeed, the main end of government is to secure these rights; consequently, Lockean governments clearly are in no position to attack private property. Although Lockean govern-

A version of this chapter was presented at the 1987 meeting of the Australasian Association of Philosophy. I would like to thank Julian Lamont, Christine Swanton, and Robert Young for their comments and criticisms.

ments will recognize a right to charity, they will not be strongly redistributive.[4]

Rousseau presents a different picture. In the state of nature one can possess but not own. Genuine property, not simply occupation but a right of ownership, characterizes our departure from the state of nature, and can only be justified by the social contract.[5] For Rousseau, then, property cannot be antecedent to political society; indeed, "the State, in relation to its members, is master of all their goods by the social contract."[6]

Whereas Lockeans insist that property rights are morally prior to the social contract and so place limits on the contractual agreement, for Rousseau no such limits exist. Consequently, those who are critical of capitalism and favor extensive redistribution are apt to adopt the Rousseauean view;[7] people are free to organize production and define ownership in any way they deem appropriate without being constrained by natural rights to property.[8]

I aim to show in this chapter that we need not, indeed cannot, simply choose Locke or Rousseau. The Lockean case is partially successful: we do possess a right to property in the state of nature that the social contract must respect. But, properly understood, this right also presupposes that the state, through the social contract, has extensive authority to redistribute property. The justification of exclusionary property rights and the market presupposes the justification of the redistributive state.

I make extensive appeal to the idea of the state of nature. Many may find this implausible. Contractual arguments are, to be sure, in vogue again, but state of nature accounts are more suspect. " 'Tis often asked as a mighty Objection, *Where are*, or ever were, there any *Men in such a State of Nature?*"[9] One of my aims is to demonstrate that the classical contractualists, as well as contemporary theorists like James Buchanan and David Gauthier,[10] rightly see the state of nature as an essential part of contractual justification. Unlike Locke or Rousseau, however, I do not see it as an historical state, and unlike Buchanan, I do not depict it as a condition of moral anarchy. Rather, my claim is that the state of nature is a necessary phase in moral justification, what I will call the *deontological basis*. Upon this deontological basis contractual theory develops a *constrained teleological* argument.

I begin in sections 2 and 3 by showing why contractual justification must employ both these phases. Section 4 then argues that the deontological basis includes a quasi-Lockean account of property rights, while section 5 shows how the full justification of these property rights requires a contractual argument justifying redistribution.

2. CONTRACTUALISM AND PUBLIC JUSTIFICATION[11]

Contractualist political theory can be understood as advancing two theses: (1) individuals are devoted to their own valuings, projects, etc., and these only provide what Derek Parfit and Thomas Nagel call *agent-relative* reasons for action,[12] and (2) political institutions are justified by appealing to the agent-relative values of each member of the public.

2.1. The Agent-Relativity of Value

The agent-relativity of value-based reasons to act is well illustrated by Hobbes's theory. Hobbes's individuals are moved solely by self-interest, and self-interest is a paradigm of an agent-relative reason to act. For a reason to be agent-relative, it must necessarily refer to the agent for whom it is a reason, that is, *"R is a reason for person P."* So, in Hobbes's state of nature, each pursues his own interest, and his interests do not necessarily provide anyone but himself with a reason to do anything. But self-interest is by no means the only sort of agent-relative reason. Indeed, what are often called "subjectivist" theories of value typically assert that all values, ends, goals, projects, etc. generate only agent-relative reasons for action. If, then, Alf loves Betty, this provides him with reasons to act in various loving ways toward Betty; but the mere fact that Alf loves Betty does not in itself provide Charlie with any reason at all to act in such ways or to help Alf secure Betty's love. So (roughly) thoroughgoing agent-relative accounts of value-based reasons assert that *V* (be it love or money) provides a reason for Alf to act only if Alf values *V*.[13]

So the task of a contractual theory is to show that this agent-relativity of value-based reasons to act somehow provides the basis for a set of rules that can regulate the actions of all. Notice how this problem evaporates if value-based reasons are *agent-*

neutral.[14] An agent-neutral reason is a reason for anyone (although some may be so situated as to be unable to act on it). If, then, Alf's pain provides an agent-neutral reason to alleviate it, *everyone* has a reason alleviate Alf's pain. According to Nagel, agent-neutral reasons "represent the values of occurrences, acts, and states of affairs themselves, not their values *for* anyone."[15] Now if all values provide agent-neutral rather than agent-relative reasons to act, then if Alf rightly values *V*, not only Alf, but everyone else, has a reason to promote *V*, assist Alf in procuring it, or whatever. But this means that, essentially, we all are aiming at the same goal: that is, the maximization of agent-neutral value.[16] So the core contractualist problem—how to generate a common set of rules from the diversity of individual goals—is replaced by a very different problem—how best to organize social life so that our common end—maximizing agent-neutral value—is best achieved.

2.2. Public Justification

Contractualist theory posits a situation in which individuals, aware of their diverse ends, agree on a set of social and moral principles. But more than that, one accepts the terms of the contract *because* it advances one's ends. That is, given one's agent-relative (but not necessarily self-interested) values, one has good reason to embrace the terms of the contract. So understood, the contractualist's proposal is striking: rather than seeing the diversity of individual ends and their essential agent-relativity as obstacles to a social and political morality, the contractualist insists that this diverse set of values can *generate* a common morality.

A contractual justification can be described as a *constrained teleology.* Michael J. Sandel suggests that we understand teleology as "a form of justification" in which first principles are derived in a manner that presupposes "final human purposes or ends."[17] Now our usual understanding of teleological justification—call it unconstrained teleology—assumes agent-neutral values. The unconstrained teleologist justifies basic principles of right by showing that they best advance what each and every person has reason to value. But when teleological justification is conjoined with agent-relative value, the result is rather different. For each has different values generating a different set of reasons to act: the teleological justification endeavors to show that the values of each can be advanced by a proposed arrangement. Alf's arguments in favor of an arrangement will be teleological (e.g., "Arrangement *A* advances value"), but his arguments will be constrained by the need to show that *A* promotes the agent-relative valuings of others, valuings that he may not share.

The justificatory force of a social contract argument is the claim that, given their agent-relative values, everyone is provided with good reasons for accepting the proposed social and political arrangement. We can say, then, that the contract asserts that the arrangement is *publicly justified* in so far as everyone has good reasons for embracing it. Consequently, the role of the consent device in contractualist theory need not be to show that, somehow, political obligation is voluntaristic. Rather, consent seems best understood as a heuristic device for demonstrating that the proposed arrangement is publicly justified: all rational agents would accept it.

This suggests an alternative interpretation of contractualism, one that leads away from fixation on consent and toward a notion of the common good. A social and political arrangement is publicly justified if from each and every valuational perspective the arrangement promotes what is rationally seen to be of value. Given the agent-relative concerns of each, a social and political arrangement is justified on the grounds that it advances a common good. By a "common good" I mean simply that a publicly justified arrangement will be one that works to the advantage of all in the sense that it promotes what each values.[18] A set of principles sanctioned by such a good (1) promotes some good (thought not necessarily the same good) from every valuational perspective and (2) takes everyone into account, and does not sacrifice any individuals to an aggregate or collective welfare.

3. VALUE AND DEONTOLOGY

3.1. The Incompleteness of Teleology

It is difficult to overestimate the attraction of teleology. To most philosophers, it is obviously the only sensible approach to ethics. "It is certainly a doubtful compliment to the right," said Ralph

Barton Perry, "to deny that it does not of itself do good." [19] Even contractual justification is at bottom teleological, although it is a constrained form of teleology demanded by the agent-relativity of value reasons. I now want to advance a crucial, and I suppose controversial, claim: The existence of a deontological morality is presupposed by our values. This being so, the philosophically popular project of a thoroughgoingly teleological justification of morality—be it constrained or unconstrained—is implausible.

All teleological justification presupposes that value is prior in justificatory argument to principles of right. Teleology, that is, requires that we can (1) identify the set of things that are of value and then (2) apply the maximization function that (3) generates moral judgments/principles of rightness and wrongness. For this project to succeed, the set of valued things identified in (1) cannot logically presuppose the validity of judgments of rightness or wrongness. That is, if some value V is only rationally sound given the validity of moral principle M, the teleologist cannot know whether V should be included in the set of values to be maximized until he knows whether principle M is sound. But if that is so, the teleologist cannot apply the maximization function until he has determined on some other grounds whether principle M is sound. Before the pure teleological project can begin, the validity of M must be determined on nonteleological grounds; and that seems to mean that the project fails before it can begin.

Many of our most important valuings are morality-based in this way. Consider, for instance, friendship. What Kant called "moral friendship" is "the confidence of two persons in revealing their secret thoughts and feelings to each other." [20] And, as Kant realized, this requires that one must be able to trust one's friend not to reveal these confidences to others. More generally, a friend must be confident that the other will take his view into account; Alf supposes that Betty will treat him with due consideration and respect and will resist any temptation to use or exploit the friendship to promote her aims and projects. Moreover, friends must trust each other in these ways even though they realize that the other has various projects and aims, some of which may be more important to the friend than the friendship. Unlike lovers, who may be able to suppose that the other values nothing so much as the beloved, and so no other values or aims could be more weighty in practical deliberation, friendship does not rest on such intensity. Yet friends do trust each other; if they are friends, Alf knows that Betty will not sacrifice him even if *all things considered,* Betty could advance her cherished projects by doing so. This is possible because friendship is informed—so deeply informed that it is easily overlooked—by notions of respect and fairness.

I have focused on perhaps a less than obvious example of a morality-grounded valuing. But more straightforward examples can be proffered: indignation at having one's body violated, resentment at having one's property taken without one's consent, outrage at the unjust treatment of minorities.[21] All these reactions seem to constitute disvaluings of states of affairs premised on the assumption that they are wrong. But if they are not wrong, or if we have no good reason to trust friends to be fair regardless of the benefits of duplicity, then the corresponding valuing or disvaluing is unsound. It is based on a false belief about rightness or wrongness. If these valuings and disvaluings are irrational, it seems that they cannot be included in the value maximization calculation. The teleologist somehow needs to filter his value inputs, but it would seem that to filter his value inputs he needs to be able to determine the rationality of their moral basis; but how can he do that until he has received the output of his calculations?

One way he can do so is to allow everything through the filter, that is, not filter at all. The teleologist may claim that the problem of the rationality of values grounded on moral principles can be put aside: if Alf values Betty's friendship, then it is a value to be taken account of in the maximization function even if it turns out that Alf's valuing is based on false beliefs. This apparently was R.B. Perry's view.[22] So it will make no difference that Alf's valuing Betty's friendship is based on his belief that she is a kind and considerate person who wouldn't hurt a flea, even though she is really a sadistic murderess, and if Alf knew this the friendship would quickly die. But as long as the friendship (or Alf) is not yet dead, the value is to be included in the maximization function. This goes far beyond the claim that value-based reasons are agent-relative to endorse, at least in the context of ethical justification, a strong sort of "subjectivism."[23]

If Alf values *V* (or "prefers" it), no matter how irrationally, it is to be included in the maximization calculation. But if, as contractualists do, we understand justification as a reason-giving activity, then whatever he may think, if it is irrational for Alf to value Betty's friendship, then he has no more good reason to endorse a social system that promotes this friendship than does a paranoid to endorse a social system that responds to his fantasies.[24]

A second, more typical, maneuver among constrained teleologists is to restrict the common good argument to a set of values that do not presuppose moral principles. Kurt Baier, for example, recognizes a wide range of value judgments as reasons for action, yet his justification of the moral enterprise focuses on advancing self-interest. That is, although Baier explicitly rejects egoism and its claim that self-interest alone moves agents,[25] he nevertheless concludes that "Hobbes' argument is sound. Moralities are systems of principles whose acceptance by everyone as overruling the dictates of self-interest is in the interest of everyone alike. . . ."[26] So for Baier the range of values that enter into the justification of morality is properly limited to self-regarding considerations. Baier is not at all unique in this regard. Gauthier appeals to only non-tuistic valuings,[27] while James Fishkin tells us that a personal plan of life—which he takes as fundamental in justification—is a "constellation of private-regarding wants and courses of action," that is, it concerns getting and doing things for oneself rather than others.[28]

Examples could be multiplied.[29] Basic to all these approaches is the aim of limiting the relevant values in justification to those that concern the agent's own welfare or interest. Under the influence of this way of thinking liberal ethics and political philosophy becomes based on a sort of self-centeredness, and indeed of a fairly radical sort. If all appeal to moralized values is to be avoided, then friendship, and I think some sorts of love, our moral outrage at being treated as mere things, our indignation at cruelty, all must apparently be excluded. And if, as seems likely indeed, these values ground yet others, affecting what jobs we prefer, our social life, and even our valuing of leisure activities, the set of values upon which justification focuses may be limited and not very significant as far as some of us are concerned. To be sure, such limitation makes the justification of liberal institutions more straightforward, but it is no less objectionable for that.[30]

3.2. Deontological Justification

If our value systems presuppose moral principles, an adequate contractual justification will not be simply a constrained teleology. The right cannot be simply defined as that which advances the good of all, for conceptions of right inform conceptions of the good. Teleological justification presupposes deontological justification. Before we can propose institutional arrangements that advance the values of all we must determine whether the fundamental moral principles upon which our value systems rest are justified.

Contractualism is a doctrine about what can be publicly justified: It seeks to show how the agent-relativity of values gives rise to agent-neutral moral principles. So it is not enough for Alf to show that some principle *M* is the bedrock of his value system. If it is not the bedrock of anyone else's value system, Alf has not shown others that they too are committed to *M*. Consequently, the deontological phase of contractualist justification will consist of an analysis of the contractors' value systems with the aim of uncovering those shared, deep moral commitments upon which all their valuational perspectives depend. If such common moral commitments are uncovered, a foundation is provided for subsequent teleological argument. Those valuings that presuppose these shared commitments, as well as those that have no moral presuppositions, can reasonably provide the basis for teleological justification.

4. The State of Nature

4.1. Natural Rights and Duties

A description of the state of nature can be interpreted as articulating the deontological foundation on which the constrained teleological argument, that is, the social contract, builds. An alternative would be to allow two sorts of argument in contractual "negotiation," arguments as to the basic moral principles we all agree upon, and arguments about what social arrangements advance the values of everyone. But this would obscure the logical priority of the deontological foundation. The claim isn't simply that deontological and teleological arguments are distinct, but that the former sets the stage for the latter by grounding some values and not others, as well as by constraining the set of possible outcomes.

In Lockean theory natural rights and natural law provide the deontological foundation; they are not justified by the social contract, but possess independent moral justification and, indeed, provide the basis for contractual negotiation. Locke, of course, essentially restricts the contract to establishing a mechanism for protecting these morally prior rights; neverthless, we must remember that the Lockean legislature is empowered to advance the public good, subject to the constraint that it does not violate natural rights, that is, rights that are morally prior to the social contract.[31] In any event, the point is that an adequate contractual theory will include two types of justificatory argument: (1) a deontological argument articulating the shared moral presuppositions of the contractors' value systems and (2) a constrained teleological argument that describes a set of moral and social principles (or a type of social arrangement) that advances the values of everyone. The first argument constitutes a description of the state of nature. It is far beyond the scope of this chapter to defend any complete description of the state of nature; very plausible, I think, are the duties of truthfulness,[32] promise-keeping[33] and fidelity to friends.[34] For our concerns, however, three rights are of particular interest: (1) the right to liberty; (2) the right to property, and (3) the right to exchange holdings.

4.2. The Basis of the Right to Natural Liberty

Consider what Locke called man's "Natural Freedom." An agent is not by nature subject "to the Will or Authority of any other Man."[35] Locke says that all men are naturally in "a *State of perfect Freedom* to order their Actions . . . as they see fit . . . without asking leave, or depending upon the Will of any other Man."[36] This starting point embodies the moral supposition that each of us is free to do as he wishes unless a justification can be advanced for restricting that freedom. That is, the claim to natural liberty provides a point of departure for all further ethical and political justification, providing a presumption against interference and placing the onus of justification squarely on those who would limit liberty. Once established, it follows that all further justificatory ethics and political philosophy becomes a defense of *liberty-limiting* principles, duties, etc.[37]

The right to natural liberty articulates a basic moral assumption of all *self-directed agents,* an assumption that can be denied only by a sort of self-destructive act. To see what a self-directed agent is, consider a contrasting sort of agent. Clifford Geertz has described Balinese social life as "at once a solemn game and a studied drama."[38] What is especially fascinating is that the main emotion helping to induce compliance with the demands of this drama isn't guilt or shame, but *lek*—a worry that one will not be able to play one's parts "with the required finesse."[39] Writes Geertz: "What is feared—mildly in most cases, intensely in a few—is that the public performance that is etiquette will be botched, that the social distance that etiquette maintains will consequently collapse, and that the personality of the individual will then break through to dissolve his standardized public identity."[40] The worry is that one may end up revealing an individualized self rather than stereotyped social role. The social roles that define personality are designed to prevent the emergence of individuated selves. As Geertz notes, this leads to an illuminating paradox: "Balinese conceptions of personhood . . . are—in our terms anyway—depersonalizing."[41]

Those acquainted with Western analyses of personality will no doubt note the basic contrast: Western analyses typically identify the person with the individuated self. This reaches an extreme in the work of Carl R. Rogers, where achievement of personhood is identified with removal of masks and roles that prevent the emergence of "the real self underneath."[42] But the focus on the self or the autonomous ego as the core of personality is hardly unique to Rogers; indeed, it is central to a large body of personality theory.[43] It even informs Erving Goffman's work. Like Geertz, Goffman employs the dramaturgical method, depicting social interactions as a series of performances. But despite the surface similarity in method, Goffman's analysis is different. Roles and performances allow us to direct and shape our self-images and plans, but they are not stereotyped scripts designed to prevent the possibility of self-revelations.[44] We might say that in Western pluralistic societies, personhood is expressed through the available cultural resources, but it is not itself conceived as a cultural artifact.

Let us use this contrast to develop two ideal types. For a *role-*

directed conception of the person agency is directed by culturally defined roles that are not devices or expressions of the self. In contrast, a *self-directed* person conceives of agency as expressing the self, whether this requires overcoming roles (Rogers) or employing them (Goffman). I now proceed to my main claim: while a role-directed person can reject the right to natural liberty, a self-directed person cannot.

Consider the role-directed person. Prima facie, it seems plausible that role-directed persons might all be committed to the principle:

RD1:   All interferences with the performances of another must be justified.

This would seem akin to the right to natural liberty: just as self-directed persons would object to any interferences with their self-directed activity, role-directed persons would object to any interferences with the performance of their roles. Of course, even RD1 falls significantly short of the right to natural liberty, as it only concerns interferences with one's role; however, it seems at least roughly analogous. But RD1 incorporates a presumption that action should reflect the intentions of the agent unless it interferes with others. Are role-directed agents committed to that presumption? Consider:

RD2:   All action must be justified by reference to the appropriate script.

This principle is free of the asymmetry of the right to natural liberty: not only interferences, but all action, must be justified by the relevant script. This principle embodies no presumption that activity should rightly flow from the self. Yet is seems appropriate for role-directed personalities; if the danger is that individuated selves may emerge, it is no less important that noninterfering action be justified by reference to the appropriate stereotyped script. Activity is not to reflect the self but must conform to the self-containing scripts presented by the culture. Given this view of the relation between the self and action, the right to natural liberty seems out of place.

The right to natural liberty articulates the basic moral outlook of self-directed agents: activity rightly expresses the self. A self-directed agent who rejected the right would be committed to allowing that another may take control of his activity, and this would be no cause of indignation. The self as director of action would be replaced by another self: one's activity becomes, strictly speaking, the expression of an alien self. Without complaint of wrongdoing, and in the absence of any justification, the self would allow another to supplant it as the source of action. But a self-directed agent will resist this: The foundation of his conception of himself is that *his* activity is properly at *his* beck and call. For another self to subvert this tie and interpose itself between an agent's self and activity threatens self-direction, hence one's status as a person. The fundamental demand of self-directing contractors will be that no one intervene in this intimate relation between the self and its activity without justifying the intervention to the self.

4.3. Quasi-Lockean Property Rights

If we focus on the right to natural liberty, Rousseau's position seems vindicated: Possession, but not exclusionary property rights, characterize the state of nature. To see this, say Alf picks up an acorn in the state of nature. Is it his? It seems plausible to maintain that the right to natural liberty would—in some circumstances at any rate—protect Alf in his possession of the acorn. At least in some cases it is certain that objects are an intrinsic part of one's ongoing activity; to wrest possession of them surely constitutes an interference with the agent's activity. And, according to the right to natural liberty, it is incumbent upon Betty to justify interventions to Alf. So the right to natural liberty can secure Alf in his possession of the acorn.

But this reasoning cannot be extended from possession to ownership. Quite the contrary: The right to natural liberty is an obstacle to justifying ownership. Let us assume that Alf is cultivating, and constantly occupying a small piece of land, such that it is reasonable to depict him as in possession of it. He then makes the proclamation that Rousseau saw as momentous: Alf asserts that the land is his, even when he is not in physical possession of it.[45] He owns it. But this is to assert that others are excluded and cannot enter, and that implies interference with their actions. The essence of ownership is to restrict the liberty of others vis à vis that which is owned; and, according to the right to natural liberty, any such exclusionary claim must be justified to those others. So the argument for the right to natural liberty does not lend itself to a transition from possession to ownership. The right provides a foundation for continued possession but an obstacle to claims to ownership.

If the right to natural liberty were the sole moral constraint in the state of nature, Rousseau's position would be unassailable: turning possession into property could occur only through the social contract. But I have emphasized that the description of the state of nature is determined by those shared moral convictions that underlie our diverse value systems, and so can include a range of rights and duties. Here Lawrence Becker's reconstruction of the Lockean argument is relevant. Becker alters the labor theory of property in a way that makes claims of desert fundamental. The "notion of desert," Becker claims, "is a constituent of morality *per se*."[46] The crux of Becker's thesis is that the concept of deservingness is a deep presupposition of the moral enterprise itself. People who act wrongly deserve blame, those who act in a worthy manner deserve praise. "To ask whether desert is an intelligible concept," says Becker, "is to call into question the whole enterprise of passing moral judgment on people for their conduct."[47] Notice that Becker's argument is precisely of the sort required if principles of desert are to be included in the description of the state of nature: that is, that the moral enterprise itself—hence all our morality-grounded valuings—presupposes the validity of desert claims.

Some have charged that, at best, all Becker shows is that reward or praise, punishment or blame, can be deserved for moral or immoral acts.[48] But I think this is to miss the point. Becker's point—and it seems to me reasonable—is that our morality presupposes the sensibility of moral statements of the sort:

> D: Alf deserves X because of some act A that Alf has performed.[49]

That is, the notion of classifying people as deserving or undeserving because of some previous act of theirs is not a notion we are free to accept or reject: our morally-informed outlook commits us to it.

The question then becomes in what ways the variables X and A are filled out. Becker believes that one deserves benefit (X) for adding value (A) to the lives of others. Hence, he says, the "following principle must be sound by definition: A person who, in some morally permissible way, and without being morally required to do so, 'adds value' to others' lives deserves some benefit for it."[50] Becker insists that it is necessary that benefit accrue to others: "Deserving a benefit for producing something which only you profit from is a strange notion."[51] Becker thus advocates grounding desert on *contribution* rather than *effort;* given the difficulties with accounts of desert based on effort this seems advisable.[52] But care needs to be exercised. Consider the following two principles of desert:

D1: Alf deserves X because Alf has produced X.

D2: Alf deserves X because Alf has contributed to the productive process and X is a suitable reward.

Becker—and this is probably the dominant position—sees D2 as the fundamental desert principle of economic systems and economic justice. Alf deserves X as a reward for contributing to the collective productive effort. But the intuition behind D1 is rather different, although the two are typically confused. David Miller, for instance, writes: "If we consider a state of nature, such as that constructed by Locke, we shall see how plausible is the view that when men produce in isolation from one another, and with land and raw materials in plentiful supply, they each deserve to retain whatever they can make by their own labour."[53] Miller depicts this desert claim as an instance of D2 (contribution); but if *contribution* to the *social productive process* is the ground of the intuition, why (as Miller rightly points out) is the intuition strongest under the assumption of isolated asocial production? The Becker-Miller account of the state of nature, I venture, is not really tapping D2 at all, but the different intuition that a person deserves what he produces or, as it used to be put, "the fruits of his labor." It seems to me misguided to suppose that this intuition is to be reduced to a reward for contributing to the lives of others. The point is different and more basic: production of X constitutes the grounds for deserving X. Pace Becker, you undoubtedly deserve what you have produced for yourself without benefiting anyone else, and it would be wrong to take it from you without justification.

That the two desert principles are typically confused is readily understandable. When people are engaged in joint productive enterprises, both D1 and D2 may sanction distribution to each according to his marginal product. According to D2 Alf should get a reward commensurate with his marginal product because this is a fitting reward for his contribution to the joint endeavour; according to D1 it is an effort to arrive at some determination of what *Alf* has produced. Miller is right that in joint enterprises determining what Alf deserves is far more difficult than in Locke's state of nature, since what constitutes the "whole product of his labour" is far more difficult to determine.[54] But this in itself testifies that it is really D1 (production) rather than D2 (contribution) that he has in mind, for contribution requires proportionate rewards but not necessarily the "whole product of one's labor."

A quasi-Lockean property right exists in the state of nature if three things are true: It must be the case that the concept of desert is universally embraced in the state of nature. If, as I think is reasonable, the notion of desert is indeed basic to the moral endeavor, desert claims would be acknowledged prior to the social contract (that is, they are part of the deontological foundation). Secondly, it must be the case that valid desert claims provide moral reasons to act. If Alf can show Betty he deserves X, he has provided Betty with (say) a reason to refrain from taking X, even if taking X would better promote Betty's values.[55] Additionally, it must be true that a self-evidently sound desert claim is that someone who produces something deserves to use and control it (within, to be sure, specific limits). Put simply, a worker deserves (in some sense) the fruits of his labor.

As Becker is well aware, justifying property rights via deserving the fruits of one's labor is very much in the spirit of John Stuart Mill. "Private property, in every defence of it," said Mill, "is supposed to mean the guarantee to individuals of the fruits of their own labour and abstinence."[56] But, Mill added:

> When the "sacredness of property" is talked of, it should always be remembered, that any such sacredness does not belong in the same degree to landed property. No man made the land. It is the original inheritance of the whole species. . . . It is no hardship to anyone to be excluded from what others have produced: they were not bound to produce it for his use, and he loses nothing by not sharing in what otherwise would not have existed at all. But it is some hardship to be born into the world and to find all nature's gifts previously engrossed, and no place left for the newcomer.[57]

If we embrace Mill's reasonable claim that no one deserves the land—or any natural resource—the desert/labor theory of property seems undermined. For if the original appropriation of a natural resource—that is, exclusionary rights over it—cannot be justified via desert, it would seem almost all subsequent desert-based property claims are undermined. Say Alf takes possession of a tree, cuts it up and claims desert-based exclusionary rights over the chair he produces. But Betty objects that he has no exclusionary rights over the tree in the first place; he never justified to her a restriction of her liberty vis à vis the tree. To this Alf may perhaps reply that he has mixed his labor with the tree, and if he deserves the fruits of his labor, he also has claims over that in which his labor is embodied. But as far as I can see, Betty need not accept this. Alf's labor on the tree may be very much like Nozick's tomato juice in the ocean: by dumping it in what was not his, he loses his labor/tomato juice, rather than gaining exclusionary rights over the tree/ocean.[58]

The intuitive appeal of desert-based theories of property begins to evaporate when we squarely face the problem of exclusionary rights over natural resources.[59] The typical response of Lockean-inspired theories is some sort of quasi-Lockean "proviso" that justifies taking resources out of the "common pool" when this does not worsen the position of others.[60] And this in turn leads to complicated compensation proposals or unconvincing arguments that Alf's extensive exclusionary right over natural resources is never to the disadvantage of Betty, who has no such rights.[61] These problems arise because whatever the stated intentions of later theorists, they follow Locke in conceiving of the state of nature as, somehow, a condition in which people can exist, if only in our imagination. As Locke said of the fruits of the earth, "there must of necessity be a means to appropriate them some way or other before they can be of use, or at all beneficial to any particular Man."[62] If desert grounds property rights, then we need some account of how these desert-based rights could function in the state of nature. After all, if they could not, the inhabitants would starve! But the state of nature is but a phase in justificatory argument. The proper response to the problem of "original acquisition" is indicated by Mill: "The essential principle of property being to assure all persons what they have produced by their labour and accumulated by their abstinence, this principle cannot apply to what is not the product of labour, the raw material of the earth."[63] Desert-based property rights, then, cannot (to any significant extent at any rate) come into being until the problem of acquisition or distribution of natural resources has been solved, and for us that will require appeal to the social contract. In the state of nature, then, people have a right to a system of private property that recognizes labor/desert as a grounding of title.[64] But because acquisition of natural resources requires contractual justification, no significant particular property rights yet emerge.

4.4. The Market in the State of Nature

Mill believed that "all the reasons that recommend that private property should exist" also recommend that one should be able to alienate it, including free gifts and bequests.[65] But this isn't obvious. If one gives away property that you deserve to another, it doesn't follow that he deserves it.[66] And even market transactions—which involve a trade of goods rather than free gifts—aren't necessarily sanctioned by desert-based arguments for property. If Alf deserves X, and so it is his property, and Betty deserves Y, and so it is hers, nothing follows as to the justifiability of exchange. Can voluntary exchange somehow transform the situation such that Alf now deserves Y and Betty X? It seems fairly obvious that a system of free exchange does not necessarily assure to each person just what he or she deserves.[67]

The problem is that market transactions pass on exclusionary rights. But it is by no means obvious that they pass on deservingness. If Alf had exclusionary rights over X because he produced X, and so deserved to own it, how can he pass on these rights to Betty, who did not produce it, and so, according to D1, does not deserve to own it? And it will not do to reply that Alf's desert-based right conjoined with his natural liberty is sufficient to justify exchange; at issue is not simply Alf's right to engage in an act with Betty, but his power to pass on exclusionary rights. The problem seems to illustrate Nozick's point that a pattern such as "to each according to his deserts" will be upset by free exchange.[68] To see our way clear of this difficulty we must first distinguish two economic desert claims:

   DJ: Alf has a property right over X if and only if he deserves X.

PR: Alf's production of *X* grounds his desert-based exclusionary right over *X*.

The first is a desert-based conception of distributive justice; it
insists on a pattern according to which each gets what he deserves. So Betty's possession of exclusionary rights over something she does not, *ex hypothesi*, deserve is excluded by DJ. But I
haven't endorsed this principle of distributive justice; I have
argued for a desert-based property right (PR) according to which
Alf deserves *X* because he produced it. So I have not endorsed
any pattern that must be maintained in the interests of justice.

Now there is certainly no logical bar to holding both (1) that
Alf rightly possesses *X* because he has performed act *A*, and (2)
he can engage in some relation with Betty that passes on to her
X even though she has never *A*-ed. For instance, Alf might be
warranted in believing in Tasmanian tigers because he (and he
alone) has seen one; but he may engage in a relation with Betty
whereby she comes to have a warrant for believing in the existence of Tasmanian tigers, even though she has never seen one.
So there is nothing crazy in thinking that desert-based property
rights might be transferred without their grounds being transferred as well. But is there any reason to think that such a right
of transfer is justified by the desert-based account of property
rights? Of three plausible bases for property rights in the state
on nature, I want to argue, the desert-based account alone
presupposes the intuitive notion of "ownership," including rights
of transfer.

Consider first contribution-based justifications (D2) à la Becker.
On this view property rights are a reward for contribution to
the social productive process. Leaving aside the tendency of this
to collapse into a theory of distributive justice (DJ), it at best
only contingently sanctions a right to transfer holdings. A reward or honor is not intrinsically transferable; although a down-
and-out actor may sell his Oscar he cannot sell his award for the
best actor of 1926. To be sure, in order to render rewards more
beneficial to the recipient we may allow them to be exchanged
for other goods, but nothing intrinsic to the concept of reward
for contribution demands that this should be so. Loyal members
of the Party may be awarded a dacha, but it may well be counterproductive to allow them to transfer it to others.

The second contrast is to a needs-based account of property.
Say, following Locke, one of the arguments for property is that

God created mankind to flourish, and this means that men *need* private property.

This can easily lead to pretty severe limits on alienation.[69] If people's needs are not always better advanced by alienation, then rights of transfer will not always be justified. Such considerations often lie behind provision in kind, rather than in cash, of welfare.

The argument I advanced in section 4.3 supports a more direct intuition that people deserve to own what they have produced. Ownership is not a reward for contribution or a way to satisfy needs; ownership of what one has produced is, in a very basic sense, fitting and appropriate.[70] And because my account points to this more direct tie, it supports appeal to something akin to what has been called "full ownership"—certainly it supports rights to possess, use, manage, consume, transfer, and destroy.[71] Conjoined with the argument for natural liberty in section 4.2, this constitutes a defense of market relations. For, given (1) that Alf has exclusionary rights over X such that it is his, and (2) Betty has exclusionary rights over Y such that it is hers, (3) that each has rights of transfer in relation to their property, as well as (4) their intention to exchange X and Y, then (5) Charlie's refusal to recognize their post-exchange property rights constitutes a violation of Alf's and Betty's property rights and (6) Charlie's demand that they refrain from engaging in the exchange constitutes an interference with their natural liberty and, so, *must be justified to them.* This isn't to say that Charlie can never provide justification: the social contract may no doubt protect Charlie against externalities arising from Alf and Betty's activities that impose costs on him. Nevertheless, the rights to own and transfer private property, conjoined with the right to natural liberty, yields a justification of market relations.

5. The Social Contract

5.1. Compromise and the Common Good

Let us assume that we have fully specified the rights and duties characterizing the state of nature. Now since, *ex hypothesi,* these articulate the moral foundations of our value systems, they articulate the limits of the contract. The contract must respect them.

For a teleological argument to ignore these rights and duties would be to advance value considerations while undermining the rationality of those values. But it does not follow that the contract is confined simply to protecting or institutionalizing these rights and duties. Once the deontological foundation of our value system is appropriately recognized, constrained teleological arguments for principles of right may commence.

Now I have said that these arguments must articulate a common good. But this seems either too weak or too strong. If it means an institution is justified if it advances everyone's values (no matter how little) vis à vis the state of nature, then it seems far too weak a requirement. For nearly any social arrangement would improve upon the state of nature; as long as a person wasn't positively exploited, he would have to acknowledge the claim that the system advances his values. On the other hand, if to justify moral principles and social institutions by appeal to the common good is to claim that they advance the values of everyone to greatest degree, that is, a system is justified only if it is *best* from *everyone's* perspective, then it seems that no successful constrained teleological justifications will be forthcoming.[72]

Between these extremes lie *compromise* justifications: All gain, but each must give up something to elicit agreement of the others. Compromise, as Martin Golding has noted, presupposes conflict in so far as none of the parties get all that they want. But compromise also requires some coincidence of interests or valuings: Each, after all, does gain something from a compromise.[73] Compromise can take place when harmony does not obtain, yet some common good exists. J. L. Mackie recognized the importance of compromise in the justification of moral principles. "We must," he said, "lower our sights a little and look not for principles which can be wholeheartedly endorsed from every point of view; but for ones which represent an acceptable compromise between different actual points of view."[74] And indeed some such compromise seems to be at the heart of contractualist justification.[75] As Rawls says, the outcome of the contract is "a pact of reconciliation"[76] that, we can add, articulates a common good.

5.2. Distributive Shares and Economic Systems

Much more could be said explicating the idea of a compromise solution. Gauthier's recent work in particular has demonstrated how the idea of a rational bargain, with the state of nature as the initial position, can be made more precise.[77] However, for present purposes the intuitive idea of a compromise solution will suffice.

I argued that, in the state of nature we have a right to a system of private property that ensures one of the fruits of one's labor. But before actual holdings can arise, people must also have exclusionary claims over natural resources. But the natural liberty of each is limited by exclusionary claims over resources. If, then, resource claims are to be justified, it must be argued that a system of property rights works to the benefit of everyone. Betty is committed to acknowledging that Alf has a right to a system of property rights that recognizes production as a ground of title, but she is not committed to accepting Alf's exclusionary claims over resources. For Alf to gain these rights he must justify to Betty limiting her right to act by granting him right to exclude her from some resource; to do this, Alf must show Betty that she has reason to embrace the restraint, that is, that she too benefits. Rawls's difference principle is a possible candidate (its first formulation is a principle about inequalities working to everyone's advantage).[78] On the other hand, Nozick could well be right; perhaps the difference principle isn't a reasonable compromise since it is the best possible option from the perspective of the least well off.[79] In any event, it seems that some principle ensuring that everyone significantly benefits from the system of property rights is essential. The failure of the Lockeans to justify a complete account of property rights in the state of nature[80] leaves the way open for followers of Rousseau to regulate holdings, through the social contract, to promote the common good.

It might seem that the partial success of the Lockeans provides no real constraint on the justifiability of economic systems. As I indicated earlier, David Miller argues at some length that desert does not provide a practical criterion for overall judgments of social justice.[81] Once we consider the complexities involved in joint products, accidents and luck, and the importance of skills and techniques one has not discovered for oneself, it may seem that the aim of giving each the whole product of his labor becomes an unsalvagable muddle. But we should be wary of rejecting a fundamental claim of justice because we cannot ever hope to apply it precisely, especially when it seems (as Miller admits) so widely accepted.[82] If we cannot make sense of giving each the full fruits of his labor, we may still pose grave objections to economic systems that entirely fail to take cognizance of the justified claims to the fruits of one's labor.

Consider, for example, Oliver Williamson's "Peer Group" system. In this system of collective ownership all the work stations in a production process are collectively owned by the workers, and reward is based on a non-marginal product principle, e.g., the workers are paid the average of the group product.[83] Now in an economy in which Peer Ownership was the only option, it is plausible that some would have significant grounds for complaint that it violates their natural right to a system that gives one exclusionary rights over the fruits of one's labor. Mandatory participation in work organizations that reward on the basis of average performance very plausibly give others control over the fruits of the labors of those who contribute well above the mean.

The argument also casts doubt on the justifiability of market socialism (Yugoslav style), a form of work organization and ownership much in vogue today.[84] Worker-managed market socialist firms certainly can reward workers differentially, recognizing the differential claims to the fruits of labor, but market socialism in effect expropriates the savings of workers invested in their firms.[85] If, as Mill said, one has a claim to the fruits of abstinence, market socialism tends systematically to ignore this. Workers who have heavily invested, especially older workers, have no exclusionary rights to these funds, entirely losing them on leaving the firm.[86]

Non-market, that is, command economies, are also challenged by the argument from the state of nature. Many socialists have aspired to reward all according to the fruits of their labor, and we can at least imagine a command economy that sought to distribute income with this in mind (e.g., according to marginal product).[87] But even if this desert-based claim informing quasi-Lockean property rights could be met in non-market systems, prohibition on market exchanges would infringe the right of transfer and constitute an interference with natural liberty.

The argument points to a market system where people have exclusionary rights over the fruits of their labor. But must the system be capitalist? Robert Dahl thinks not; indeed he indicates that "corporate capitalism" cannot be justified. "Whatever one many think of the validity of Locke's notion of labor as justifying private property . . . ," he says, "it cannot justify the ownership of a corporation by stockholders. For on Locke's justification only those who labor to produce goods and services, the workers and employees, would be entitled to own the goods and services produced by the firm."[88] Thus it might seem that a system of worker cooperatives—which was Mill's dream—is required by the argument.[89] Now certainly a cooperative system is consistent with my argument, but it is not at all clear that corporate capitalism is precluded. Because we have rejected the desert-based conception of distributive justice (DJ) in favor of a desert-based theory of property rights including the power to transfer title (section 4.4), Dahl's main claim—that those who do not labor cannot have justified title—can also be rejected. Although I certainly have not demonstrated that it is impossible to show that in some way corporate capitalism is inherently immoral, my argument does demonstrate (1) that any prohibition of capitalist acts between consenting adults is a violation of natural liberty and so stands in need of justification and (2) abolishing the right to transfer justified holdings is a violation of the right to property and the social contract cannot legitimately ignore this natural right. But the capitalism that is justified is a distinctly redistributive sort, ensuring that all gain to the extent required by the principle of fair compromise.[90] Moreover, nothing in the quasi-Lockean argument precludes public regulation of the private sector. The quasi-Lockean argument from the state of nature provides parameters for the social contract, but within these a variety of economic systems might be justified.

6. Conclusion

I have sketched a contractual justification of an economic system characterized by the market, private property, and significant redistribution of income and wealth by the state. The combination of market, private property, and redistribution, of course, is not at all novel. It was the heart of the program of the "new liberalism" that arose around the turn of this century,[91] and it has recently been defended by a number of liberal political philosophers. But it has long been doubted whether this widely accepted triad of institutions can be justified from a single coherent moral perspective. Beginning with an individualist liberal theory that provides solid grounding for private property and the market, redistributive capitalism (it is said) then overlays a collectivist theory that aserts existence of a state empowered to distribute a pool of social assets. This leads to the charge of incoherence.[92] If society is essentially a system of mutual advantage among individuals entertaining diverse and often competing ends, from where does the pool of collective assets come? How can the liberal state, devoted to the protection of individual freedom of choice, be transformed into a collectivist enterprise pursuing social goals? I have tried to show here that redistributive capitalism articulates a morally unified outlook: The contractual argument that justifies private property also justifies redistribution.

NOTES

1. John Locke, *Second Treatise of Government*, in *Two Treatises of Government*, ed. Peter Laslett (Cambridge: Cambridge University Press, 1960), 368–69, sec. 124.

2. See, for example, James Tully, *A Discourse on Property: John Locke and his Adversaries* (Cambridge: Cambridge University Press, 1980); John Christman, "Can Ownership be Justified by Natural Rights?" *Philosophy and Public Affairs* 15 (Spring 1986): 156–77.

3. I am following here Stephen Buckle, "The Natural History of Property: Natural Law Theories from Grotius to Hume" (Ph.D. diss., Australian National University, 1987), chap. 3, sec. 3. My thinking on these matters was spurred by Buckle's work. It might be argued that until the invention of money, Locke's theory does not justify extensive holdings, and, of course, Locke maintains that the use of money presupposes a "tacit Agreement" (*Second Treatise*, 311, sec. 36). I cannot pause to consider such problems here, but note that the use of money does not presuppose the social contract; the "tacit Agreement" to which Locke

refers does not in any way lead him toward the Rousseauean argument that I describe in the next paragraph.

4. "Charity," said Locke, "gives every Man a Title to so much out of another's Plenty, as will keep him from extreme want, where he has no other means to subsist otherwise." (*First Treatise of Government*, in *Two Treatises of Government*, ed. Laslett, 188, sec. 42). See also Alan Ryan, *Property and Political Theory* (Oxford: Basic Blackwell, 1984), 34; Buckle, "Natural History of Property," chap. 3, sec. 3.

5. See Ryan, *Property and Political Theory*, 54ff.

6. Jean-Jacques Rousseau, *The Social Contract*, in *The Social Contract and Discourses*, trans. and ed. G. D. H. Cole (London: Dent, 1973), book 1, chap. 9, 179. See Ryan, *Property and Political Theory*, chap. 2. Locke held that "in Governments the Laws regulate the right to private property"; but he also insisted that the *"Fundamental Law of Property"* was that government could not take property without the consent of the people (*Second Treatise*, 320, sec. 50; 380, sec. 140).

7. Not that Rousseau favored collective ownership. "It is", he said, "certain that the right of property is the most sacred of all the rights of citizenship, even more important in some respects than liberty itself. . . ." See *A Discourse on Political Economy*, in *The Social Contract and Discourses*, trans. and ed. Cole, 138.

8. This is essentially the view of Robert A. Dahl, *A Preface to Economic Democracy* (Berkeley: University of California Press, 1985), 65ff. What I have characterized as Rousseau's view Dahl associates with Jefferson; he too describes the alternative as a Lockean conception.

9. Locke, *Second Treatise*, 294, sec. 14.

10. James M. Buchanan, *The Limits of Liberty* (Chicago: University of Chicago Press, 1975), chap. 2; David Gauthier, *Morals by Agreement* (Oxford: Oxford University Press, 1986), chap. 7. Robert Nozick, of course, employs the idea of the state of nature, but he is not a contract theorist. See his *Anarchy, State and Utopia* (New York: Basic Books, 1974), chaps. 1 and 2.

11. In this section I am summarizing arguments more fully developed elsewhere. See my "On Community and Justice: A Reply to Professor Golding," *Bulletin of the Australian Society of Legal Philosophy* 9 (Oct. 1985): 197–204; "Subjective Value and Justificatory Political Theory," in *Justification*, ed. J. Roland Pennock and John W. Chapman, NOMOS 27 (New York: New York University Press, 1986), 241–69; S. I. Benn and G. F. Gaus, "Practical Rationality and Commitment," *American Philosophical Quarterly* 23 (July 1986): 255–66; "The Commitment to the Common Good," paper presented at the 1986 Annual Meeting of the American Political Science Association, in *New Essays on Political Obligation* ed. Paul Harris (London: Routledge and Kegan Paul, 1988).

12. See Derek Parfit, *Reasons and Persons* (Oxford: Clarendon Press, 1984), 143; Thomas Nagel, *The View from Nowhere* (New York: Oxford University Press, 1986), 152ff. See also Kurt Baier, *The Moral Point of View*, abridged ed. (New York: Random House, 1965), 28–34.

13. We have to be cautious about hidden indexicals. Everyone may value money, and so everyone may have reason to obtain it. But this would not mean that the value implies agent-neutral reasons. For, more exactly, Alf values *his* possession of money, which provides *him* with a reason to obtain money for *himself;* Betty values *her* own possession of money, which provides *her* with a reason to obtain it for *herself,* etc. Compare this to the example of Alf's pain in the next paragraph. Thomas Nagel has argued that this provides a truly agent-neutral reason; I have disputed this. See my "Subjective Value and Justificatory Political Theory," 252–55.

14. This term also derives from Parfit. See the references to Parfit and Nagel in note 12 above.

15. Thomas Nagel, *The Possibility of Altruism* (Princeton: Princeton University Press, 1978), 119–20. In this earlier work, Nagel used the terms "subjective" and "objective" reasons. He notes his adoption of Parfit's terminology on p. 152 n. of *The View from Nowhere.*

16. For simplicity's sake, I will not distinguish between (1) agent-neutral value-based reasons for acting and (2) agent-neutral value. Strictly speaking, my interest is (1), but often the point can be put more simply in terms of (2). Mutatis mutandis, the same applies to agent-relative value/reasons for action.

17. Michael J. Sandel, *Liberalism and the Limits of Justice* (Cambridge: Cambridge University Press, 1982), 3. Sandel is characterizing deontology in this passage, contrasting it to teleology; consequently, the characterization of teleology is implied rather than explicit. For characterizations of teleology along similar lines, see Robert O. Olson, "Teleological Ethics," in *The Encyclopedia of Philosophy,* ed. Paul Edwards (New York: Macmillan and Free Press, 1967); William K. Frankena, *Ethics,* 2d ed. (Englewood Cliffs, N.J.: Prentice-Hall, 1973), 14–16.

18. B. J. Diggs is, I think, one of the few to notice that the idea of the common good is central to contractualism. See "The Common Good as Reason for Political Action," *Ethics* 83 (July 1973): 283–93, esp. 293. For analyses that would tend to dispute this, see Bruce Douglass, "The Common Good and the Public Interest," *Political Theory* 8 (Feb. 1980): 103–17; Baier, *The Moral Point of View* 106–9.

19. Ralph Barton Perry, *Realms of Value* (Cambridge: Harvard University Press, 1954), 107.

20. Immanuel Kant, *The Doctrine of Virtue,* trans. Mary J. Gregor (Philadelphia: University of Pennsylvania Press, 1964), 144, sec. 47.

21. On the moral emotions of indignation and resentment, see S. I. Benn, "Freedom, Autonomy and the Concept of a Person," *Proceedings of the Aristotelian Society* (1976): 109–30, 120–21; Nagel, *The Possibility of Altruism*, 84–85; David A. J. Richards, *A Theory of Reasons for Action* (Oxford: Clarendon Press, 1971), 250ff; Charles Fried, *An Anatomy of Values* (Cambridge: Harvard University Press, 1970); John Rawls, *A Theory of Justice* (Cambridge: Belknap Press of Harvard University Press, 1971), secs. 73, 74; P. F. Strawson, "Freedom and Resentment" in his *Freedom and Resentment and Other Essays* (London: Methuen, 1970), chap. 1.

22. Ralph Barton Perry, *General Theory of Value* (New York: Longman's, Green, 1954), 614.

23. I have argued that a subjective theory of value need not make such a radical claim. See my "Subjective Value and Justificatory Political Theory."

24. This points out the implausibility of Bruce A. Ackerman's neutrality principle. Pace Ackerman, if citizen Alf has a paranoid conception of the good founded on an irrational belief system, then Betty can provide Alf with good reasons that his conception of the good *is* inferior, and that social institutions can rightly view it as such. See his *Social Justice in the Liberal State* (New Haven: Yale University Press, 1980), 11.

25. This is especially clear in Baier's "Moral Reasons and ℞easons to be Moral," in *Values and Morals*, ed. Alvin I. Goldman and jaegwon Kim (Dordrecht: Reidel, 1978), 231–56, 240ff.

26. Baier, *The Moral Point of View*, 154.

27. "Morals by agreement," Gauthier writes, "have a non-tuistic rationale" (328). Indeed, as he sees it, to allow altruistic considerations to enter into the justification of morality would pave the way for exploitation. "[T]he contractarian sees sociability as enriching human life; for him, it becomes a source of exploitation if it induces persons to acquiesce in institutions and practices that but for their fellow-feeling would be costly to them. Feminist thought has surely made this, perhaps the core form of exploitation, clear to us." See *Morals by Agreement*, 11 (the claim is repeated on 351). This, I must confess, strikes me as bizarre. How could we arrive at an adequate justification of friendship without considering the value friends place on each others' welfare? Cf. Kant's remark that "friendship cannot be a union aimed at mutual advantage," in *The Doctrine of Virtue*, 142, sec. 46.

28. James S. Fishkin, *Tyranny and Legitimacy* (Baltimore: The Johns Hopkins Press, 1979), 29. Wheras Baier is willing to affirm that "generally speaking, self-regarding reasons are better than other-regarding ones" (*The Moral Point of View*, 146), Fishkin denies that "the personal part of a life is necessarily the most important part. A person may be so devoted to altruistic causes that it is his public-regarding wants that are

most important to him. Nevertheless, since it is *his* plan, he must figure in it somewhere" (29). It isn't clear how this last sentence supports his characterization of life plans in terms of private-regarding wants.

29. See, for example, Ronald Dworkin, *Taking Rights Seriously* (Cambridge: Harvard University Press, 1978), 234ff; Rawls, *A Theory of Justice*, 13–14.

30. Kenneth Arrow notes and criticizes this feature of contemporary liberal theory in his "Values and Collective Decision-Making," in *Philosophy, Politics and Society,* series, ed. Peter Laslett and W. G. Runcimann, 3d ed. (Oxford: Basil Blackwell, 1967), 215–32, 222–23.

31. See Locke, *The Second Treatise*, 375, sec. 135.

32. In another context Stanley Benn and I have argued that, regardless of what one values or desires, one has a reason to tell the truth. This points the way toward a justification of this duty. See our "Practical Rationality and Commitment," 256–57.

33. Joseph Raz argues that some conceptions of promising "present promises as creating a relation between promisor and promisee—which is taken out of the general competition of conflicting reasons. It creates a special bond, binding the promisor to be, in the matter of the promise, partial to the promisee. . . . Hence [such conceptions of promising] . . . can only be justified if the creation of such special relationships between people is held to be valuable." This seems essentially right, but we want to be careful about suggesting that the promise is a means to such relations. More accurate is that the value of such special relations informs our way of looking at the world, and obligatory nature of promising is a presupposition of this valuing. See Raz's "Promises and Obligations," in *Law, Morality and Society*, ed. P. M. S. Hacker and J. Raz (Oxford: Clarendon Press, 1977), 210–28, 228. If the duty to keep promises characterizes the state of nature, one of Hume's main criticisms of contractualism is undermined. See "Of the Original Contract" in his *Essays Moral, Political and Literary* (Oxford: Oxford University Press, 1963), 452–73, 468.

34. This, of course, is suggested by the argument in sec. 3.1 above. See "Commitment to the Common Good" for a more detailed argument.

35. Locke, *Second Treatise*, 322, sec. 54.

36. Ibid., 287, sec. 4.

37. For analyses of liberalism that also focus on the presumption in favor of liberty, see Joel Feinberg, *The Moral Limits of the Criminal Law*, vol. 1; idem, *Harm to Others* (New York: Oxford University Press, 1984), 14; S. I. Benn, *A Theory of Freedom* (Cambridge: Cambridge University Press, 1988), chaps. 5 and 6. Joseph Raz criticizes "the presumption of liberty" in *The Morality of Freedom* (Oxford: Clarendon Press, 1986), 8–12.

118

38. Clifford Geertz, "Person, Time and Conduct in Bali," in *The Interpretation of Cultures*, ed. Clifford Geertz (New York: Basic Books, 1973), 360–411, 400.

39. Ibid., 402.

40. Ibid.

41. Ibid., 390.

42. Carl Rogers, "What It Is to Become a Person," in *The Self*, ed. Clark E. Moustakas (New York: Harper and Row, 1956), 195–211, 197.

43. For just a few examples, see Heinz Hartmann, *Essays on Ego Psychology* (London: Hogarth, 1964), esp. "Comments on the Psychoanalytic Theory of the Ego," 113–41; Karen Horney, *Neurosis and Human Growth* (New York: Norton, 1959); Abraham Maslow, *Motivation and Personality* (New York: Harper and Row, 1954); Anthony Storr, *The Integrity of Personality* (Harmondsworth: Penguin, 1961); Gordon W. Allport, *Pattern and Growth in Personality* (New York: Holt, Rinehart and Winston, 1961).

44. See Erving Goffman, *The Presentation of Self in Everyday Life* (Harmondsworth: Penguin, 1971). Alan Ryan explores the possibility that the self may be exhausted by these performances and require some time backstage. See his "Private Selves and Public Parts," in *Public and Private in Social Life*, ed. S. I. Benn and G. F. Gaus (New York: St. Martin's Press, 1983), 134–54, esp. 150–53.

45. "The first man who, having enclosed a piece of ground, to whom it occurred to say *this is mine* and found people sufficiently simple enough to believe him, was the true founder of civil society." See Jean-Jacques Rousseau, *Discourse on the Origin and the Foundations of Inequality among Men*, in *The First and Second Discourses*, ed. Victor Gourevitch (New York: Harper and Row, 1986), 170 (first sentence of second part).

46. Lawrence C. Becker, *Property Rights* (London: Routledge and Kegan Paul, 1977), 49.

47. Ibid.

48. See Christman, "Can Ownership Be Justified by Natural Rights?" 167.

49. "Desert, then denotes a relationship between an individual and his conduct, and modes of treatment which are liked or disliked." See David Miller, *Social Justice* (Oxford: Clarendon Press, 1976), 92.

50. Becker, *Property Rights*, 51.

51. Ibid., 55.

52. See Miller, *Social Justice*, 102ff. For the distinction between contribution and effort-based accounts, see also Michael A. Slote, "Desert, Consent and Justice," *Philosophy and Public Affairs* (Summer 1973): 323–47.

53. Miller, *Social Justice*, 104.

54. Ibid.

55. As Joel Feinberg says, "This is simply another way of saying that person's desert of *X* is always a reason for giving *X* to him, but not always a conclusive reason." See "Justice and Personal Desert," in his *Doing and Deserving* (Princeton: Princeton University Press, 1970) 55–87, 60.

56. John Stuart Mill, *Principles of Political Economy* (Fairfield, N.J.: Augustus M. Kelly, 1976), 209 (book 2, chap. 1, sec. 3).

57. Ibid., 233 (book 2, chap. 2, sec. 6).

58. Nozick, *Anarchy, State and Utopia*, 174–75.

59. John Christman apparently disagrees; he argues that Lockean provisos do not cohere well with desert-based accounts of property rights since desert claims are not "limited by the distribution of benefits generally." If one deserves it, one deserves it, whether or not it leaves enough for others. But my argument is that the desert claim is undermined because one had no exclusionary rights over the resource, not because honoring the desert claim results in a certain sort of distribution. See "Can Ownership be Justified by Natural Rights?" 168.

60. See, for example, Locke, *Second Treatise*, chap. 5; Nozick, *Anarchy, State and Utopia*, 178ff; Gauthier, *Morals By Agreement*, chap. 8. See also John Bogart, "Lockean Provisos and State of Nature Theories," *Ethics* 95 (July 1985): 828–36.

61. Cf. Locke's remark that "a King of a large and fruitful Territory there [i.e., in America where land has still not been appropriated] feeds, lodges, and is clad worse than a day Labourer in England [who has no exclusionary rights over land in a state where all the land has been removed from the state of nature]." Hence even those left out are better off then they would be in the state of nature. See *Second Treatise*, 315, sec. 41. Compare the very similar argument given by Adam Smith in *The Wealth of Nations*, ed. Edwin Cannon (Chicago: University of Chicago Press, 1976), vol. 1, 14. (book 1, chap. 1).

62. Locke, *Second Treatise*, 304–5, sec. 26.

63. Mill, *Principles of Political Economy*, 229–30 (book 2, chap. 2, sec. 5).

64. This is a modification of a suggestion made by Alan Ryan. See his "Public and Private Property," in *Public and Private in Social Life*, ed. Benn and Gaus, 223–45, 226ff.

65. Mill, *Principles of Political Economy*, 226 (book 1, chap. 2, sec. 4).

66. As Becker notes, some of Mill's own arguments imply as much. See *Property Rights*, note 7 at 36. Cf. Mill's *Principles of Political Economy*, 209 (book 2, chap. 2, sec. 3).

67. This problem is discussed by Allen Buchanan, *Ethics, Efficiency and the Market* (Oxford: Clarendon Press, 1985), 51–53.

68. Nozick, *Anarchy, State and Utopia*, 155ff.

69. Locke, *Second Treatise*, 288, sec. 6, 301–3, 305–6, sec. 27. I have greatly benefited here from Steven Buckle, "The Natural History of Property," chap. 3, sec. 3.

70. See Feinberg, "Justice and Personal Desert," 56ff.

71. See Becker, *Property Rights*, 18ff.

72. Gauthier suggests in *Morals by Agreement* that the market can fulfill this strong condition. The idea of a perfectly competitive market, he tells us, reveals "a structure in which the divergent and seemingly opposed interests of different individuals fully harmonize" (83). But market transactions include bargains, and within a range of possible mutual gains, the gains can be distributed differently. Witness the phenomenon of consumer's surplus: some consumers would pay more than the marginal price, but they don't, and so they receive a surplus.

73. Martin Golding, "The Nature of Compromise: A Preliminary Inquiry," in *Compromise in Ethics, Law and Politics*, ed. J. Roland Pennock and John W. Chapman, NOMOS 21 (New York: New York University Press, 1979), 3–25.

74. J. L. Mackie, *Ethics: Inventing Right and Wrong* (Harmondsworth: Penguin, 1977), 93.

75. This is shown by Arthur Kuflik, "Morality and Compromise," in *Compromise*, ed. Pennock and Chapman, 38–65, 55–64.

76. Rawls, *A Theory of Justice*, 221. Cf. Rawls's remark that "the principles of justice are the result of a fair agreement or bargain" (p. 12).

77. Gauthier persuasively argues that a rational bargain is one that minimizes the maximum relative concession. See *Morals by Agreement*, chap. 5.

78. Rawls, *A Theory of Justice*, 60.

79. Nozick, *Anarchy, State and Utopia*, 192ff. It should be pointed out, however, that minimax relative concession (see note 77 above) is concerned only with minimizing the maximum concession; it is thus possible that under minimax relative concession some parties make no concession at all. Nevertheless, it may be argued that the difference principle requires overly large concessions from the advantaged.

80. See also Christman, "Can Ownership be Justified by Natural Rights?"

81. See Miller, *Social Justice*, 114–21.

82. Miller, *Social Justice*: "There is in any case no doubt that most people in present-day Britain, say, hold a view of social justice which gives a large place to making incomes correspond to personal deserts" (p. 120).

83. Oliver E. Williamson, *The Economic Institutions of Capitalism* (New York: Free Press, 1985), 217–18.

84. See, for example, Charles Lindblom, *Politics and Markets* (New

York: Basic Books, 1977), chap. 24. See also Buchanan, *Ethics, Efficiency and the Market,* chap. 4.

85. It might be possible to create a bond scheme that could overcome this difficulty. See P. J. D. Wiles, *Economic Institutions Compared* (New York: Wiley, 1977), 348–49.

86. Younger workers can recieve the fruits of their investment through increased profitability. Hence the time horizon of workers is crucial in understanding the investment decisions of Yugoslav firms. See Erik G. Furubotn and Svetozar Pejovich, "Property Rights and the Behavior of the Firm in a Socialist State: The Example of Yugoslavia," in their edited volume, *The Economics of Property Rights* (Cambridge, Mass.: Ballinger, 1974), 227–56, 239ff.

87. See Wiles, *Economic Institutions Compared,* chap. 11.

88. Dahl, *Preface to Economic Democracy,* 78. Dahl rejects the Lockean treatment of property in favor of a more Rousseauean approach; that is, he rejects natural property rights, which put moral constraints on what economic system the people may choose.

89. On Mill and cooperatives, see *Principles of Political Economy,* 764–94 (book 4, chap. 7, secs. 5–7). Dahl too looks forward to a cooperative organization. See *A Preface to Economy Democracy,* esp. 148ff. Perhaps the most successful current cooperative is the Mondragon group in Spain, a case on which Dahl draws. However, in an important study—which Dahl does not cite—it has been shown that it generates adequate levels of investment only because of its very special circumstances, in particular its nonmobile labor force. See Keith Bradley and Alan Gelb, "The Replication and Sustainability of the Mondragon Experiment," *British Journal of Industrial Relations* 20 (1982): 20–33.

90. This, I think, constitutes a response to Dahl's claim that "corporate property [does not] fare any better on Mill's justification, for . . . Mill's justification not only excludes property in land but, like Locke, limits initial acquisition to producers." See *A Preface to Economic Democracy,* 78.

91. See Michael Freeden, *The New Liberalism: An Ideology of Social Reform* (Oxford: Clarendon Press, 1978); Gerald F. Gaus, *The Modern Liberal Theory of Man* (New York: St. Martin's Press, 1983), chap. 7.

92. Edward Shils, "The Antinomies of Liberalism," in *The Relevance of Liberalism,* ed. Zbigniew Brzezinski et al. (Boulder: Westview, 1978), 135–200, 139. Cf. Michael Oakeshott, *On Human Conduct* (Oxford: Clarendon Press, 1975), parts 2 and 3; John W. Chapman, "Justice, Freedom and Property," in *Property,* ed. J. Roland Pennock and John W. Chapman, NOMOS 22 (New York: New York University Press, 1980), 289–324; F. A. Hayek, *The Mirage of Social Justice* (Chicago: University of Chicago Press, 1976).

5

JUSTICE UNDER CAPITALISM

JONATHAN RILEY

I

Many observers share Alan Ryan's view that "capitalism is not
... morally very engaging."[1] Socialists in particular often claim
that distributive injustice is inherent in capitalism. Michael
Harrington's assertions in this regard are fairly typical: "Capitalism ... is outrageously unjust: it requires a continuing maldistribution of wealth in order to exist. But more than that, it is
also self-destructive. This is why we live in the twilight of an
epoch."[2] Even if the finger of doom is not pointing in the
direction Harrington thinks, all virtuous citizens must surely be
socialists if capitalism necessarily involves gross inequality in the
distribution of personal wealth with attendant poverty, exploitation of labor, worker alienation, and class antagonism.

Remarkably, admirers of capitalism usually concede that it is

I am very grateful to Richard Krouse and Michael S. McPherson for stimulating
my interest in this topic. In particular, I have benefited from their interpretation
of Mill offered in a paper, "The Logic of Liberal Equality: John Stuart Mill and
the Origins of the Political Theory of Welfare-State Liberalism," delivered at
the Poverty, Charity and Welfare conference held at Tulane University, Febru-
ary 14–16, 1986. Conference proceedings are published in J. Donald Moon,
ed., *Responsibility, Rights and Welfare* (Boulder, Colo.: Westview Press, 1988).
Nevertheless, I defend a quite different interpretation of Mill in the present
chapter. My thanks also go to David Braybrooke, John Chapman, and Roland
Pennock for helpful comments and suggestions. Responsibility for the views
expressed remains mine alone.

indifferent to claims of distributive justice. Strong admirers focus instead on its putative virtues of economic efficiency and liberty. Milton Friedman, Friedrich Hayek, and Robert Nozick, for example, variously defend free enterprise but essentially ignore the charge that it gives rise to an unjust pattern of economic inequality.[3] Weak admirers temper their admiration by insisting that capitalism must be supplemented by substantial redistribution of income and wealth. Kenneth Arrow and Amartya Sen, for example, want more economic equality (however defined) despite their admiration for the efficiency of capitalist markets.[4] The important point is that these observers apparently agree that claims of distributive justice are foreign to capitalism. Many have come to think that unconstrained capitalism is inherently unjust. It runs on personal greed, demands laissez-faire to generate efficient resource allocations, and, unless constrained by government, destroys every semblance of economic equality.

If capitalism is inherently unjust, then writers of every ideological persuasion must feel surprise at the degree of support voiced by a majority of Americans for private property and economic individualism. Most seem to be disturbed by the degree of economic inequality in the U.S. yet are apparently unwilling to abandon capitalism or to authorize redistribution of property without adequate compensation.[5] The grossly inegalitarian nature of the American economy has been fairly clear for some time. According to the available data (much of it sketchy and unreliable), economic growth during the four decades leading up to the Civil War gave rise to marked inequality that in large measure seems to persist up to the present day despite some twentieth-century levelling.[6]

Income inequality is significant and seems inflexible in important respects. In 1985, for example, the poorest 20 percent of U.S. households received about 5 percent of total money income before taxes and the next poorest quintile received about 11 percent of total pretax income. The richest 20 percent and 5 percent of households received about 44 percent and 17 percent of total pretax income, respectively.[7] The shares of the two poorest quintiles have remained roughly constant for the last fifty years even though about 10 percent of total pretax income has been redistributed from the richest quintile to the middle classes during the same period. This performance is sometimes described as a "revolutionary" levelling of incomes but does not seem to have involved much pretax income redistribution toward the poor and near-poor. Moreover, the share of the richest 5 percent of households declined only slightly during the same period, from about 19 percent of total pretax income in 1929 to 17 percent in 1985. The data imply that the average income of the top 20 percent is still nearly nine times that of the bottom 20 percent.[8]

Lester Thurow notes that the distribution of pretax income masks a more unequal distribution of market earnings. In 1985, the bottom quintile of individuals earned less than 2 percent of total wages and salaries and the next poorest quintile earned less than 8 percent. The richest 20 percent of individuals earned about 48 percent. The average pay of the top 20 percent is more than 25 times that of the bottom 20 percent.[9] Moreover, the earnings distribution has been gradually becoming more unequal since World War II, although rising government transfer payments and labor force participation rates for women have offset the rising inequality in earnings up to now.[10]

The details of personal wealth distribution are more problematic but available data suggest remarkable wealth inequality. In 1973, for example, about 35 percent of all families apparently held no measurable wealth and indeed the bottom 80 percent of families owned only about 15 percent of total net wealth. The top 5 percent and 1 percent of families held about 55 percent and 33 percent of total net wealth respectively.[11] Some evidence suggests that the wealth shares of the richest groups have been largely stable since about 1945, although wealth seems to have been even more concentrated during the hundred years prior to World War II.[12] Moreover, the portion of wealth that might be called "riches" or "capital wealth" is even more unequally distributed.[13] Riches include bonds and securities, corporate stocks, commercial real estate and rental property, trust fund equity and, more generally, all wealth "over and above those assets [such as consumer durables and owner-occupied housing] which are necessary to reproduce [any person's] labor power from day to day, rested, fed, and at [his] customary place of work."[14] In 1973, for example, the richest 5 percent and 1 percent of families owned about 85 percent and 60 percent respectively of all privately held corporate stock in America.[15]

Related to gross economic inequality is what Jennifer Hochschild labels "the hollowness of the equal opportunity claim" in the U.S.[16] Access to occupations is largely determined by socioeconomic background, race, and sex, even if relative pay rates are influenced by market forces for those workers who have access to the particular occupation.[17] Moreover, upward mobility within the wealth distribution appears to be at best modest. According to Thurow, "about 50 percent of the great fortunes are gotten through inheritance."[18] The richest families can preserve their privileged status by relying on legal loopholes to avoid estate and inheritance taxation on their massive inter-generational transfers of wealth.[19] The other 50 percent of the great fortunes are apparently made through risky investments in financial assets such as corporate stocks. Stock values may increase wildly when the corporation is expected (perhaps without much evidence) to experience excess profits for one reason or another. Thurow suggests that these giant capital gains are largely a matter of luck, and notes that legal loopholes again permit the rich to pay little or no capital gains taxes.[20] In short, the U.S. economy apparently shows little tendency to mitigate earnings inequality by breaking down the barriers of racial and sexual discrimination and providing all workers with a more or less equal opportunity to acquire skills; and shows even less tendency to reduce the concentration of wealth through taxation of the rich.

The extent of measured economic inequality in the U.S. can only strengthen the conviction that capitalism is inherently unjust.[21] Gross inequality, in addition to other problems, has prompted speculations that capitalism is destroying the traditional moral values that bind American society together and indirectly legitimate capitalism itself. Even analysts not disposed to criticize capitalism are prepared to grant that it is inherently incapable of legitimating itself and "singularly devoid of plausible myths [or ideals] . . . that command a high degree of commitment and sacrifice on the part of those who believe in them."[22] And yet capitalism in some form has always seemed to inspire many Americans, to wit, all those who admire the familiar "American dream" that "you can make it if you try" through hard work, sacrifice, and a little luck. It is easy to dismiss the relevance of these ideals given the contemporary American reality. But dreams apparently die hard. Indeed, Robert Nisbet sug-

gests that a rather ambiguous capitalist ideal is inseparable
from what he calls "the American Religion": "One need only
scan the speeches of the pioneering industrialists—Carnegie,
Rockefeller, Ford and others—to discover quickly that they had
all of the European socialist's contempt [for] . . . class inequalities and other hereditary obstacles to the freest possible rise of
the common man. But they [also] had something the European
socialist didn't have: conviction that the good society could and
would be achieved by individual freedom rather than collective
action."[23] Rich capitalists might be expected to display a firm
conviction that no necessary contradiction eixts between distributive justice and economic freedom. But American workers
seem to have been similarly convinced: "Every working man a
capitalist, every capitalist a working man at heart: this was a part
of the American Religion."[24] Even if, as Nisbet fears, "the
American Religion" may not prosper in the future, the possibility of distributive justice under capitalism seems to have been
taken for granted in America up to now.

We are presented with a paradox. Gross economic inequality
arguably confirms the injustice of capitalism, yet most Americans cling to their traditional faith that capitalism and economic
freedom can somehow be reconciled with distributive justice.
Perhaps most of the people really can be fooled all of the time.
But I will argue for a different resolution of the paradox:
Capitalism properly understood is not inherently unjust. Instead, pure capitalism is grounded on a principle of distributive
justice that is at odds with marked inequality among self-interested agents capable of work and abstinence. An implication of
my argument is that Americans who seem to embrace a capitalist ideal are not being inconsistent when they condemn the
contemporary pattern of inequality. Capitalism itself, properly
understood, is not compatible with the apparent extent and
intergenerational stability of wealth inequality.

My argument relies at several crucial points on the writings of
J. S. Mill. He is remarkably suggestive not only about the meaning of justice under capitalism but also about the sorts of government intervention required to promote its achievement.
Moreover, his claims need repeating that capitalism is the type
of economy most likely "for a long period to come" to yield
distributive justice.[25] Recent commentators suggest, however,

that he ultimately dismisses capitalism in favor of socialism as a means of attaining equality and real economic freedom.[26]

II

As Mill remarks, "mankind have many ideas, and but few words."[27] Some ambiguity is unavoidable in any discussion of justice under capitalism because key words like "capitalism" and "justice" are contested concepts.

By "capitalism" I mean an economy in which private agents, including corporations, are assigned legal rights to own production goods, that is, the factor inputs or means of production. Of course, individuals are also assigned rights to own consumption goods but that does not distinguish capitalism from socialism: "Socialism by no means excludes private ownership of articles of consumption; the exclusive right of each to his or her share of the produce when received, either to enjoy, to give, or to exchange it . . . The distinctive feature of socialism is . . . that the instruments of production are held as common property."[28] The distinctive feature of capitalism, then, is that production inputs (including labor, capital, and land) are held as private property.

"Property" is a term that refers to the rights of ownership granted by society with respect to both production and consumption goods. The meaning of the term varies across societies because different societies assign different bundles of proprietary rights. Mill writes, "The idea of property is not some one thing, identical throughout history and incapable of alteration . . . ; at any given time it is a brief expression denoting the rights over things conferred by the law or custom of some given society at that time . . . ; but these powers of exclusive use and control are very various and differ greatly in different countries and in different states of society."[29] "Private property" refers to the proprietary rights held by private agents. "Public property" refers to the rights held by government or its agents in the public interest. Both private and public property owners may assign to nonowners various rights or permissions relating to some nonexclusive use of the relevant assets. Even though socialism comprehends private property in articles of consumption, it is convenient to focus on the means of production in order to speak as if the institution of private property were restricted to capitalism. If capitalism is unjust, then it must be because private ownership of productive assets is inherently unjust.

Among the proprietary rights that are esential to the idea of private property is the right of contract. According to Mill, "The idea of private property . . . includes . . . the freedom of acquiring by contract. The right of each to what he has produced, implies a right to what has been produced by others, if obtained by their free consent; since the producers must either have given it from good will, or exchanged it for what they esteemed an equivalent, and to prevent them from doing so would be to infringe their right of property in the product of their own industry."[30] Given that private property implies freedom of contract, capitalism involves markets whenever property owners choose to transact through well-defined contractual arrangements. A market is any decentralized mechanism that enables buyers and sellers to implement contracts. A market may be a price system or a bargaining process. In either case, participants generally know only their own production and consumption plans and seek to maximize their self-interest by competing with one another for the best possible terms of exchange.

The relation of capitalism to the market requires clarification in at least three respects. First, the market does not necessarily presuppose private property. Markets are logically conceivable under socialism. But most observers agree with Mill that a moral revolution is necessary before socialist managers will have sufficient incentives to promote economic efficiency.[31] Given the present state of moral education, incentives of public spirit, conscience, and honor cannot be depended upon to motivate most people. Rather, "with men as they now are," the sole reliable incentive is "the prospect of bettering their own economic condition and that of their family." Moreover, any moral improvement is likely to be gradual. "We must therefore expect, unless we are operating upon a select portion of the population, that personal interest will for a long time be a more effective stimulus to the most vigorous and careful conduct of the industrial business of society than motives of a higher character."[32] The general conclusion is that capitalism is required to avoid market failure. If predominantly self-interested managers are to generate economic efficiency, then they must either own capital in the enterprise or be accountable to those who do.[33]

Second, capitalism does not necessarily rely on markets to achieve economic efficiency because markets sometimes fail.[34] As Oliver Williamson among others points out, capitalists may remove certain types of transactions from the market into vertically integrated firms to promote economic efficiency.[35] Markets tend to be efficient only if transactions are discrete and precise and so amenable to well-defined contractual agreements. Ideally, market exchange is anonymous, takes place among parties without any continuing relation and involves non-specific assets with high values in alternative uses. Non-market capitalist institutions are arguably more efficient for transactions that are not suited to straightforward contracting. For example, a vertically integrated firm is likely to reduce transactions costs if exchange is personal, the parties need to make sizeable investments in expectation of a continuing relation, and the goods traded are "idiosyncratic" asets (highly specific to particular purposes) with virtually no value in any alternative use. Capitalism may in principle rely as much on planning as does socialism. Nevertheless, planning by the managers of large-scale private corporations does not involve any departure from the principle of laissez-faire. No government intervention in the economy is implied.

Third, even if capitalist institutions, including the market, generate efficiency, this efficiency "is faint praise indeed" from the perspective of distributive justice.[36] All that economic efficiency, sometimes termed Pareto optimality, implies is that nobody can be made better off without making someone else worse off. "A state in which some people are starving and suffering from acute deprivation while others are tasting the good life can still be Pareto optimal if the poor cannot be made better off without cutting into the pleasures of the rich—no matter by how small an amount."[37] This distinction between efficiency and distributive justice is not contingent on the existence of large-scale private firms but remains valid even if we imagine that capitalism is characterized by many small-scale owner-managed firms operating in competitive markets. The moral standing of the market must be distinguished from its vaunted efficiency. Indeed, the view that the invisible hand somehow brings about justice by resolving conflicts among selfish agents in a way that no agent intends, is simply misplaced. As Sen has made clear, the market is not concerned with resolving conflicts at all. Instead, it permits different agents to realize their shared intentions to transact on the best possible terms given their respective positions in the (perhaps highly inegalitarian) distribution of wealth. In short, "the market division of benefits tends to reflect, roughly speaking, the economic 'power balance' of different individuals and groups."[38] If the given distribution of wealth and economic power is judged to be unfair in terms of some theory of justice, then government intervention to redistribute wealth becomes justified according to that theory—even if the economy is otherwise efficient. My argument will be that capitalism properly understood contains a theory of justice on the basis of which marked economic inequality may be rectified by government. Capitalism itself authorizes departures from the principle of laissez-faire in the name of distributive justice.

"Justice" also requires clarification. Unfortunately, justice involves potentially contradictory ideas whatever theory is adopted of its ultimate foundations or first principles. Arrow, for example, broadly following John Rawls, suggests that justice values both liberty and equality of results. But he admits that liberty and equality are "basically complementary" only if the idea of equality of outcome is left imprecise and "the right to engage in business and to set prices freely" is not essential to the idea of liberty.[39] More generally, Mill suggests that justice commonly includes such diverse ideas as conformity to legal rules; respect for moral rights that the law fails to recognize; the distribution of personal benefits and harms according to desert; the keeping of our promises, either express or implied, and satisfaction of any expectations that we "knowingly and voluntarily" raise in other persons; impartiality in the sense of refusing "to show favour or preference to one person over another, in matters to which favour and preference do not properly apply"; and, closely related to impartiality, some kind of equality, the idea that "in the eyes of many persons constitutes [the] essence [of justice]."[40] Evidently, these various ideas are incompatible with each other in many contexts. Justice becomes problematic unless some order of priority is established among the component ideas. Many alternative orderings are conceivable, however, depending upon our particular theory of the ultimate foundations of justice. Both Arrow and Mill defend versions of a utilitarian theory of justice according to which different ideas or "secondary principles" of justice should be evaluated and compared on the basis of their expected consequences for general utility.[41] Sen, on the other hand, adopts a pluralist theory of justice that rejects the feasibility let alone the appeal of any complete ordering of the various components of justice.[42]

We can ignore the vexed question of the ultimate foundations of justice. General agreement obtains that justice properly consists of various impartial assignments of legal and moral rights, some of which may perhaps conflict with others in particular circumstances. Whatever order of priority, if any, is established among the different sorts of rights, each person's collection of rights is deserving of equal protection by society. More to the point, three sorts of personal rights-assignments are associated with capitalism: rights to economic liberty, that is, rights to engage in business; property rights; and welfare rights. My strategy will be to isolate the three ideas or "secondary principles" of justice that respectively give rise to these three sorts of rights-assignments. Following Mill, I argue that rights to economic freedom are at best property rights by another name and have no basis in his famous "principle of liberty"; that property rights are based on a principle of desert that is essential to justice under capitalism; and that welfare rights are based on a principle of need that, though not essential to capitalist justice, is compatible with the principle of desert. In short, capitalist justice implies property rights grounded on the principle that producers deserve the fruits of their exertions. But these property rights can be supplemented by welfare rights grounded on the notion that persons incapable of productive labor need help; and also by rights to liberty grounded on Mill's idea that every person has a purely private sphere—outside the economy— where he should be free to do as he likes because his conduct affects no other persons against their wishes. The resulting mixture of property rights, welfare rights, and rights to be left alone might ultimately be justified by any of several alternative theories of justice.[43]

III

Justice under capitalism properly does not involve individual rights to liberty with respect to the allocation of scarce resources. Mill, for example, makes clear that his famous "principle of liberty"—a secondary principle of justice prescribing impartial assignments of rights to act as one likes in purely private matters—has nothing to do with the economic doctrine of "laissez-faire" or "free trade": "[T]rade is a social act. Whoever undertakes to sell any description of goods to the public, does what affects the interest of other persons, and of society in general; and thus his conduct, in principle, comes within the jurisdiction of society. . . . [T]he so-called doctrine of free trade . . . rests on grounds different from . . . the principle of individual liberty."[44] Economic transactions are by their very nature public concerns rather than purely private actions. Business freedom is not protected as a matter of right. As Arrow says, "business freedom by its very nature affects others, since it determines the terms on which they receive goods: hence, it can be justified only if others benefit, not if it inflicts serious injury. Indeed, most, though not all, of those who argue for business freedom accept that it must be restricted in such cases as monopolization and fraud."[45]

The freedom to engage in business is properly grounded not on justice but on general expediency. In particular, society might adopt a policy of laissez-faire to promote efficiency. Mill defends laissez-faire on efficiency grounds: "Laissez-faire . . . should be the general practice: every departure from it, unless required by some great good, is a certain evil."[46] Most modern economists agree that "there is indeed a strong argument for competitive price-setting and for freedom of entry into business as a contribution to efficiency in the allocation of resources."[47] But any person's freedom to compete is not the same thing as a right to liberty. As Arrow complains, "to compare [business] freedom with those of freedom of expression, of life-style, or of personal consumption seems to me to be a very strange setting of priorities."[48] The latter freedoms are rights whereas business freedom is properly a mere permission. In this regard, Mill emphasizes that libertarian rights are absolute moral claims that other persons, including government officials, have perfect moral duties to respect. Interference with any individual's right to liberty can never be legitimate given a proper definition of his purely private sphere. By contrast, a permission is merely a claim that is derived from the absence of any moral obligation on the part of the agent to refrain from competing with others, who similarly have no moral obligations to refrain from competition. Society may legitimately revoke any permission whenever to do so seems generally expedient:

> Restrictions on trade, or on production for purposes of trade, are indeed restraints; and all restraint *qua* restraint, is an evil: but the restraints in question affect only that part of conduct which society is competent to restrain; and are wrong solely because they do not really produce the results which it is desired to produce by them. . . . [L]eaving people to themselves is always better, *ceteris paribus,* than controlling them: but *that they may be legitimately* controlled for these ends, is in principle undeniable.[49]

Economic freedom is a matter of general expedience rather than justice and moral right. If, as Mill thinks, purely private spheres can be identified where the agent's conduct does not directly injure others, then equal rights to liberty can be assigned in harmony to all agents with respect to their private spheres. But economic transactions do not belong in private spheres. Any agent's transactions inevitably affect the plans of others whether they like it or not, by influencing prices. Precisely because of interdependence among competitors for scarce resources, it is generally not feasible to give every agent an equal moral right to set prices as he likes. Agents must bargain for a common price at which to carry out their transactions, not claim that everyone else has a moral duty to accept some arbitrary price. Indeed, the idea that any agent has a right to set prices lacks appeal because liberty in this context is inseparable from power over others.

Unequal bargaining power among agents plays a significant role in the real-world exchange for at least two reasons. First, when competitive markets fail, pursuit of efficiency can call for non-market institutions, large corporations and government, to allocate resources.[50] Second, even if markets are efficient, it seems fair to say with Sen that prices generally reflect the balance of bargaining power that is implicit in the more or less unequal initial distribution of wealth. If the distribution of resources is highly inegalitarian, then a policy of laissez-faire may well exacerbate the problems of distributive injustice, lack of bargaining power, and lack of economic freedom. As Arrow points out, to the extent that people are impoverished, economic efficiency and freedom are associated with injustice: "What one's income is, is not determined here by justice, but by a complicated system of interactions whose ethical meaning is hard to define. The idealization of freedom through the market completely ignores the fact that this freedom can be, to a large number of people, very limited in scope."[51] Hence, justice under capitalism cannot be based on rights to engage in business and set prices. A principle must be found to limit inequality of wealth and power. No "principle of economic liberty" can do this.

IV

What is uniquely characteristic of justice under capitalism is the assignment of individual property rights in production goods. The secondary principle of justice underlying these property rights is an "equitable principle of proportion between remuneration and exertion."[52] As Mill explains:

> Private property . . . is supposed to mean, the guarantee to individuals of the fruits of their own labour and abstinence. . . . The institution . . . , when limited to its essential elements, consists in the recognition, in each person, of a right to the exclusive disposal of what he or she have produced by their own exertions, or received either by gift or by fair agreement, without force or fraud, from those who produced it. The foundation of the whole is, the right of producers to what they themselves have produced.[53]

Justice under capitalism stipulates that individuals deserve rewards that are proportional to their productive labor. Mill goes on to argue that this principle of desert does not justify the actual economic inequality in any modern economy. In his view, "the principle of private property has never yet had a fair trial in any country."[54] If the principle were given a fair trial through suitable reform of property, he suggests, then any remaining inequality of results "could not justly give umbrage" in societies whose members are capable of work: "That all should indeed start on perfectly equal terms, is inconsistent with any law of private property: but if . . . the tendency of legislation has been to favour the diffusion, instead of the concentration of wealth . . . ; the principle of individual property would have been found to have no necessary connexion with the physical and social evils which almost all socialist writers assume to be inseparable from it."[55]

The principle that individuals deserve the fruits of their own exertions remains controversial, however, and requires clarification. It must be distinguished from any positive analysis of how personal incomes are determined in an exchange economy. The desert principle holds that producers deserve to have exclusive control over the physical products of their own exertions. Strictly speaking, the principle does not depend for its definition on any antecedent rules of social exchange: A producer can be properly said to deserve the fruits of his own labor even if exchange with other producers never takes place. The issue of fair exchange values is relevant only insofar as producers wish to participate in an exchange economy. The determination of prices and incomes under competitive conditions is the subject of general competitive analysis.

Competitive analysis takes for granted that production inputs are uniformly related to outputs. Consider labor, for example. A physical unit of labor is defined; one "manpower" is generally supposed equal to one-tenth horsepower. Some such unit of effort or exertion is perfectly conceivable although measurement problems should not be minimized. Any unit of labor, when added to given quantities of inputs in a production process, yields additional output (or "marginal product") in a quantity that mankind does not freely choose but discovers as a natural constraint. The latter point is important because it implies that efficiency in production is not simply a matter of arbitrary judgement or power. Knowledge of the laws and conditions of production is required. Says Mill, "Whatever mankind produce, must be produced in the modes, and under the conditions, imposed by the constitution of external things, and by the inherent properties of their own bodily and mental structure."[56] Given a medium of exchange, the competitive reward to any input is then deduced to be the value of its marginal product: Labor, for example, earns a wage rate equal to the value of the marginal product of work in that kind of occupation. The competitive price of any final product is simply the sum of the competitive rewards earned by the various inputs that go into its production at the margin. It should be noted that competitive analysis does not require production technology to be represented by neoclassical "aggregate production functions." As a result of the well-known Cambridge controversies, such production functions are now known to depend on highly restrictive assumptions needed to aggregate the different kinds of capital and labor. But competitive equilibrium does not presuppose that aggregate production is some function of homogeneous inputs termed "labor," "capital," and "land." Even if production must be described in disaggregated terms, it remains possible to refer to the marginal product of each different kind of input and to explain any agent's income as the sum of the various competitive rewards to his various kinds of capital assets, labor skills and talents, and land holdings.[57] Because there is no presumption that the different types of inputs can be aggregated, however, the notion of a uniform rate of return to any aggregate input like "capital" loses meaning. Moreover, the explanation of factor shares is seen to be a complex exercise that does not necessarily involve homogeneous classes of capitalists, laborers, and landowners.

The principle of desert identifies which portions of personal income and wealth are morally deserved. It does so by stipulating which sorts of competitive factor rewards should be guaranteed by right to any individual. As already noted, personal income and wealth inequality may well be closely related to inequalities in bargaining power among individuals and groups. The competitive model essentially ignores such considerations, however, by assuming that no individual or coalition has any power to set prices. This assumption is problematic for explanatory purposes, but it has appeal as a normative device for two reasons. First, it implies an absence of arbitrary impediments to efficiency in production and exchange. Second, it also implies that all agents have equal bargaining power and this equality seems closely related to equality of results. Even as a normative device, however, the competitive model arguably suffers from internal tensions except at a so-called "long run" equilibrium where all factor inputs are in variable supply, production everywhere exhibits constant returns to scale, factor prices equal the values of the marginal products (also average products) of the relevant inputs, and excess profits are zero. Unless these special long-run competitive assumptions hold, some types of inputs are in arbitrarily fixed supply. This destroys equality of bargaining power and seems at odds with the basic competitive premise that all agents accept prices as given. For example, any non-produced input or natural resource brings long-run economic rent (i.e., excess profit) to its possessors, thereby giving them a permanent reward from competitors who do not possess the resource and cannot make it themselves. This advantage to mere possession is hard to square with the competitive idea that agents are powerless to establish prices that differ from marginal costs in the long run. Possessors of the natural resource apparently have power to set prices (uniform or otherwise) that enable them to receive rewards for mere possession. Similarly, economists commonly refer to "short run" competitive equilibria where, for example, some particular type of capital or labor is temporarily in fixed supply for the economy as a whole. Owners of the limited supplies of these produced inputs receive short-run economic rents or "quasi-rents" (i.e., excess profits) because they apparently enjoy a temporary bargaining advantage until competitors can produce additional supplies of the inputs. For the moment, I want to make use of our special long-run competitive model to clarify the desert principle for a modern economy. Unequal control over fixed inputs creates complications for the application of the desert principle but does not destroy the principle itself. I will return to such complications in due course.[58]

According to the principle of desert, any person's remuneration should be proportional to his work or effort. That is, he should have rights over the products of his labor, including the right to exchange his products for anything he deems to be of equivalent value. Any reasonable person will so deem the remuneration he receives for his labor in our imaginary long-run competitive equilibrium. His wage rate equals the value of the marginal product (and average product) of his type of labor. In other words, his salary is society's evaluation of the contribution made by his labor to the creation of the relevant product in circumstances where personal bargaining power is equally distributed and the laws of production are given. Thus, any person deserves the long-run competitive incomes associated with his labor; and also deserves any wealth he manages to accumulate from such income.

Scholars continue to debate whether people have a desert-based claim for a rate of return to any type of capital.[59] In this regard, capital is often confused with money, the medium of exchange. But as Mill emphasizes, capital properly includes all property created by past labor for the support of present labor:

> Capital . . . [is] a stock, previously accumulated, of the products of former labour. . . . What capital does for production, is to afford the shelter, protection, tools and materials which the work requires, and to feed and otherwise maintain the labourers during the process. These are the services which present labour requires from past, and from the produce of past, labour. . . . [A]ll property, however ill adapted in itself for the use of labourers, is a part of capital, so soon as it, or the value to be received from it, is set apart for productive reinvestment.[60]

Unlike labor or land, capital literally has no productive powers of its own. Without capital, however, labor cannot exert its productive powers. And without production, society is left with an extremely primitive form of economy involving consumption and perhaps exchange of whatever natural resources can be found. Every production economy, not only capitalism, relies on capital. Workers simply cannot subsist without assets, however minimal, provided in advance of production "though the capital needs not necessarily be furnished by a person called a capitalist."[61] Moreover, since capital is the product of past labor, any person in possession of capital deserves its long-run competitive rate of return provided he has created the capital himself or has acquired it in a series of competitive transactions involving the persons who did create it. The principle of desert justifies property rights in capital because capital, as much as any final consumption good or service, is the fruit of labor.[62]

The long-run competitive rate of return to any type of capital is an interest rate whose level depends on the life of the capital good, excess profits being zero at competitive equilibrium.[63] The interest rate received by any owner of capital equals the value of the marginal (and average) product of that type of capital during the period of time covered by the interest rate. In other words, the capitalist's interest income is society's evaluation of the contribution made by *past labor* (used in creating that type of capital) to present production in a competitive environment where personal bargaining power is equal and capital is necessary for production. Commentators often refer to interest as "a reward for waiting" in the sense that abstaining from present consumption implies a sacrifice. But this obscures the fact that interest income is a reward for past labor, not for mere idle biding of time. A person who saves deserves interest only to the extent that his savings are reinvested in present production. By investing his savings in capital produced by past labor, the person acquires the property rights originally held by the workers who created the capital goods. Strictly speaking, time per se is irrelevant from the perspective of desert. If capital goods could be created immediately and also used to help produce some final product on the spot, owners of capital would still receive and deserve a competitive reward for its use in production. But there would now be no point in distinguishing between present labor and capital produced by past labor. Instead, we might as well speak only of different types of labor, each type earning a competitive wage rate in present production.

Whereas long-run competitive rewards to labor and capital are justified by the principle of desert, rewards to uncultivated land (or, more generally, natural resources) cannot be similarly justified. Land, like labor, has productive powers of its own. In primitive economies with little or no capital, individuals owe their subsistence to the natural fruits of the earth. Moreover, land and its wild products are scarce resources with value in competitive economies. But no individual deserves the economic rents associated with land in its natural state because "no man made the land."[64] Land is not created by labor "but . . . exists by nature."[65] Property rights in land cannot be grounded on the desert principle: "The essential principle of property being to assure to all persons what they have produced by their labour and accumulated by their abstinence, this principle cannot apply to what is not the produce of labour, the raw material of the earth."[66] The competitive incomes of idle landlords who "grow richer, as it were in their sleep" as the economy grows, should be redistributed through taxation: "This would not properly be taking anything from anybody; it would merely be applying an accession of wealth, created by circumstances, to the benefit of society, instead of allowing it to become an unearned appendage to the riches of a particular class."[67]

Recall that our special long-run competitive model cannot accommodate a non-produced input like land. Owners of land have a permanent bargaining advantage over non-owners that is at odds with the normative ideal of the model. The desert principle is compatible with the ideal because rewards for mere possession of land are not justified by the principle. But although no person deserves the rents that accrue to natural resources like uncultivated land, these resources are indispensable to productive labor in primary industries including agriculture, oil and gas, mining, and forestry. Indeed, even in secondary manufacturing and tertiary service industries, productive labor merely further transforms or "improves" what was originally some raw material of the earth, thereby creating "value-added." Strictly speaking, then, the competitive incomes of all workers will involve some component of economic rent unless the relevant natural materials are not scarce resources (in which case they are free inputs) or the rents are appropriated at the primary stage by government through the tax system. If labor makes use of natural resources that (for all practical purposes) are not scarce, then Locke's famous proviso is satisfied: sufficient quantities of the same type of natural resources remain for other individuals. But if the relevant natural materials are limited in supply and thus command a price, as surely must often be the case in large-scale industrial societies, then the Lockean proviso cannot be satisfied. Thus, we face a problem: Any worker may well deserve to own the fruits of his own labor and saving but he does not deserve to own the raw materials required for most types of labor to take place at all under modern industrial circumstances.[68]

Nevertheless, any advanced industrial society evidently must permit some agents rather than others to make use of scarce natural resources. Society's permission may be, though it need not be, given in the form of limited legal rights to control particular natural resources for particular purposes and only for those purposes. These limited property rights must evidently be assigned on some generally expedient basis other than the desert principle. Ideally, they should not guarantee any remuneration to mere possession of the natural resources per se. No reward to labor is required to bring the natural resources into existence so their owners do not deserve any income from mere possession. Moreover, these limited property rights are properly contingent on society's approval of the sort of the labor that the right-holder intends to employ in combination with the raw materials. After all, something like land is a "common inheritance" whose supply is fixed by nature: Any person should be permitted to exclude others from using the land only if his use is approved by the community and requires the exclusion of other uses. In Mill's view, for example, "when land is not intended to be cultivated, no good reason can in general be given for its being private property at all"; and even a person granted limited property rights to cultivate the land, should be required by law to recognize other persons' rights to the same land for purposes of access where such access does not damage his produce or invade the privacy of his home.[69] In any case, if society assigns limited property rights in natural resources (necessarily on the basis of some principle other than that of desert), then individuals properly deserve the fruits of their own labor and capital used in combination with the natural resources with the caveat that no reward is deserved for mere possession of the latter, in which case all natural-resource rents should in principle be confiscated by government.

The principle of desert prescribes property rights in the products of labor, that is, all man-made alterations to natural resources. But the natural resources themselves are not products of labor. Owners of labor and capital thus have desert-based moral rights to their long-run competitive rewards where possessors of natural resources have no such moral claims.

Nevertheless, society may legally permit limited retention of natural resource rents to encourage selfish agents *efficiently* to develop the resources for public purposes. This policy is prescribed by efficiency rather than justice. Limits are implicit in the normative ideal of our special long-run competitive model: Equality of bargaining power is as much a long-run goal as is efficiency. It should also be emphasized that society cannot rely exclusively on markets to allocate limited property rights in natural resources. For example, if society permits any person to use his labor and capital to cultivate a piece of land, then the person deserves a fair market return for his work and savings though not for his mere possession of the undeveloped land. The cultivator should also be able to sell his limited property rights to anyone else who similarly agrees to use the land in the manner originally approved by society. But the cultivator has no moral right to sell the land without society's permission to, say, a real-estate broker planning to develop a shopping center. Society properly limits the extent of the market by vetoing certain types of exchanges. Moreover, no approved buyer should be forced to pay a generally inexpedient rent to the cultivator for the mere transfer of ownership of the land. Society properly has authority to tax away any portion of rent accruing to idle land and redistribute it to the buyer after deducting a minimal transfer fee to cover the costs of the transaction.

A serious complication for the desert principle is occasioned by the fact that no person deserves the rents that accrue to his natural endowments like talents and ambitions.[70] Again, these non-produced inputs are incompatible with the normative ideal of our imaginary long-run competitive equilibrium because their owners enjoy permanent bargaining advantages over the rest of us. But undeserved personal endowments are indispensable to productive labor in all sorts of occupations, and "there seems to be no way to discount for [the] greater good fortune [of the better endowed]."[71] Evidently, every society faces a dilemma in this context. On the one hand, society can refuse to assign property rights in talents and try to redistribute the products of talent on the basis of some higher equitable principle like perfect equality. But in practice this more or less substitutes some higher egalitarian standard of justice for the principle of desert altogether because the separate contribution of talent to output cannot be identified. On the other hand, society can assign limited property rights in talents, necessarily on the basis of some principle other than that of desert, to facilitate socially approved labor by the talented, then try to redistribute that portion of output that is due to talent. But again the separate contribution of talent cannot be identified, so we are more or less left with our original property rights grounded on the principle of desert.

Mill himself recognizes that a principle of "sharing the remuneration equally, without regard to the quantity of work done by the individual . . . , appeals to a higher standard of justice" than does the principle of desert associated with private property. The latter principle is better adapted to the prevailing "selfish type of character," however, "and until education shall have been entirely regenerated, is far more likely to prove immediately successful, than an attempt at a higher ideal."[72] Equality of remuneration may well be a higher principle of justice because it "makes compensation" to any person who is less talented or skilled through "no fault of his own." But any such principle requires a corresponding sacrifice of leisure from the more talented such that their personal satisfaction is generally less than that of the less talented.[73] This inequality of personal satisfaction encourages self-interested workers with talent to be unproductive and to feel resentment at what they claim to be society's robbery of their personal endowments. Indeed, given different personal skills and talents, equality of remuneration will not be accepted unless talented individuals learn to replace their subjective desires for personal consumption and leisure with higher moral desires for equality of results.

If perfect equality of results is an impossible standard of justice given the selfish motivations of most individuals, then the principle of desert associated with capitalism is the best *possible* standard of justice, even though it is second-best when compared to any higher moral ideal not currently feasible. Nevertheless, the desert principle runs into further complications if produced inputs like labor and capital are temporarily in fixed supply for one reason or another. In this short-run context, owners of some types of labor and capital (not merely land) may receive quasi-rents in addition to the relevant marginal value products. For example, by investing in a particular type of capital good before his competitors do, a capitalist-entrepreneur may receive quasi-rents to his type of capital until other investors can increase its supply. These quasi-rents are usually interpreted to be excess profits. Similarly, by learning a particular type of skill before his competitors do, a worker-entrepreneur may receive quasi-rents to his type of labor until other workers can acquire the same skill. Such quasi-rents are also properly interpreted to be a form of excess profits (to human capital investment). But do workers and capitalists deserve these quasi-rents? Do producers deserve any pure profits, or losses, included in the income from their own labor and saving?

The answer is clearly in the negative. According to the principle of desert, remuneration must be proportional to exertion: producers deserve competitive rewards equal to the marginal value products of their labor and capital, provided the capital is produced by their own labor or purchased with savings from the rewards to their own labor. Quasi-rents to labor and capital are not deserved because the same quantities of labor and capital would exist in the short run even without quasi-rents. These excess profits do not reward work or saving, therefore, but something else. What that something else is, depends very much on how we interpret the nature of the economy. Consider the quasi-rent to a particular type of capital good, for example. On the one hand, we might emphasize that freedom to invest promotes long-run competitive efficiency in a world of risk and uncertainty: excess profits are temporarily received by any capitalist-entrepreneur who spots a more productive use for that type of capital before other investors do. Any quasi-rent to capital is then interpreted to be a reward to the capitalist-entrepreneur for promoting efficient resource allocation, a reward, that is, for contributing benefit to society.[74] On the other hand, we might emphasize instead that private ownership of capital allows the rich to dominate the poor in a world of personal wealth inequality: excess profits are income transfers that capitalist-entrepreneurs have the power to demand indefinitely from the rest of society. A quasi-rent to capital is now seen to be a reward to the capitalist-entrepreneur for domination, a reward for inflicting harm on society.[75] Similarly, the quasi-rent to a particular type of labor can be given two interpretations, each of which perhaps contains some part of the truth.

Quasi-rents are not deserved but any society must decide whether or not to permit them to be retained by capitalists and workers. Considerations of economic efficiency rather than of justice arguably support a general policy of laissez-faire: Producers generally should be given permission to retain quasi-rents with no suggestion that they have a moral right to do so. As a practical matter, of course, quasi-rents are not easily distinguished from the marginal value products of capital and labor anyway. But the key argument is one of principle: laissez-faire as a general rule promotes efficiency if economic power is more or less widely dispersed through the assignment of property rights grounded on desert. In this regard, we may recall Oliver Williamson's argument that laissez-faire generally facilitates the development of a wide variety of efficient market and non-market institutions under risk and uncertainty, different institutions serving to minimize the costs of different types of transactions.[76] Mill too claims that laissez-faire must be the general rule. In his view, when conducting a private business or entering into a personal contract, "most persons take a juster and more intelligent view of their own interest, and of the means of promoting it, than can either be prescribed to them by a general enactment of the legislature, or pointed out in a particular case by a public functionary."[77]

Nevertheless, Mill also admits a rather large class of exceptions to the general rule of laissez-faire. Government intervention may be called for to protect an indigent or incompetent agent, to void contracts in perpetuity, to regulate large-scale private enterprises, or to solve "free-rider problems," among other things.[78] Indeed, government intervention is called for to promote efficiency in complex modern capital markets. The stock market essentially vanishes at our long-run competitive equilibrium, for example, suggesting that the most efficient stock brokerage industry is no stock brokerage industry. But in the real world, active stock markets arise because "investment resources simply do not flow quickly across firms and industries thereby equalizing real rates of return."[79] Moreover, the present value of a company's expected excess profit stream can be a staggering sum. For example, if a corporation is forecast to receive excess profits of $5 million per year indefinitely, then the present value of these profits is $50 million if the annual rate of interest on riskless investments is 10 percent. This present value is in principle reflected in the stock value of the company. Fluctuations in interest rates or in the company's expected profit stream can generate massive wealth for a few lucky stockholders. In our example, if the interest rate falls to 5 percent, then the present value of the same excess profit stream increases to $100 million, an instant $50 million bonanza for the stockholders that has nothing to do with the desert principle.[80] Government measures to improve the efficiency of capital markets are properly beyond the scope of this chapter. But measures might include tax incentives to encourage private managers rapidly to reinvest their company's retained earnings in other higher-profit firms and industries as opportunities arise; direct government equity investments in the latter with a view to increasing net public revenues; and virtual confiscation of all personal capital gains above some suitable threshold level.[81]

Any discussion of the desert principle would be incomplete without noting that property rights in gifts and inheritances canot be justified on this basis. This kind of property is not the product of labor or saving by the beneficiary, except perhaps to the extent that family and friends are regarded as market investments. Moreover, at least beyond a certain scale, gifts and inheritances are incompatible with the normative ideal of more or less equal bargaining power implicit in our imaginary long-run competitive model. The legal terms and conditions of inheritance are thus properly a matter of general expedience rather than of moral desert. As Rowley and Peacock argue, Mill's proposals in this regard continue to have appeal: "The appropriate solution . . . (following Mill), is to disallow total inheritances (by will and by gifts *inter vivos*) from all sources by any individual *in excess* of strictly specified amounts (with the limit designed to eliminate the idle rich at each point of death), but to allow each individual to disperse his wealth privately to chosen inheritors as long as this limit is not violated. Wealth that is not so dispersed might be transferred to suitable charities.[82]

Strictly speaking, the principle of desert prescribes individual rights to own the products of one's own labor and saving, including whatever one can get for the products in a truly competitive market. If the laws of property are designed in conformity to the desert principle, then—abstracting for a moment from excess profits and inheritances—personal wealth inequality is due only to differences in personal efforts, savings rates, and talents. These personal differences are largely a matter of voluntary choice when individuals have equal access to education and job training. At the extreme, inequality of talent is the only inequality imposed by nature. Different talents, though undeserved, cannot justly "give umbrage" to self-interested individuals capable of work in this context. Any capable person is endowed with *some* talents and—given an equal opportunity— can more than make up for any relative lack of talent by working harder and saving more. Admissible economic inequality is thereby rather narrowly circumscribed under any just form of capitalism. "Nothing is imlied in property but the right of each to his [or her] own faculties, to what he can produce by them, and to whatever he can get for them in a fair market."[83]

Rights to excess profits (land rents and quasi-rents) and inheritances are not esential to capitalist justice. But, within limits, these sorts of legal rights may have to be permitted by society as a means of promoting long-run efficiency. Limits are implicit in the normative ideal of our long-run competitive model: We should not depart too much from equal bargaining power and the equality of wealth it seems to presuppose. Limited property rights in excess profits and inheritances exacerbate the problem of inequality. Yet the added inequality is not properly chargeable to the principle of private property itself. Rather, the extra inequality is permitted only because it is judged to be inseparable from the attainment of efficiency by any economy whose participants are motivated primarily by self-interest. Nevertheless, luck does play a role along with desert in generating economic inequality in any real-world capitalist economy. As Mill summarizes: "The inequalities of property which arise from unequal industry, frugality, perseverance, talents, *and to a certain extent even opportunities,* are inseparable from the principle of private property, and if we accept the principle, we must bear with these consequences of it [emphasis added]."[84]

Clearly, the property rights associated with capitalist justice safeguard any person's capacity to earn a living for himself and his dependents by means of his own exertions. Corresponding to any producer's property rights are duties held by all other persons to refrain from seizing the producer's property. The system of property rights and duties secures expectations relating to the production and exchange of scarce resources. This security is especially valuable when most members of society are primarily motivated by self-interest. No person capable of work can depend on the voluntary charity of others. As Mill says, "since the human race has no means of enjoyable existence, or of existence at all, but what it derives from its own labour and abstinence, there would be no ground for complaint against society if everyone who was willing to undergo a fair share of this labour and abstinence could attain a fair share of the fruits."[85] The feeling of security afforded by property rights is properly part of any justification of private property. Indeed, Mill seems to consider security of expectations to be paramount in his utilitarian justification of private property: "I do not, indeed, quite agree . . . that, from the utilitarian point of view, the right of private ownership is founded solely on the motives it affords to the increase of public wealth; because independently of those motives, *the feeling of security* of possession and enjoyment, which could not (in the state of advancement mankind have yet reached) be had without private ownership, *is of the very greatest importance as an element of human happiness.*"[86]

Evidently, property rights grounded on desert do not apply to anyone who is incapable of productive labor. Another secondary principle of justice is required to secure subsistence for him.

V

Capitalist justice grounded on desert can be supplemented by a principle of need that prescribes welfare rights to any indigent person. No one deserves his personal endowments or lack thereof. Even a predominantly selfish society can recognize the need to compensate to those disabled by nature. Moreover, no producer deserves to be impoverished by losses suffered on his risky and uncertain investments. An individual willing to work may have invested most of her resources in acquiring skills that she has no opportunity to exercise through no fault of her own. Even a predominantly selfish society can recognize the need temporarily to support her while she acquires marketable skills.

Mill emphasizes that "the claim to help . . . created by destitution, is one of the strongest which can exist"; and that "the certainty [or security] of subsistence should be held out by law to the destitute . . . rather than . . . their relief . . . depend on voluntary charity."[87] Moreover, individual rights "to be supported at the cost of other people" are grounded on a principle of need: "Apart from any metaphysical considerations respecting the foundations of morals or of the social union, it will be admitted to be right that human beings should help one another; and the more so, in proportion to the urgency of the need: and none needs help so urgently as one who is starving."[88] Strictly speaking, welfare rights should not be held by able-bodied persons unwilling to work. They deserve to be impoverished. But government cannot easily distinguish the disabled in all cases, and must "act by general rule." As a result, welfare rights must be assigned independently of considerations of desert: "The state . . . cannot undertake to discriminate between the deserving and the undeserving indigent. . . . Private charity [alone] can make these distinctions."[89]

That government must impartially assign individual welfare rights creates obvious incentive problems in any society of predominantly selfish individuals unless steps are taken to ensure that "the condition of those who are supported by legal charity [is] kept considerably less desirable than the condition of those who find support for themselves."[90] As Krouse and McPherson remark, Mill's own approach seems extraordinarily harsh by modern standards. He limits welfare rights to some minimum level of assistance needed for bare subsistence: "[T]he administrators of a public fund ought not to be required to do more for anybody, than that minimum which is due even to the worst. If they are, the indulgence very speedily becomes the rule."[91] Moreover, he recommends exceptional legal penalties against welfare recipients to encourage them to support themselves by their own labor if they can. In particular, welfare recipients would be denied the franchise as well as permission to procreate, neither of which Mill regards as a moral right.[92]

Mill's extreme concern to safeguard the priority of the principle of desert indicates his commitment to private property as well as his estimate of the predominantly selfish character of his contemporary society. Perhaps the same degree of concern is no longer required in a wealthy modern society like the United States. In any case, the point is that even a predominantly selfish society can consistently recognize a perfect moral duty to support people incapable of work. The duty of every wealthy producer to provide subsistence for the indigent is legally enforced through the tax system, of course, because government intervention is required to resolve the "free-rider problem."[93] Welfare relief, like police protection, becomes another generally accepted function of government. Indeed, given that government must have the authority to tax producers if it is to exist at all, the focus of attention shifts to principles of just taxation under capitalism. In this regard, Mill generally argues for proportional taxation of all earned income above subsistence from labor and saving, with sharply progressive taxation of all unearned income (gifts, inheritances, land rents, capital gains, and the like). Whatever its other merits, his argument seems to be more or less fair in terms of the principles of desert and of need since it requires more or less equal "sacrifices"—in terms of labor and abstinence—from all taxpayers living above subsistence.[94]

VI

My argument is that capitalism in its best form involves property rights grounded on the principle that producers deserve the fruits of their labor and saving. A capitalist economy can admit welfare rights grounded on the principle that the destitute need help from the wealthy who can afford to support them through an equitable tax system. Rights to liberty in purely private matters outside the economy can also be assigned on the basis of Mill's principle of liberty. Economic inequality continues to exist in this ideal context but is largely the result of voluntary decisions including work-leisure choices, consumption-savings decision, human capital investment choices and so on. Nevertheless, differences in natural talents and in opportunities for excess profit generate more inequality than desert alone requires. The added inequality cannot justly "give umbrage" to predominantly self-interested individuals, however, provided it is a necessary by-product of the pursuit of long-run competitive efficiency.

The picture that emerges is of a more or less classless version of capitalism where most are at once workers and owners of capital. Commentators sometimes suggest that capitalism implies a division of society into distinct classes of, say, productive workers and idle owners of capital. Indeed, Alan Ryan goes so far as to claim that "one reasonable test for socialism would be the aspiration for a classless society."[95] But private ownership of capital need not result in a class-divided society. Indeed, if the laws of property are made to conform to the principle of desert, then labor and abstinence are required to accumulate wealth, even though opportunities to collect limited excess profits also obtain. Moreover, intergenerational transmission of wealth is subject to severe limitation because inheritance rights are not grounded in desert and are no necessary part of private property. Idle owners of natural resources collect no rewards from mere possession and are reduced to welfare relief unless they otherwise exert themselves. In short, wealth inequality is likely to be minimal. Individuals remain at liberty to retire from productive labor but will rarely enjoy the good fortune to combine leisure with unusual riches.

Various economic institutions are compatible with these ideal capitalist principles. The capital stock of an enterprise might be owned by its employees who—in addition to receiving salaries in proportion to their types of labor—share any profits including interest, and, with limited liability, losses in proportion to their individual investments. Alternatively, the stock of any enterprise might be owned, at least in part, by workers of other firms, each worker perhaps investing in a number of private corporations.[96] The important consideration is that capital ownership must be relatively diffuse if not more or less egalitarian when the distribution of property is predominantly governed by the desert principle. Self-interested owners of capital are led to cooperate as partners. Otherwise, no large-scale productive activities, with associated opportunities for profit, can be undertaken.

As Mill argues, a cooperative version of capitalism carries far more appeal than the more familiar versions that are plagued by inequality and class hostility: "[T]he industrial economy which divides society absolutely into two portions, the payers of wages and the receivers of them . . . is neither fit for, nor capable of, indefinite duration: and the possibility of changing this system for one of combination without dependence, and unity of interest instead of organized hostility, depends altogether upon the future developments of the partnership principle."[97] Indeed, he holds out the hope that cooperation might eventually bring about "the moral revolution in society" required for socialism. He remarks that a decentralized version of socialism involving self-governing enterprises "would be the nearest approach to social justice, and the most beneficial ordering of industrial affairs for the universal good, which it is possible at present to foresee."[98] The employees of the enterprise would have equal voices in its government and equal claims to profits.[99] But Mill also emphasizes that the higher moral ideal underlying social-ism is not yet feasible. Given that society consists of predomi-nantly self-interested individuals, a situation likely to persist "for a considerable length of time," most persons simply will not accept equal profit-sharing with coworkers who bring less capi-tal and/or talents and skills to the enterprise.[100]

The cooperative capitalist ideal provides a benchmark to guide the reform of actual "mixed economies" like the U.S. In partic-ular, the pattern of inequality in America is unjustified from this ideal capitalist perspective. Suitable reform of property in accord with the desert principle would radically redistribute personal wealth within a generation or two. Gifts and inheri-tances above some minimum level should be subject to sharply progressive taxation as should rents accruing to uncultivated land, particularly in urban areas, and to other natural resources. Virtual confiscation of personal capital gains above some mini-mum level also seems defensible as an imperfect way of getting at unearned quasi-rents as well as perhaps rent to talents.[101] A program of these and other measures, particularly education and job training, could eventually abolish undue concentration of personal wealth and inequality of economic opportunities. But this program would require at least a generation to have its effect. Given the overriding significance of security of expecta-tions for any justification of property rights, reform of property would be self-defeating if the reform itself destroyed security. Society must respect existing individual titles to uncultivated land and other natural resources as well as titles to property already received as gifts, inheritances, or capital gains.[102] If any existing titles are to be abrogated, then fair compensation must be paid by the taxpayer to the former owners. This just com-pensation requirement defeats any possibility of significant wealth redistribution within a generation.[103]

The possibility of capitalist justice seems to have always been taken seriously by most Americans and may even be part of some loosely defined "American Creed." I have tried to clarify the nature of capitalist justice and to show that its achievement would require a radical attack against the pattern of inequality in today's America. My argument may seem paradoxical to both defenders and critics of capitalism, including those who see an inherent contradiction between capitalism and democracy. But the claim that democratic equality and private property are necessarily at odds is itself problematic, as most Americans apparently believe. The desert principle justifying capitalism encourages a diffusion of wealth that dovetails nicely with the democratic principle justifying a more or less equal opportunity for every citizen to participate effectively in the political system. Indeed, Thomas Jefferson captures this aspect of the American Creed when in his First Inaugural Address he remarks that the popular happiness requires a democratic government protective of property rights grounded on desert: "[T]he sum of good government [is] a wise and frugal government, which shall restrain men from injuring one another, shall leave them otherwise free to regulate their own pursuits of industry and improvements, and shall not take from the mouth of labor the bread it has earned."[104]

NOTES

1. Alan Ryan, *Property and Political Theory* (Oxford: Blackwell, 1984), 187.

2. Michael Harrington, *The Twilight of Capitalism* (New York: Simon and Schuster, 1976), 320.

3. Milton Friedman, *Capitalism and Freedom* (Chicago: University of Chicago Press, 1962); idem, *Free to Choose* (New York: Avon, 1979); Friedrich Hayek, *Law, Legislation and Liberty* (London: Routledge & Kegan Paul, 1982), vols. 1–3; Robert Nozick, *Anarchy, State and Utopia* (Oxford: Blackwell, 1974).

4. Kenneth Arrow, *The Limits of Organization* (New York: Norton, 1974); idem, "The Viability and Equity of Capitalism," E. S. Woodward Lecture (Vancouver: University of British Columbia Department of Economics, 1976); idem, "A Cautious Case for Socialism," in *Beyond the Welfare State*, ed. I. Howe (New York: Schocken Books, 1982), 261–76; Amartya Sen, *On Economic Inequality* (Oxford: Clarendon Press, 1973); idem, *Poverty*

and Famines (Oxford: Clarendon Press, 1981); idem, *Commodities and Capabilities* (Amsterdam: North-Holland, 1985); and idem, *On Ethics and Economics* (Oxford: Blackwell, 1987). Neither Arrow nor Sen dismisses the appeal of socialism.

5. For some evidence that most Americans, rich and poor alike, remain reluctant to abandon capitalism in principle despite their discontent at the pronounced degree of inequality found in the modern American economy, see Jennifer L. Hochschild, *What's Fair? American Beliefs about Distributive Justice* (Cambridge: Harvard University Press, 1981); Robert E. Lane, "Market Justice, Political Justice," *American Political Science Review* 80 (1986): 383–402; and Herbert McClosky and John Zaller, *The American Ethos: Public Attitudes Towards Capitalism and Democracy* (Cambridge: Harvard University Press, 1985). On American atitudes toward individualism, see also Robert N. Bellah et al. *Habits of the Heart* (New York: Harper & Row, 1985), esp. 142–63. It should be noted that the actual U.S. economy is what might be termed "mixed welfare state capitalism," i.e., a welfare state (redistributive taxation) and elements of socialism (public ownership of productive assets) are combined with the predominant emphasis on capitalism.

6. Jeffrey G. Williamson and Peter H. Lindert claim in their *American Inequality* (New York: Academic Press, 1980) that U.S. experience confirms the well-known Kuznets hypothesis. Kuznets hypothesized that economic growth produces first an increase then a decrease in inequality as average incomes rise. See Simon Kuznets, "Economic Growth and Income Inequality," *American Economic Review* 45 (1955): 1–28. See also Jeffrey G. Williamson, "Is Inequality Inevitable Under Capitalism? The American Case," in *Modern Capitalism*, ed. P. L. Berger (London: Hamilton Press, 1987), 1: 48–83.

7. U.S. Department of Commerce, Bureau of the Census, *Statistical Abstract of the United States, 1987,* 437.

8. For discussion, see Hochschild, *What's Fair?* 3–6; Lars Osberg, *Economic Inequality in the United States* (Armonk, N.Y.: M. E. Sharpe, 1984); and Williamson and Lindert, *American Inequality*, 65–95. It should be noted that the overall distributional impact of the complex and ever-changing tax system is difficult to assess. See, for example, Lester C. Thurow, *The Zero-Sum Society* (New York: Penguin, 1981), 167–77; and Thurow, *The Zero-Sum Solution* (New York: Simon & Schuster, 1985), 110–31, 207–61.

9. U.S. Department of Commerce, Bureau of the Census, *Current Population Reports: Consumer Income*, series P-60, no. 156 (Aug. 1987), 141, 146–51.

10. Thurow, *The Zero-Sum Society*, 156–57.

11. Daphne Greenwood, "An Estimation of U.S. Family Wealth and

Its Distribution from Micro Data, 1973," *The Review of Income and Wealth* 29 (1983): 35–36. For a balanced discussion of alternative estimates and of limitations in the data relating to this controversial topic, see Osberg, *Economic Inequality in the United States*, 38–47.

12. Hochschild, *What's Fair?* 6–8; Osberg, *Economic Inequality in the United States*, 47–49; and Williamson and Lindert, *American Inequality*, 9–63.

13. See Edward N. Wolff, "The Size Distribution of Household Disposable Wealth in the United States," *The Review of Income and Wealth* 29 (1983): 125–46; and Osberg, *Economic Inequality in the United States*, 45–47.

14. Osberg, *Economic Inequality in the United States*, 47.

15. Greenwood, "An Estimation of U.S. Family Wealth and Its Distribution from Micro Data, 1973," 35.

16. Hochschild, *What's Fair?* 13.

17. For discussion of the evidence and its limitations, see Osberg, *Economic Inequality in the United States*, 85–194, 256–66; Henry Phelps Brown, *The Inequality of Pay* (Berkeley: University of California Press, 1977); and Thurow, *The Zero-Sum Society*, 178–214. More generally, see Berger, *Modern Capitalism*, vol. 1.

18. Thurow, *The Zero-Sum Society*, 172.

19. For relevant discussion, see John A. Brittain, *Inheritance and the Inequality of Material Wealth* (Washington, D.C.: Brookings Institution, 1978); Gordon Cooper, *A Voluntary Tax? New Perspectives on Sophisticated Estate Tax Avoidance* (Washington, D.C.: Brookings Institution, 1979); Osberg, *Economic Inequality in the United States*, 195–219; and Robert A. Pollak, "A Transactions Cost Approach to Families and Households," *Journal of Economic Literature* 23 (1985): 581–608.

20. Thurow, *The Zero-Sum Society*, 167–78.

21. Strictly speaking, a measure of inequality does not logically imply any *evaluation* of the relevant distribution. To judge whether there is too much inequality in society, it is necessary to specify distributional norms and then evaluate the measured distributions of income and wealth against those norms. My point is that the pattern of wealth inequality in America is at odds with any reasonable distributional norms, including the desert norm that I will suggest properly underlies capitalism.

22. Peter L. Berger, *The Capitalist Revolution* (New York: Basic Books, 1986), 195. Even so, Berger doubts that there is any so-called "legitimation crisis" in Western societies and emphasizes the remarkable degree to which capitalism seems to be accepted by the majority in these societies (194–209). The self-destructive tendency of capitalism has been explored from a variety of perspectives. See Daniel Bell, *The Cultural Contradictions of Capitalism* (New York: Basic Books, 1976); Samuel Bowles

and Herbert Gintis, *Democracy and Capitalism* (New York: Basic Books, 1986); Robert A. Dahl, *A Preface to Economic Democracy* (Berkeley: University of California Press, 1985); Jurgen Habermas, *Legitimation Crisis* (Boston: Beacon Press, 1973); Harrington, *The Twilight of Capitalism;* Robert Heilbroner, *The Nature and Logic of Capitalism* (New York: Norton, 1985); and Joseph A. Schumpeter, *Capitalism, Socialism and Democracy* (New York: Harper & Row, 1942).

23. Robert Nisbet, "America as Utopia," *Reason* 18 (Mar. 1987): 38. On the notion of an "American Religion" or "American Creed," see also Samuel P. Huntington, *American Politics: The Promise of Disharmony* (Cambridge: Belknap Press, 1981), and references cited therein.

24. Huntington, *American Politics*. On the reluctance of American workers to embrace socialism, see, for example, Seymour M. Lipset, "Why No Socialism in the United States?" in *Sources of Contemporary Radicalism*, ed. S. Bialer and S. Sluzar (Boulder: Westview Press, 1977), 31–149.

25. J. S. Mill, "Chapters on Socialism," in *Collected Works of John Stuart Mill*, ed. J. M. Robson (London: Routledge & Kegan Paul: Toronto: University of Toronto Press, 1965–), 5:750. See also Mill, *Principles of Political Economy*, in *Collected Works*, ed. Robson, 2:214.

26. See, for example, Ryan, *Property and Political Theory*, 142–74.

27. Mill, "Use and Abuse of Political Terms," in *Collected Works*, ed. Robson, 18: 6.

28. Mill, "Chapters on Socialism," 738.

29. Ibid., 753, 750. For a similar idea of property, see Lawrence C. Becker, *Property Rights: Philosophic Foundations* (London: Routledge & Kegan Paul, 1977), 7–23. More generally, see also C. B. Macpherson, ed., *Property* (Toronto: University of Toronto Press, 1978); and J. R. Pennock and J. W. Chapman, eds., *Nomos 22: Property* (New York: New York University Press, 1980).

30. Mill, *Principles of Political Economy*, 215, 217.

31. Mill, "Chapters on Socialism," 737–42. Mill's doubts about the efficiency of market socialism relative to capitalism largely concern the incentives of socialist managers, not those of ordinary workers. He admits that fixed-wage earners as opposed to capitalists have few incentives to perform efficiently. Moreover, his point extends to private managers who are hired at a fixed salary and own no stock. Nevertheless, as discussed below in section 6, Mill refuses to concede any advantage to socialism on this score not least because he imagines an ideal version of capitalism in which salaries are supplemented by profit-sharing arrangements for every member of every enterprise. See Mill, "Chapters on Socialism," 742–49; *Principles of Political Economy*, 201–9, 954–56.

32. Mill, "Chapters on Socialism," 740.

33. For an argument that moral incentives can in principle give rise to market efficiency, see Joseph H. Carens. *Equality, Moral Incentives and the Market* (Chicago: University of Chicago Press, 1981).

34. For discussion of the various sources of market inefficiency, see, for example, Kenneth Arrow, "The Organization of Economic Activity: Issues Pertinent to the Choice of Market versus Nonmarket Allocation," in *The Analysis and Evaluation of Public Expenditure,* vol. 1, U.S. Joint Economic Committee Report, 91st Congress, 1st Session (Washington: USGPO, 1969), 59–73; Frank Hahn, "Reflections on the Invisible Hand," *Lloyds Bank Review* 144 (1982): 1–21; Leonid Hurwicz, "On Informationally Decentralized Systems," in *Decision and Organization,* ed. C. B. McGuire and R. Radner (Amsterdam: North-Holland, 1972), 297–336; Hurwicz, "The Design of Mechanisms for Resource Allocation," *American Economic Review* 63 (1973): 1–30; and Hurwicz, "Incentive Aspects of Decentralization," in *Handbook of Mathematical Economics,* ed. K. J. Arrow and M. D. Intriligator (Amsterdam: North-Holland, 1986), 3: 1441–82.

35. Oliver Williamson, *Markets and Hierarchies* (New York: Free Press, 1975); idem, "The Modern Corporation: Origins, Evolution, Attributes," *Journal of Economic Literature* 19 (1981): 1537–68; and idem, *The Economic Institutions of Capitalism* (New York: Free Press, 1985). See also Arrow, *The Limits of Organization;* and Alfred D. Chandler, Jr., *The Visible Hand* (Cambridge: Harvard University Press, 1977).

36. Sen, "The Profit Motive," *Lloyds Bank Review* 147 (1983): 6.

37. Ibid.

38. Ibid., 7. See also Sen, "The Moral Standing of the Market," in *Ethics and Economics,* ed. E. F. Paul, F. D. Miller, and J. Paul (Oxford: Blackwell, 1985), 3–23.

39. Arrow, *The Viability and Equity of Capitalism,* 9–17; Rawls, *A Theory of Justice* (Cambridge: Belknap Press, 1971).

40. Mill, *Utilitarianism,* in *Collected Works,* ed. Robson, 10:240–44.

41. For Arrow's defence of a "purely ordinalist" utilitarian approach to justice despite his "strong agreement" with the "broad thrust" of Rawls's neo-Kantian theory of justice, see, especially, Arrow, "Some Ordinalist-Utilitarian Notes on Rawls's Theory of Justice," *Journal of Philosophy* (1973): 245–63. For Mill's complex version of the classical utilitarian theory of justice, see Mill, *Utilitarianism,* 240–59.

42. See, especially, Sen, *Commodities and Capabilities.*

43. Many writers claim that Mill's three secondary principles of justice are in conflict. See, e.g., Krouse and McPherson, "The Logic of Liberal Equality." As I try to make clear in subsequent sections, I do not find the claim persuasive although difficulties of applying the principles should not be minimized.

44. Mill, *On Liberty,* in *Collected Works,* ed. Robson, 18: 293. Mill's idea

of privacy must be distinguished from the view that whatever is not done by government is private.

45. Arrow, *The Viability and Equity of Capitalism*, 13.

46. Mill, *Principles of Political Economy*, 945.

47. Arrow, *The Viability and Equity of Capitalism*, 12.

48. Ibid.

49. Mill, *On Liberty*, 293. For Mill's view that libertarian rights are absolute moral claims, see *On Liberty*, 223–26, 260–61, 276–91. For his view that these rights correlate to perfect moral duties, see "Use and Abuse of Political Terms," 8–9; and *Utilitarianism*, 247–48. For his distinction between a moral right and a merely expedient permission (two claims often conflated under the same term "right"), see "Use and Abuse of Political Terms," 9–10. For his exceptions to the general rule of laissez-faire, see *Principles of Political Economy*, 944–71.

50. See Arrow, *The Limits of Organization*, 45–79. Despite the inseparability of power over others from the pursuit of efficiency in this context, scholars debate whether power or efficiency should be the main focus of research. For perspectives on the debate, see, for example, Arthur Francis, "Markets and Hierarchies: Efficiency or Domination?" in *Power, Efficiency and Institutions*, ed. A. Francis, J. Turk, and P. Willman (London: Heinemann, 1983), 105–16; and Stephen A. Marglin, "Knowledge and Power," in *Firms, Organization and Labour*, ed. F. H. Stephen (New York: St. Martin's Press, 1984), 146–64.

51. Arrow, *The Limits of Organization*, 21.

52. Mill, *Principles of Political Economy*, 208.

53. Ibid., 208, 215.

54. Ibid., 207.

55. Ibid., 207–8. See also 810–11.

56. Ibid., 199.

57. For discussion of the Cambridge controversies, see Christopher J. Bliss, *Capital Theory and the Distribution of Income* (Amsterdam: North-Holland, 1975). See also Arrow and Hahn, *General Competitive Analysis* (San Francisco: Holden-Day, 1971); and Gerard Debreu, "Existence of Competitive Equilibrium," in Arrow and Intriligator, *Handbook of Mathematical Economics*, 2:697–743.

58. For clarification of the subtle distinction between "long-run" and "short-run" analysis, see Hal R. Varian, *Microeconomic Analysis*, 2d ed. (New York: W. W. Norton, 1984). In my view, the only true competitive equilibrium is a long-run equilibrium with all factors in variable supply. Fixed factors give their possessors more bargaining power than nonpossessors. Inequality of power is at odds with the competitive hypothesis that all agents take prices as given.

59. See, for example, N. Scott Arnold, "Capitalists and the Ethics of

Contribution," *Canadian Journal of Philosophy* 15 (1985): 87–102; Arnold, "Why Profits Are Deserved," *Ethics* 97 (1987): 387–402, 411–31; Edward Nell, "On Deserving Profits," *Ethics* 97 (1987): 403–410; and David Schweickart, *Capitalism or Worker Control?* (New York: Praeger, 1980).

60. Mill, *Principles of Political Economy*, 55, 57. Mill remarks that "money cannot itself perform any part of the office of capital, since it can afford no assistance to production" (55). Money by itself does not create the food and equipment required by labor.

61. Ibid., 59.

62. See Mill, "Thornton on Labour and Its Claims," in *Collected Works*, ed. Robson, 5:653.

63. Mill includes interest (reward for abstinence), insurance (indemnity for risk), and compensation for managerial skills (wages of superintendence) in gross profits. But "the current rate of interest on the best security" is properly the only component of profit that rewards "the use of the capital itself." The insurance component of profit properly only arises outside of competitive equilibrium and the managerial compensation component is properly a type of labor cost. All three components may be paid either to the same person or to different persons. For convenience, I distinguish between the capitalist (owner or riskless lender of capital), the entrepreneur (risk-taking borrower or lender of capital), and the manager (superintendent of the enterprise). See Mill, *Principles of Political Economy*, 400–15, 647–59, 698–701.

64. Ibid., 230.

65. Ibid., 58.

66. Ibid., 227.

67. Ibid., 819.

68. For critical discussion of the Lockean proviso, see, e.g., Nozick, *Anarchy, State and Utopia;* Becker, *Property Rights,* esp. 32–56; and Andrew Reeve, *Property* (London: Macmillan, 1986), esp. 112–51. Nozick argues that a weak version of the proviso will not be violated by private enterprise. Becker and Reeve both give compelling reasons for thinking otherwise. It should be noted that Locke separately requires any user of a natural resource to work efficiently, i.e., not permit anything to spoil in his possession.

69. Mill, *Principles of Political Economy*, 232. See also Mill, "The Right of Property in Land," in *Collected Works*, ed. Robson, 25:1235–243.

70. See Arrow, *The Viability and Equity of Capitalism*, 15–17; Ronald Dworkin, "What is Equality? Parts 1 and 2," *Philosophy and Public Affairs* 10 (1981): 185–246, 283–345; Frank Knight, *The Ethics of Competition* (New York: Harper, 1935), 54–57; Marglin, "Knowledge and Power"; Rawls, *A Theory of Justice*, 103–4, 310–15; and Sen, *Commodities and Capabilities.*

71. Rawls, *A Theory of Justice*, 312.

72. Mill, *Principles of Political Economy*, 210. See also Mill, *Utilitarianism*, 253–54.

73. See John E. Roemer, "Equality of Talent," *Economics and Philosophy* 1 (1985): 151–86.

74. See Arnold, "Why Profits Are Deserved." Arnold goes further and suggests that entrepreneurs *deserve* their excess profit because profits are a reward for spotting misallocations of resources and the size of the reward is proportional to the degree of misallocation. But his notion of desert is defined relative to the goal of economic efficiency rather than to that of distributive justice.

75. See, e.g., Marglin, "What Do Bosses Do? The Origins and Functions of Hierarchy in Capitalist Production," *Review of Radical Political Economy* 6: 33–60; and Nell, "On Deserving Profits."

76. See references cited above at note 33.

77. Mill, *Principles of Political Economy*, 951.

78. Ibid., 947–71.

79. Thurow, *The Zero-Sum Society*, 174.

80. Ibid., 172–74.

81. For relevant discussion, see Mill, *Principles of Political Economy*, 954–56; Thurow, *The Zero-Sum Society*, 174–77; and Thurow, *The Zero-Sum Solution*, 207–98.

82. Charles K. Rowley and Alan T. Peacock, *Welfare Economics: A Liberal Restatement* (New York: Wiley, 1975), 157, emphasis in original. See also Mill, *Principles of Political Economy*, 218–26, 887–95.

83. Mill, *Principles of Political Economy*, 218.

84. Ibid., 225.

85. Mill, "Chapters on Socialism," 714.

86. Mill, letter to Charles Elliot Norton dated June 26, 1870, reprinted as Letter 1569, in *Collected Works*, ed. Robson, 17:1739–40. On the importance that Mill assigns to security of possession in the process of economic growth and advancing civilization, see *Principles of Political Economy*, 880–86. See also Samuel H. Hollander, *The Economics of J. S. Mill* (Toronto: University of Toronto Press, 1985), 1:198–204; and Ryan, *Property and Political Theory*, 91–117.

87. Mill, *Principles of Political Economy*, 960, 962. See also 355–79. For an illuminating critique of Mill's approach to welfare rights, see Krouse and McPherson, "The Logic of Liberal Equality," sections II–III.

88. Mill, *Principles of Political Economy*, 360, 960.

89. Ibid., 962.

90. Ibid., 961.

91. Ibid., 962. Inherent ambiguities in the idea of "disability" have arguably prevented public administrators from holding the line, leading

to what some observers refer to as a fiscal and moral "crisis" in the modern welfare state. For a balanced discussion, see Deborah A. Stone, *The Disabled State* (Philadelphia: Temple University Press, 1985).

92. Both voting and having children are other-regarding actions so that neither action is protected by Mill's principle of liberty. Instead, society properly considers whether or not to interfere with them under certain circumstances. Clearly, Mill argues that general expedience requires interfering with the voting and childbearing of anyone who is a welfare recipient, but not otherwise. For the case of voting, see Mill, *Considerations on Representative Government,* in *Collected Works,* ed. Robson, 19: 467–74, 488–90. For the case of childbearing, see *Principles of Political Economy,* 357–60; and *On Liberty,* 304–5.

93. Mill, *Principles of Political Economy,* 960–62.

94. Ibid., 805–72.

95. Ryan, *Property and Political Theory,* 157. Some writers similarly distinguish between capitalism and an "egalitarian" private property economy. See, e.g., Krouse and McPherson, "The Logic of Liberal Equality," drawing on James E. Meade, *Efficiency, Equality and the Ownership of Property* (London: Allen & Unwin, 1964). But it seems arbitrary to restrict the term "capitalism" to highly inegalitarian or class-divided private-property economies. After all, capitalists, idle or otherwise, must also exist in any "egalitarian" private-property economy. See, e.g., Mill, *Principles of Political Economy,* 235–38.

96. In either case, any worker remains free to transfer his capital between corporations or to consume it himself.

97. Mill, *Principles of Political Economy,* 896–97. See also 895–906.

98. Ibid., 794.

99. Ibid., 775–94, 903–4. A similar version of democratic socialism is discussed by Dahl, *Preface to Economic Democracy.* See also Bowles and Gintis, *Democracy and Capitalism;* and Charles E. Linblom, *Politics and Markets* (New York: Basic Books, 1977).

100. Given the predominantly selfish characters of most individuals, Mill doubts not only the productive efficiency of socialism but also its compatibility with individuality. Even within a self-governing enterprise, the majority may well tyrannize over some competent group of entrepreneurs. See, e.g., *Principles of Political Economy,* 201–14; and "Chapters on Socialism," esp. 727–50.

101. Mill suggests all of these sorts of measures. See *Principles of Political Economy,* 218–26, 819–37. For recent discussion of such proposals, see, e.g., Brittain, *Inheritance and the Inequality of Material Wealth;* Cooper, *A Voluntary Tax?;* Anthony Downs, *The Revolution in Real Estate Finance* (Washington, D.C. Brookings Institution, 1985); and Osberg, *Economic Inequality in the United States,* 195–219.

102. For similar reasons, Mill argues that individual title should be given by prescription after a certain period. See *Principles of Political Economy*, 217–18.

103. For Mill's insistence on just compensation, see *Principles of Political Economy*, 230, 1238–39; "Chapters on Socialism," 753. See also Krouse and McPherson, "The Logic of Liberal Equality," sec. 3.

104. Thomas Jefferson, "First Inaugural Address," in *Thomas Jefferson: Writings,* ed. Merrill D. Peterson (New York: The Library of America, 1984), 494. For an example of the argument that "the Jeffersonian synthesis of property and democracy [is] archaic," see Bowles and Gintis, *Democracy and Capitalism,* 47–55, 174–213. In their view, liberal capitalism should be abolished in favor of a "postliberal democracy" involving self-governing socialist enterprises. See also Dahl, *A Preface to Economic Democracy.* On Jefferson and the American Creed, see Peterson, *The Jeffersonian Image in the American Mind* (New York: Oxford University Press, 1960).

PART III

MARKETS AND CHARACTER

6

JUSTICE AND
THE MARKET DOMAIN

MARGARET JANE RADIN

I. Introduction: The Metaphor of the Wall

It has been traditional to view some aspects of social life as inappropriate for the market. We speak of a metaphorical wall between the market and other realms of social life, much as we speak of a wall between church and state. There is a traditional understanding that important political activities, like voting, are on the nonmarket side of the wall. There is also an understanding that certain special kinds of interactions between persons are on the nonmarket side of the wall—that is, are morally required to be kept there—even if some people desire to "marketize" them. It is this latter understanding that I wish to explore and question here. Does justice require that we delineate and protect a nonmarket domain? In general, how might a theory of social justice take into account the question of the domain of the market?

A traditional liberal view is that the market appropriately encompasses most desired transactions between people, with a few special exceptions. Those few exceptions—for example, the way we acquire a spouse or a child—are morally and legally protected from the market. I want to suggest that the traditional view is wrong in granting too much ground to the market. The metaphor of a wall between a market and nonmarket realm is inapposite because it wrongly suggests a large realm of pure free-market transactions to which special kinds of personal interactions form a special exception. It wrongly suggests that a laissez-faire market regime is prima facie just.

I shall leave aside here one way that the wall metaphor is evidently inapposite. To think of a wall between politics and markets, and also a wall between special kinds of personal interactions and markets, obscures the fact that they are not the same kind of wall. The wall between certain personal interactions and markets is thought to bar sales only, whereas the wall between politics and markets is thought to wall off nonmonetary transactions as well as sales. In political elections we are not to give other people proxies to vote for us, whether they pay us or not; elected officials are not to relinquish their power to another's discretion, whether they are bribed or not. In nonmarket personal transactions, like adoption or organ donation, by contrast, giving is not prohibited. Indeed, fostering giving may be a reason for the market ban. This discrepancy between the kinds of walls at least shows that the wall metaphor is oversimplified. Nevertheless, I do not pursue this, nor do I pursue the problem of how we should think about the supposed wall between politics and the market.[1] Instead, I want to pursue the debate over nonmarket personal interactions. How should we conceive, for example, of attempted sales of human organs?

In order to frame this discussion it is necessary to notice that there is another way to deny the appositeness of the wall metaphor, and that is to say that in principle there is no limit to the market. Someone who holds this view thinks of the market as encompassing the social world. She thinks not only that social justice does not require us to protect a nonmarket domain, but also that social justice requires a universal market structure. This is the approach taken by some of the contemporary theorists who bring economics to bear on political and legal theory. Hence, it is possible to see an imaginary battle being waged. The traditional liberal view, asserting that there must be a realm of personal interactions walled off from the market, is striving to hold some territory against the oncoming forces of economics and the notion that everything is grist for the market mill.

In my view, both sides are wrong, and so is the battle. Instead of trying to defend the small piece of ground representing the list of special nonmarket personal interactions, it would be better to try to reclaim for peaceful co-existence some of the territory the traditional liberal view concedes to the market. The traditional liberal view is wrong because it assumes that not much is on the nonmarket side of the wall, and the battle lines prevent us from appreciating the nonmarket aspects of many of our market relations. They prevent us from seeing fragments of a nonmarket social order embedded or latent in the market society. They prevent us from thinking about social justice in terms of fostering this latent co-existent nonmarket order.

II. Universal Commodification vs. the Wall

A. *The Market as Methodological Archetype*

Let us first consider a sketch of an archetype representing the economic view, and then consider the reasons given by its opponents for walling off a few special things from the market. Some law-and-economics theorists can be understood to endorse a methodological archetype that is sometimes referred to as market-imperialism, but which I prefer to call universal commodification. Under universal commodification, all things desired or valued—from personal attributes to good government—are goods or commodities.[2] Commodities are usually pictured as objects separate from the self and social relations. Hence, universal commodification is a form of objectification. It assimilates personal attributes, relations, and desired states of affairs to the realm of objects. Universal commodification implies that all things can and should be separable from persons and exchanged through the free market, whenever some people are willing to sell and others are willing to buy. All human attributes are conceived of as possessions bearing a value characterizable in money terms, and all human interactions are conceived as exchanges understandable in terms of gains from trade.

The language in which this conceptual scheme is couched is the rhetoric of the market. Under universal commodification, the human universe of social interaction—from government to love and sexuality—is conceived and described in the rhetoric of trading objects for money. Hobbes conceived of the value of a person in market rhetoric: "the *Value* or WORTH of a man, is as of all other things, his Price; that is to say, so much as would be given for the use of his Power."[3] In Hobbes's conception, everything about a person that others need, desire, or value is a possession that is priced. The Hobbesian person fits into the archetype of universal commodification. The Hobbesian conception of the political order likewise conceives of politics in market rhetoric. Modern Hobbesians view political activity as fully describable in terms of "rent seeking" by those who can achieve monetary gain from the capture of portions of Leviathan's power.[4]

The method of justifying actions and states of affairs under universal commodification is monetary cost-benefit analysis. For whatever we do not normally buy and sell, universal commodification uses monetary cost-benefit analysis either to justify or criticize the anomaly. Thus, in the universal commodification methodology, the only exceptions to the rule of laissez-faire are for situations in which laissez-faire cannot arrive at an efficient result. These are the situations called market failure.[5]

For one who is willing to conceive of everything (corneas for transplant, sexuality, babies for adoption) in market rhetoric, the only explanation for why some things might be held out of the market is market failure: free riders and holdouts, administrative costs, information costs, and so on. Judge Richard Posner, for example, apparently views a ban on selling oneself into slavery as justified by information costs.[6] Finding no apparent market failures that would suggest noncommodification of children, he suggests that a free market in babies would be a good idea.[7]

B. Three Attempts to Maintain the Wall

Those who advocate the traditional wall to claim a few things for a domain that is in principle off limits to the market rely on reasons other than market failure. Three prevalent kinds of arguments are deployed in trying to keep something—babies, blood, kidneys—on the nonmarket side of a metaphorical wall. The first is an argument based upon the degradation and invasion of personhood occasioned by allowing sales. The second is an argument based upon creating or preserving opportunities for altruism. The third is a slippery slope argument that I call a domino theory, claiming that to allow sales for some people who choose them will foreclose nonmarket sharing for those who don't choose the market regime. As we shall see, the second and third arguments are related, because the argument based upon opportunities for altruism assumes the domino theory is true. But the two arguments are not coextensive, for, as we shall see, the domino theory is also applied to cases that do not fit the argument about altruism.

I shall argue that these arguments are too general for the task they have been put to, that is, to show that universal commodification is wrong because there must remain certain specific pockets of nonmarket social interactions. Instead, they seem to point toward a more generalized nonmarket perspective. That is, these arguments have been aimed at shoring up a wall between the market and nonmarket domains, but in fact they undermine the wall metaphor. These arguments fail to capture what is wrong about universal commodification.

Personhood prophylaxis. The first strand of argument is often thought of in connection with organ transplants, especially from living people. The argument holds that we must prevent poor people from being forced to sell their kidneys and corneas. The general idea is that it is somehow degrading to be selling off one's body parts, and that this is an injury to personhood that society should prevent. Thus I characterize the argument as aimed at personhood prophylaxis. In this strand of argument it is also thought that in some sense such sales are the result of coercion and do not represent a voluntary act on the seller's part.

Of course, it is problematic whether this kind of action that results from poverty should count as coerced. Does poverty "coerce" someone into selling a kidney, or does someone, because she is poor, choose to sell a kidney? A hard choice is not a non-choice. But the main problem with the personhood prophylaxis form of argument is that it seems cruelly smug. Under what circumstances do people need money badly enough to sell a kidney? Perhaps to feed, clothe, and house their children, or to support elderly or handicapped relatives. It may appear to observers that selling a kidney is degrading, but if these are the circumstances, it seems more degrading instead to have to endure the state of affairs that the sale was supposed to ameliorate.[8]

Notwithstanding the problems with the prophylaxis argument as it stands, it seems clearly to harbor a compelling thought. There is something going on that troubles us with respect to the integrity of the person when we observe someone trying to sell off parts of the body. As I shall argue later, this suggests that we think through more clearly in general how we can structure society to respect persons, not that we try to wall off a few troublesome transactions.

Preserving opportunities for altruism. According to the second strand of argument, something should be held off the market when permitting sales would foreclose, or fail to create, opportunities for altruism that ought to be open. With regard to human blood, for example, Richard Titmuss claimed that altruism is encouraged if society permits only donation, and discouraged if society permits both gifts and sales.[9] In the Titmuss style of argument, altruism is encouraged by donation rather than sale because giving is thought to be communitarian and to emphasize interdependence, whereas market transactions are thought to be individualistic and to emphasize isolation. A donor's experience in being responsible for saving a stranger's life is said to bring us closer together, cement our community, in a way that buying and selling cannot.[10] Interdependence is also emphasized by the possibility of reciprocity. A donor's sense of obligation today could be partially founded on the recognition that she might well need to become a recipient tomorrow. A recipient's sense of gratitude and acknowledgment of dependence upon others' altruism rather than upon her own wealth creates solidarity and interdependence.[11]

According to this argument, altruism is foreclosed if both donations and sales are permitted. If sales are not allowed, donations have no market value and remain unmonetized. If sales are allowed, then even gifts have a market equivalent. My giving a pint of blood is like giving $50 of my money. According to this argument, such monetization discourages giving. We are more willing to give health, perhaps life itself, to strangers than we are to give them $50 of our money.

Something like this argument can be made for certain cases of human organ donation, as well. Imagine the case of grief-stricken parents being asked to donate the heart of a brain-dead child to a newborn victim of congenital heart disease in a distant hospital. The act of donating the heart may be one of those distinctively human moments of terrible glory in which one gives up a significant aspect of oneself so that others may live and flourish. The parents are being asked to give up the symbolic integrity of their child and face immediately the brute fact of death.

But now imagine the experience if the grieving parents know that the market price of hearts is $50,000. There seems to be a sense that the heroic moment now cannot be, neither for them to experience nor for us to observe, in respect and perhaps recognition. If the parents take the money, then the money is the reason for their action; or at best, neither we nor they themselves will ever know that the money was not the reason for the action. But if they don't take the money, then their act can seem like transferring "their" money to someone else. It can seem so, that is, if the domino theory is true, and once something is monetized for some it is monetized for all.

If the domino theory is true, no matter what choice the parents make, the opportunity for a pure act of caring is foreclosed. I think many people would intuitively object, however, to the domino idea that whatever is monetized for some people is necessarily monetized for themselves as well. As I shall argue later, this objection has a deeper theoretical basis. For the domino theory to hold, we must "naturally" tend to commodify, and this "natural" tendency seems to be merely a debatable ideological postulate.

A domino-style argument can also be made about adoption. People (sometimes) give up children in pain and in hope that they will have a better life elsewhere. There is at least some human glory in being able to do this. Perhaps it disappears if the child bears a market value. If money is paid, it would contaminate the experience of the adoptive parents as well as that of the natural parents, since they will be aware that they valued the child as much as a car, perhaps, but not as much as a house. The adopted child herself, if she finds out what price was paid for her, may always wonder whether a higher asking price would have left her without parents. Even if the natural parent doesn't accept the money, doesn't take the price that the market will bear, perhaps knowledge of the price could contaminate the experience, making it seem as though the natural parent is giving the adopting parent $10,000 out of her pocket. In addition, if children have a market value, then even parents who do not put their children up for adoption will know what their children are worth, and how much money they are losing by not doing so. All children will also know how much they are worth and how much their parents are losing by keeping them. We will all know how much we cost our parents. We will all conceive of ourselves as objects bearing monetary value. But this worry too assumes the domino theory is true, which we have yet to investigate.

Although the example of organ donation involved donation of a child's heart, it seems that the argument about opportunities for altruism also fits the case of donation of one's own organs, especially donation to strangers. But it may not fit the case of donation to one's friends and relatives. That depends upon whether this situation can properly be described as altruism. Perhaps altruism means giving unselfishly in the context of a presupposition of selfishness; altruism is to go against one's "natural" selfishness. Perhaps, at any rate, altruism means this in the context of liberal individualism.[12] Ties of family and friendship already overcome one's "natural" selfishness. So, perhaps, actions expressing those ties, although unselfish, would not count as altruistic, since there is no selfishness to overcome in doing them.

If we grant *arguendo* the assumption that permitting any commodification engenders a domino effect, the main problem with the argument about opportunities for altruism, which I think turns out in the end to be a virtue, is that it is too general to carve out a few exceptional kinds of interactions that must remain unmonetized. Suppose we grant that opportunities for altruism must be kept open, most likely because we think altruism is required for proper human flourishing and community cohesion. Still, how are we supposed to know which, and how many, opportunities must be kept open? Why focus on blood, for example? Many (perhaps even most) kinds of work present opportunities for altruism—social worker, teacher, police officer, etc.

Maybe those who make the argument would cabin it by suggesting that, given our pervasive "natural" selfishness, only things that can be given without special training or on a one-shot basis are practicable avenues for altruism in the market society. It is not quite clear why this should be so, however. Can we not say that people ought to give their services when they can? But the problem is that we cannot argue that any of these services must remain completely unmonetized. If we must invest our capital in learning skills or developing our talents, then we must expect (in a market society) to be paid for them once they are developed, in order to supply ourselves with those things we need in order to keep on living and working—food, shelter, and so on. If the domino effect that is implicit in the argument about opportunities for altruism really does hold, then all such services given altruistically will in fact feel like transferring money from donors to recipients, because the services bear a market value. Altruism requires nonmonetized vehicles.

Even accepting a need to find gift objects that must remain completely unmonetized, it still seems that the argument about opportunities for altruism is more general than its proponents have thought. Many kinds of gift objects or volunteer services that can be given on a one-shot basis and do not require much special training might still fit the argument: gifts of old clothes or books; services like reading to blind people, being a subject for experimentation, driving voters to the polls, census-taking, and so on. Why do we not think of keeping these things completely unmonetized? Maybe those who make the argument about opportunities for altruism would further try to cabin it by suggesting that, in addition to being things that can be given on a one-shot basis, the things that must be kept unmonetized are extremely important, perhaps meaning the difference between life or death, to the recipient. But such an attempt to cabin the argument must fail, because it is unclear why the level of importance should matter in this way. There seems to be no reason why we must make altruism dramatic in order to preserve it.

The domino theory. The third strand of argument, the domino theory, holds that there is a slippery slope leading from toleration of any sales (of something) to an exclusive market regime (for that thing). Although it is a necessary supposition of the argument about opportunities for altruism, the domino theory is more often brought up in connection with prostitution and sale of babies. The domino theory implicitly makes two claims: first, as a background normative premise, that it is important for a nonmarket regime to exist; and second, as an empirical premise, that a nonmarket regime cannot co-exist with a market regime. The market drives out the nonmarket version, hence the market regime must be banned.

The domino theory covers more than just the territory sup-

posedly conducive to altruism, since those who argue that sexuality must remain nonmonetized do not argue that the reason
is so that it may be altruistically given. Indeed, as I suggested
earlier, it seems that the concept of altruism already presupposes more distance, remoteness, or impersonality between people than we wish to countenance in our ideals of sexuality.
Those who are against monetized sex are probably against altruistic sex also.

Preserving opportunities for altruism does not, then, seem to
be the main reason for asserting that noncommercial sex must
remain possible. Nor does it seem to be the main reason at work
in the inclination to ban baby selling, although it can play a part,
as my earlier discussion indicated. Rather, it appears that the
uncommodified version must remain possible because commodification somehow destroys or deeply disfigures the possible
value of sex itself or the value of the baby itself.

With babies this does not seem difficult to understand. Super-
ficially, at least, it seems to fail to treat children as persons to
make them all realize that they have a definite commercial value,
and that this is all their value amounts to, even if their parents
did not choose to sell them or did not obtain them by purchase;[13] the domino theory asserts that this will be the result of
permitting sales for those who choose them. Is it similarly an
injury to personhood to commercialize sex? If noncommercial
sex becomes impossible, as we are here assuming, the argument
that the answer is yes asserts that we shall all be deprived of a
significant form of human bonding and interrelation. If disrespect for personhood has an individualistic flavor, perhaps this
would be better put as disrespect for humanity or human relations. Under this analysis, noncommercial sex is a component of
human flourishing, like the need for opportunities to express
altruism. Commercial friendship is a contradiction in terms, as
is commercial love. If opportunities for noncommercial friendship and love were not available, we would not be human. The
argument we are reviewing asks us to see sexuality analogously.

But let us finally focus on the domino part of the theory. Is it
the case that if some people are allowed to sell babies or sexual
services, those things will be thereby commercialized for everyone? The argument that the answer is yes assumes that once the
fact of market value enters our discourse, it must be present in,

and dominate, every transaction. The fact of pricing brings with it the conceptual scheme of commodification. We cannot know the price of something and know at the same time that it is priceless. Once something has a price, money must be a part of the interaction, and the reason or explanation for the interaction, when that something changes hands. A sale cannot simultaneously be a gift. If our children know that the going rate of babies is $10,000, they will know that they are worth $10,000. They will know that they are worth as much as an economy car, but not as much as a house. Worse, if they know that the market price of "good" babies is $10,000, whereas the price of "medium-grade" babies is only $8,000, they will be anxiously comparing themselves with the "good" grade of child in hopes that they measure up. One can fill in the analogous argument regarding sexuality.

III. Incomplete Commodification: The Metaphor of Coexistence

A. Coexistence of Market and Nonmarket Interaction

The domino theory assumes that we cannot both know the price of something and know that it is priceless. We cannot have a sale that is also, and "really," a gift. Is this assumption correct? Or does it grant too much to universal commodification at the outset, by assuming that thinking in money terms is what comes most "naturally" to us? Perhaps it is not true that an interaction cannot be both a sale and a gift at the same time; that we cannot both know the price of something, and know that it is unmonetizable or priceless. This kind of critique of the domino theory would see a nonmarket aspect to much of the market. I shall elaborate it somewhat by considering work and our ideals about work.

Because this is a market society, most people must be paid for their work if they are to live, yet the kind of work we all hope to have—I think—is that which we would do anyway, without money, if somehow by other means our necessities of life were taken care of. Our ideals about work—at least for many of us—do not turn on capitalist rationality. What we hope to get out of working is not all money, nor understandable in money terms (unless the archetype of universal commodification describes our conceptual scheme).

Inspired by Hannah Arendt, I think it is helpful here to introduce a distinction between work and labor, though it is not the same one she had in mind.[14] It is possible to think of work as always containing a noncommodified human element; and to think of the fully commodified version as labor. I think we can understand the difference between working and laboring the way we understand the difference between playing notes and playing music. Laborers play notes, workers play the music. Laborers are sellers; fully motivated by money, exhausting the value of their activity in the measure of its exchange value, and understanding their labor as separate from their real lives and selves. Workers take money, but are also at the same time givers. Money does not fully motivate them to work, nor does it exhaust the value of their activity. Work is understood not as separate from life and self, but rather as a part of the worker, and indeed constitutive of her. Nor is work understood as separate from relations with other people.

Many teachers and scholars identify this way with their work. So, of course, do many performers, artists, and writers; and editors and publishers. So do many doctors, and nurses, and people who care for children, the elderly, the retarded, the handicapped; and people who counsel students, or married couples, or those who have trouble with drugs or alcohol. Fire-fighters, paramedics, and law enforcement officers can do their work as givers to others while being paid. So can military people and judges. Certainly that is what we hope for from political officials.

The nonmarket aspect to work is not limited to the arts, public servants, teaching, and the helping professions. (Even if it were, it would be significant enough to recognize that so many activities can be in the market but not of it.) The concept of the personal touch in one's work, of doing a good job for the sake of pride in one's work, and for the sake of the user or recipient, and for the sake of one's community as a whole, is intelligible for much of the market economy. Plumbers, housecleaners, carpenters, financial advisers, and clerks can all work with personal care for those who need their services. Those who sell products can genuinely care about the needs of people they are selling to. It is possible to fix a vacuum cleaner and care whether it works; it is possible to sell shoes and care whether they fit. However mechanized and technological and rational is the market society, it is still true that the worker we consider the good worker is working and not just laboring.

These are prevalent ideals about work; they are seen played out in practice sometimes. It is true, of course, that the market also contains grinding assembly-line jobs that hardly anyone could treat as humane work. With few exceptions those who labor at these jobs do not feel that they are living while working, but only do the labor so that they may have some time to live during the hours they are not on the job. But I think these jobs run counter to deep-seated ideals about work based upon a pervasive conception of human flourishing; I think that basically we agree with Marx that this is inhumane commodification of people.[15]

Many people have the sense, however, that these ideals about work are declining. As market rationality takes over, there is less and less room for working with care. Many kinds of work are becoming impersonal, some say. (Health care is a primary example.)[16] What does it mean to say they are becoming impersonal? That seems to be simply to say that market rhetoric fully characterizes the process of interaction between seller and buyer. This is to say that to the participants in the interaction the services or things are completely commodified. The relation between health-care provider and patient, for example, is no different from that between the proverbial seller and buyer of widgets.

Putting it this way suggests that complete noncommodification—complete removal from the market—is not the only alternative to complete commodification. Incomplete commodification is also possible. Incomplete commodification describes a situation in which things are sold but the interaction between the participants in the transaction cannot be fully or perspicuously described as the sale of things. If many kinds of sales retain a personal aspect even though money changes hands, those interactions are not fully described as sales of commodities. There is an irreducibly nonmarket or nonmonetized aspect of human interaction going on between seller and recipient; to them the things sold are incompletely commodified. That there

should be the opportunity for work to be personal in this sense
does seem to be part of our conception of human flourishing—
which is why those who see increasing depersonalization de-
plore it. Complete commodification of work—pure labor—does
violence to our notion of what it is to be a well-developed
person.

B. Incomplete Commodification and the Ideals of Personhood and Community

Now it may be clear why I think it gives up the ball game to
argue that certain specific items (for example, blood) must remain completely noncommodified so as to keep open opportunities for altruism, especially if those who argue this way hope
that these sporadic opportunities may lead the way to a less
commodified society. The way to a less commodified society is
to see and foster the nonmarket aspect of much of what we buy
and sell, rather than to erect a wall to keep a certain few things
completely off the market and abandon everything else to market rationality.

If social justice would be improved by a less commodified
society, then, rather than walling off a few transactions from
the pure free market, we should seek to deepen and consolidate
the nonmarket countercurrents that cut across the market. One
way that we already do this to some extent is, of course, with
regulation. At least, that is one way of interpreting what regulation means. Such an interpretation would be consistent with
prevalent critiques of liberal notions of the individual and society.

Liberal conceptions of personhood and community (individuality and sociality) have been criticized for expressing and
creating an alienated, crassly commercial form of life.[17] Liberal
personhood has seemed to postulate an abstract, isolated subject
radically separate from a world of objects (and other subjects).
Liberal sociality has seemed to postulate that the whole is nothing other than the sum of its parts. In this conception of sociality, community is an aggregate of self-interested individuals
each striving for her own autonomous ends, and cooperation is
normatively conceived of as resulting from an n-person prisoner's dilemma.[18] If we accept to some extent the criticisms
leveled against the liberal conceptions of personhood and community, we shall conceive of the person as more integrally con-

nected to the world of things and other people.[19] And we shall conceive of community as crucially founded on human interdependence, as a network of processes and relations that expresses and creates value and significance not normatively reducible to an aggregate of self-contained individuals.

Incomplete commodification as an expression of a nonmarket order co-existent with a market order can be related to this shift in conception of the ideals of personhood and community. The kinds of goods that deviate most from laissez-faire are those related to human beings' homes, work, food, environment, education, communication, health, bodily integrity, sexuality, family life, and political life. For these goods it is easiest to see that preservation and fostering of the nonmarket aspect of their provision and use is related to human flourishing and social justice—to personhood and community as reconceived to meet the critique of liberalism. Once we accept that pervasive incomplete commodification is related to appropriate ideals of personhood and community, it is clear why the arguments for piecemeal noncommodification of specific items are unsatisfactory. It seems that the values of personhood and community require not that certain specific exceptional things be insulated by a wall while everything else is governed by market forces; rather, it seems that the values of personhood and community pervasively interact with the market and alter many goods from their pure free-market form.

IV. Some Ramifications for a Theory of Justice

Now I shall offer a few reflections on how what I have said so far might bear on how we think about justice. I cannot offer a theory of social justice integrating incomplete commodification and the demise of the wall metaphor. But I think it may be useful, nevertheless, to reflect in a preliminary way on how this view of the question of the market domain would influence the general form of an appropriate theory of social justice.

A. Walzer's Liberal Theory of Separation

It should be clear that in my view it is misguided to conceive of social justice in terms of erecting and maintaining a wall separating market from nonmarket realms. Michael Walzer's theory of separation is the most distinguished example of the spatial metaphor I believe we should reject.[20] In Walzer's work, the metaphor is of spheres rather than walls. Nevertheless, we can see in his work the concessions of a modern liberal toward universal commodification.

Walzer posits eleven separate "spheres of justice," with the market as only one of them. Walzer's separation thesis is that justice consists in complex equality. By this he means that the hierarchization that occurs in each sphere—due to differences in biological endowments, energy, and luck—is not wrong so long as preeminence in one realm does not spill over, giving the top dogs in one realm automatic dominance in others. In other words, justice lies in keeping the spheres separate. Thus, Walzer assumes that complete commodification in a large sphere is prima facie just.[21]

In light of this separation thesis, one of Walzer's primary tasks, perhaps his most crucial one, is to show how money and power in the free-market sphere can indeed be self-contained in the market realm. Otherwise money and power in the market sphere spill over and give market top dogs unjust dominance in the realms of education, free time, security, recognition, public office, and political power. (Thus, Walzer accepts a domino theory: the market, if unchecked, will tend to overstep its bounds.) In order to show how the market may be contained, Walzer must first tell us where the market sphere (normatively) ends and other realms begin. That is, he must map the limits of the sphere. This he does not satisfactorily accomplish.

Walzer's term for the transforming of every social good into a commodity (which I have called universal commodification) is "market imperialism."[22] Here is how he poses the problem of market imperialism and proposes a principle for containing it:

> What is at issue now is the dominance of money outside its sphere, the ability of wealthy men and women to trade in indulgences, purchase state offices, corrupt the courts, exercise political power. Commonly enough, the market has its occupied territories, and we can think of redistribution as a kind of moral irredentism, a process of boundary revision. Different principles guide the process at different points in time and space. For my immediate purposes the

most important principle has this (rough) form: the exercise of power belongs to the sphere of politics, while what goes on in the market should at least approximate an exchange between equals (a free exchange).[23]

As an attempt to delimit a market sphere, the power/free exchange distinction is not useful. That only free exchanges should be allowed is no more than the negative liberty that "market imperialists" themselves claim. A contract made under duress is not a valid contract.

Apparently Walzer wants us to understand "free" expansively, so that poverty by itself can count as coercion and negate free exchange. Perhaps Walzer just means to argue that without welfare rights or a minimum income or standard of living we cannot count any exchange as free. Does he mean, then, that selling to poor people is an act of political power while selling to middle-class people is an appropriate act in the market realm? The concept of economic coercion seems to straddle the supposed boundary between politics (power) and the market (free exchange), so I do not see how Walzer can use that concept to help draw it.[24]

Walzer lists fourteen types of things that are "blocked exchanges" (off limits to the market). One of them is "desperate exchanges," by which he means exchanges in the labor market that are motivated by poverty.[25] This "blocked" category of "desperate exchanges" raises theoretical problems that are relevant to the issues surrounding use of the spatial metaphor. Walzer uses this rubric to justify the eight-hour day, minimum wage regulation, and health and safety regulation. About this Walzer comments, "This is a restraint of market liberty for the sake of some communal conception of personal liberty, a reassertion, at lower levels of loss, of the ban on slavery."[26]

It is unclear whether market liberty and the communal conception of personal liberty are synonymous with negative and positive liberty, respectively. In general, it is not clear whether Walzer means to reject the idea of negative liberty at all, and, if so, to what extent. The ideological force of negative liberty tends to pull liberal separationist views like Walzer's toward universal commodification.[27] It would be helpful to know, then, how Walzer would treat the libertarian hard question that the idea of "desperate exchanges" doesn't get to: are we justified in prohibiting someone who really freely chooses for reasons of her own to work long hours in dangerous conditions from doing so? Would Walzer say that this free choice would be an exercise of "market liberty," but one we reject in the name of "personal liberty"?

Perhaps Walzer means to argue that the choice is not "liberty" at all, but coercion.[28] Perhaps he would want to say that the argument about free choice raised by the notion of "market liberty" is a red herring. We should not preoccupy ourselves with the case of some middle-class, well-off, sane, well-educated person suddenly taking it into her head, fully cognizant of what she is doing, to subject herself to hazardous work for long hours at subsistence wages, because this person and these conditions just do not in life confront each other. Those who choose to sell their labor under these conditions—or to sell their kidneys— are poor and oppressed. But even if we think of the exchange as coerced, and not usefully characterized as an exercise of liberty, we are still left with the problem that to the desperate person the desperate exchange must have appeared better than her previous straits, and in banning the exchange we haven't done anything about the straits. That is the same problem we noticed with the liberal prophylactic personhood argument I described earlier. It seems to add insult to injury to ban desperate exchanges by deeming them coerced by terrible circumstances, without changing the circumstances.

Walzer's argument seems unsatisfactory because the distinction between market liberty and personal liberty assumes the divide Walzer wants to use it to delineate. Market liberty for Walzer characterizes the permissible sphere of commodification and personal liberty characterizes a realm that is off-limits to the market. If we assume that it is intuitively obvious or a matter of definition which kind of liberty an asserted transaction belongs to, then we have solved the normative issue of the limits of the market. Otherwise, as I think is the case, the categories personal liberty and market liberty must be the conclusions of a moral argument rather than the basis of one. In my view, that moral argument will turn on our substantive commitments to a theory of proper human flourishing within a properly constituted community. Also in my view, those substantive commitments will lead not to a wall, but rather to a more generalized modification of the market (commodity) scheme.

B. *Incomplete Commodification and the Form of a Theory of Justice*

Now I wish to explore whether we can think more satisfactorily about social justice and the market if we abandon the metaphor of walls (and spheres). Before proceeding, it will be useful to take note of prevalent forms of theorizing about social justice. In one kind of theorizing, we concentrate on justice for the community as a whole. This is often conceptualized in terms of distribution of goods or wealth. A theory of justice in this form can (though of course it need not) cohere with a universal commodifying view of the social order. For example, Robert Nozick's unpatterned entitlement theory replicates the market in its global reliance on entitlement (private property) and just transfer (free contract).[29] Hobbesian theories likewise conceive distributive justice to be the outcomes of unfettered market trades, with adjustments for market failures that mimic what a free market would have achieved.[30]

In another kind of theorizing, we concentrate on social justice as just deserts for individuals, or respect for personhood. This kind of theory too can be captured by universal commodification; for example, when the person's deserts are conceived of as negative freedom to buy and sell all things in markets. Although it would oversimplify matters to attribute such a conception to Rawls, it is possible to see Rawls's theory as tending in this direction.[31] For Rawls, a version of negative liberty is the primary requirement of social justice. All the bases of self-respect necessary to respect persons are conceived of as primary "goods," which at least perpetuates the rhetoric of fungible possessions and objectification.

Whether we are theorizing about justice for the community or for individuals, the still-prevalent liberal metaphor of social contract seems itself to perpetuate market rhetoric. Modern contractualists do not always mean the language of contract to imply monetary exchange or implicit monetizability of all individual and social value.[32] Yet contract is a linchpin of universal commodification, and in the liberal tradition the contract metaphor must draw its power from the normative power of promises to exchange commodities. It is hence possible to see theories of justice that are couched in contract rhetoric as tending toward universal commodification—reduction to monetary terms of the broader normative ideas of social commitment, agreement, and consensus.

Positing the propriety of pervasive coexistence of market and nonmarket aspects to human interactions is an alternative both to theories that imply or can be understood to countenance universal commodification and to "wall" theories of social justice like Walzer's. Incomplete commodification would be reflected both in a theory of overall distributive fairness and a theory of proper treatment of individuals. Key principles for both these aspects of justice in such an alternative theory are that who should get what things of value depends upon the appropriate relation between persons and things, and between persons and other people.

For example, if we accept as appropriate a close connection between persons and their housing,[33] then housing should be socially provided in such a way not only that everyone may have the shelter necessary for physical survival, but also that everyone may have the continuity of residence (often) necessary for proper self-development. Housing, both rented and owned, is appropriately incompletely commodified: it has special nonmarket significance to participants in market interactions regarding it, and it is appropriately socially regulated in recognition of the propriety of this self-investment. This is not because, as Walzer might have it, housing belongs to the "sphere" of security and welfare, in which distribution should be according to the principle of need, rather than to the "sphere" of money and commodities, in which distribution is appropriately according to the principle of free exchange.[34] Rather it is because, although we value the efficiency of the market, at the same time housing must be incompletely commodified in recognition of its connection with personhood.

Who gets what depends upon appropriate relations between persons and other people, and not just between persons and things. People engaged in market interactions are not just acquiring things, they are relating to each other. A theory of social justice should recognize that these interactions often are (and ought to be able to be) valued for themselves and specifically, and not merely instrumentally and fungibly. As critics of Rawls (for example) have often noted,[35] many kinds of solidarity and interrelations between people are central to our conception of human flourishing and hence must not be excluded from a theory of social justice.

C. Incomplete Commodification and the Issue of Nonideal Justice

Once we abandon the wall metaphor, does this mean that all things formerly thought to be exceptional can be treated as incompletely commodified, enabling them to be bought and sold? That would be frightening to anyone who accepts the domino theory, for it would mean that incomplete commodification would necessarily give way to complete commodification. Yet if personhood and community are better fostered by generalized incomplete commodification than by the traditional wall, then perhaps even babies, sexuality, etc., could be bought and sold without being thought of as objects or as fungible. But before we conclude that this is correct, we must address two further kinds of questions. First, in our nonideal world, should we credit the domino theory, at least for things important to personhood, because it is too risky not to? Second, even under ideal circumstances, are there some things that just cannot be commodified, even incompletely, consistently with our conceptions of personhood and community?

The second question is hard to address for anyone who thinks, as I do, that our circumstances—our situatedness—matter deeply for our central normative conceptions. We cannot jump outside our present world to see whether partial commodification (of babies, for example) would be a wrong in itself in some other world. If we view the question as asking us to focus on our ideals as currently formulated (and not, so to speak, on ideal ideals), then it seems to me that we cannot say that the mere fact that money changes hands is a wrong, once that fact is divorced from the various bad implications of commodification.

But perhaps that is a divorce we cannot now imagine in detail, much less socially implement. In our nonideal world, the mere fact that money changes hands might be rightly treated as having bad implications, or at least bad possibilities, for some especially sensitive cases like sale of babies. (A sensitive case is one in

which complete commodification would destroy or deeply undermine personhood or community as we conceive them.) This
would be to answer the first question I posed above in the
affirmative for such cases. Whether or not babies could be priced
and yet not be inappropriately commodified depends on how
important noncommodification of people is and how risky it
might be to allow buying and selling given our estimate of the
current state of our tendencies to think in terms of commodification. It is one thing to say that in some imagined world to sell
babies is not necessarily to commodify them unduly, and another thing to say that that is so in our world. In other words,
there is still room for complete noncommodification of some
special things, not because they are to be walled off from a
laissez-faire market realm, but rather because in our nonideal
world even partial commodification could lead to foreclosing
the nonmarket conceptions of personhood and community.

The problem brings up the issue of non-ideal or second-best
(or perhaps just practical) justice. There is always a gap between
the ideals we can formulate and the progress we can realize.
Hence there is always an ambiguity about theorizing about (and
seeking) justice: does justice refer to the best general ideals we
can formulate, or does it refer to a theoretical working out of
what changes would now count as social improvements? To
avoid all significant harms to personhood and community may
be an ideal of justice; yet it may also be the case that justice (at
least for here and now) instead means only that we should
choose the best alternative from among those available to us. If
that is what justice means, then whatever harms to personhood
and community are present in the best alternative cannot be
thought of as unjust, although they may come to be unjust when
a better alternative becomes available.

D. Further Implication for Justice as
Respect for Personhood

Pursuing a bit further the idea that both the overall distribution
pattern and individual desert depend upon appropriate connections between persons and their contexts of things and other
people, I shall comment on three kinds of connections between
what I have said about the considerations counseling rejection
of the wall metaphor, and the notion of justice as respect for

personhood. Here I mean to discuss, first, the significance for social justice of the dilemma created when it seems we cannot respect personhood by choosing either the market or the non-market solution to a problem. Second, I want to note the significance of incomplete commodification, based on respect for personhood and the fostering of community, for the justification of regulation. Finally, I want to bring up the ultimate question of market rhetoric: Is it possible that it is unjust to think and talk about some things in the discourse of commodification?

The dilemma of commodification. First, there is the observation that the prophylactic personhood argument—that people should not be allowed to sell their organs, etc., because that is degrading to personhood—calls attention to a more pervasive problem of social justice. If people are so desperate for money that they are trying to sell things we think cannot be separated from them without significant injury to personhood, we do not cure the desperation by banning sales. Nor do we avoid the injury to personhood. Perhaps the desperation is the social problem we should be looking at, rather than the market ban. Perhaps worse injury to personhood is suffered from the desperation that caused the attempt to sell a kidney or cornea than would be suffered from actually selling it. The would-be sellers apparently think so. Then justice is not served by a ban on "desperate exchanges."

These considerations change the arena of argument from considerations of appropriateness to the market to explicit considerations of social justice. If neither commodification nor noncommodification can put to rest our disquiet about harm to personhood in conjunction with certain specific kinds of transactions—if neither commodification nor noncommodification can satisfy our aspirations for a society exhibiting equal respect for persons—then we must rethink the larger social context in which this dilemma is embedded. We must think about wealth and power redistribution.

In other words, sale of one's body parts presents a dilemma because it seems we cannot honor our intuitions of what is required for society to respect personhood, either by permitting sales or by banning them. I am suggesting that the dilemma should be treated as Wittgenstein suggests we treat philosophical questions: as the symptom of an illness.[36] The dilemma

throws into relief the results of inequalities of wealth distribution, and should make us consider the justice of the surrounding circumstances that create the dilemma.

One's body is bound up with one's personhood, which is why
when organs are donated it is a significant expression of human
interrelation. But to preserve organ donation as an opportunity
for altruism is also one way of keeping from our view the
desperation of poor people. Hence, one who thinks social progress can be brought about by forcing unjust conditions upon
our attention might agree with the universal commodifier that
sales should be permitted. The progressive thinks, in other
words, that fellow feeling is better served by permitting sales so
that the spectacle will awaken fellow feeling in the rest of us, to
eliminate poverty. The universal commodifier, on the other
hand, thinks that even altruism is monetizable, and, in cases
where there are willing buyers and willing sellers, it must be
worth less than sales. This type of alliance between the far right
and the far left is a sure sign that something is incoherent about
the middle way.[37]

If it appears that we cannot respect personhood either with
commodification or noncommodification, given the surrounding social circumstances, for example with organ-selling, and if
we agree that this means we ought to change the surrounding
circumstances, we are still faced with the question of whether or
not we should permit commodification while we try to do that.
If we opt to permit sales for those who choose, as the libertarian
and radical might both recommend, we risk complete commodification—if the domino theory correctly predicts the resulting
social consciousness, given the level of commodification already
present. Complete commodification makes the supposed goal of
greater respect for persons in a less commodified future even
less imaginable. But perhaps this risk is not as bad as the degradation of personhood and reinforcement of powerlessness
brought about by the regime of enforced noncommodification.
Obviously, I have no handy algorithm for making this decision.[38]

Regulation and community. A second connection between justice
and my discussion of the arguments surrounding the wall metaphor is the question of nonefficiency justification for regulation—that is, socially mandated deviations from the laissez-faire

market regime for many things that are bought and sold. If everything is appropriately fully commodified unless efficiency dictates otherwise, then exceptions from the laissez-faire regime are justified only where the market for some reason cannot achieve efficient outcomes. This in fact is the position of many economists on regulation. It makes many types of regulation (for example, residential rent control) difficult to justify; when these types of regulation are frequently imposed anyway by the political order, they are seen as obvious examples of selfish rent-seeking by powerful interest groups. But as I have argued above, there is another way to view regulation of many things that are important to human personhood and community, and that is as incomplete commodification. If we stubbornly intuit that these things that are very important to human life, health, and self- and community development ought not to be completely monetized, then regulation that does not (theoretically) meet an efficiency test is in principle justified. Then the response of the political order in imposing the constraints on commodification may be seen as a good-faith working out of community values, so that persons and the community may properly flourish, rather than interest-group rent-seeking.

Can market rhetoric be unjust? The third question that I would like to raise here has to do with whether social justice (as respect for persons) and the rhetoric of universal commodification are connected. I think that conceiving of politics as mere rent-seeking, and essential human attributes as mere scarce commodities, expresses and fosters a conception of human flourishing inferior to that expressed and fostered by a discourse that recognizes personhood and community as essentially unmonetized and not fungible. But is it unjust to think of these aspects of human life in terms of commodities? Does Richard Posner act unjustly in trying to convince us that the right way to think of children is as commodities, and that the right way to think of much that legislatures do is in terms of rent-seeking?[39]

I want to be especially tentative here because I do not suppose I understand the connection between justice and a discourse that embodies an inferior conception of human flourishing. At present it seems to me that three things can be said about it.

First, there is a serious risk of error to interests important to personhood and community. Even if the universal commodifier thinks that these interests are in principle monetizable and tradeable, it is very easy to make mistakes in one's cost-benefit analysis, and in particular to ignore these "costs" that are difficult to monetize. This pattern of ignoring "costs" to personhood and community can be thought of as a wrong, and perhaps as an injustice.

Second, in some cases market rhetoric itself can be viewed as an act injurious to personhood. Thinking about children in market rhetoric makes a person's uniqueness into a fungible item of exchange: This seems insulting to personhood, and injurious to personhood insofar as it is even partly internalized by the persons affected. Again, this is a wrong, and perhaps can be characterized as an injustice in an ideal theory of justice having respect for personhood as a central element. Even in a nonideal theory, it does not seem plausible that countenancing this kind of wrong is our best alternative, all things considered.

Third (and this may be a generalization of the above), it may be that market rhetoric, the discourse of commodification, in which all things valued by and in human beings are goods for sale, is a conceptual scheme that keeps us from becoming well-developed persons.[40] To the extent the rhetoric is internalized, it alienates us from our true selves as persons; or, to put this another way, hampers self-development. For example, if universal commodification rhetoric were to succeed in creating internal perceptions of ourselves as laborers rather than workers, or as bearers of fungible commodities rather than personal attributes, then some of the human potential included in our conception of personhood would be lost to us. (Of course, if this transformation were fully to take place, perhaps we would drop the conception of personhood that counts this as a loss, and substitute instead a commodifier conception of personhood that would not recognize it.)

If there is no such thing as better or worse conceptions of human flourishing, and therefore no such thing as better or worse discourses embodying them, then there is no problem of wrong or injustice posed in setting up such a dissonance within the self; the dissonance is at best a psychological malaise. Nor is it wrong to eliminate the dissonance by converting us completely to a commodified self-conception. But it seems to me that it must be otherwise if we do accept that there can be better or worse conceptions of human flourishing, and better or worse discourse that creates and expresses them. If we accept that universal market rhetoric is an inferior discourse because it creates and expresses a conception of flourishing inferior to one that holds that certain aspects of personhood and community must remain unmonetized and not fungible; and if we accept that part of a theory of social justice is that we must treat persons as persons, or as persons deserve, or with respect for persons; then it seems that it is at least wrong to commodify everything in rhetoric. It seems at least open to us to argue that this kind of wrong is an injustice from the ideal point of view, and perhaps from the nonideal point of view if it does not plausibly seem to be our best available alternative.[41]

V. Conclusion

I would like to leave matters here for now, except to point out that the title of this chapter, "Justice and the Market Domain," must now be taken as a warning rather than a prescription. The warning is against trying to construct a theory of justice by drawing out limits or boundaries or a wall—or even, in Walzer's metaphor, a sphere—around a free-market bailiwick that is laissez-faire in principle. Instead, I think that we should think about justice in terms of a nonmarket perspective that permeates many of our market interactions, at least in the way we think about them ideally. At the same time, we can recognize, I think, that this perspective is played out in practice to some extent in large areas of incomplete commodification. If I am right that these intuitions can be related to central ideals of personhood and community, then further reflection on personhood and community should yield a better understanding of incomplete commodification, both of its role in a good theory of social justice and of the extent to which it should prevail in practice.

NOTES

1. I am aware that this bifurcation of the topic may assume a distinction that is problematic for the views I recommend. Our chosen regime

for the transfer of human organs may be just as political as voting. I think that all this means, however, is that in pursuing the debate over nonmarket personal interactions versus the market, I am making a start on the debate over politics versus the market as well.

2. There are clearly affinities between the connotations of the term "commodity" as I use it, and Marx's use of the term "commodity" to mean a good traded under laissez-faire market circumstances. For Marx a commodity is valued for its exchange value (which we now call market value) and all commodities are commensurate with money, which he called the universal equivalent. There are other ways of viewing the word commodity that antedate the advent of capitalism and the notions of exchange value and laissez-faire markets. Nevertheless, I prefer to use it in the sense I define, so that it can make clear the import of treating the human world as if it were one giant market, which I am calling universal commodification.

A more detailed characterization of universal commodification and a discussion of the meaning of the term "commodity" will be found in Margaret Jane Radin, "Market-Inalienability," *Harvard Law Review* 100 (June 1987): 1849. In that article, which is a companion piece to the present chapter, I explore the notion of making some things inalienable through market transactions. There I contrast universal commodification to an opposing archetype, universal noncommodification, and reject both these extremes in favor of a nonideal evolutionary coexistence of market and nonmarket schemes. More detailed discussions of some of the themes referred to below will be found there: in particular, market rhetoric and market methodology; the link between universal commodification and an inferior conception of human flourishing; incomplete commodification in its participant and social aspects; the critique of the prophylactic personhood defense of market-inalienability; the domino theory (holding that once any market transactions are permitted, market rhetoric and methodology will dominate all transactions); the double bind (representing a perception that for some things both commodification and enforced noncommodification seem harmful).

3. Hobbes, *Leviathan* 10, 16, 42; cf. C. B. Macpherson, *The Political Theory of Possessive Individualism* (Oxford: Oxford University Press, 1962), 17–87.

As an example of market rhetoric, consider this passage by Judge Richard Posner:

> The household commodity that places the greatest demands on the wife's time is rearing children, so an increase in the opportunity cost of that time is immediately translated into an increase in the shadow price of children to the household. A rise in the price

of children can be expected to reduce the quantity of children demanded; and since rearing children is not only one of the most difficult to conduct at comparable cost outside of the household, a decline in the demand for children should result—and evidently has resulted—in a decline in the demand for marriage. But even without any increase in women's net market income, there would be a reduction in the number of children per household, for with dramatically reduced child mortality a couple needs fewer children in order to be reasonably confident of having as many (grown) children as desired. . . . The pleasure we get from our children's presence is the result of "consuming" the intangible "services" that they render us.

Richard Posner, *Economic Analysis of Law*, 3d ed. (Boston: Little, Brown, 1986), 129–30.

4. See, e.g., James M. Buchanan, Robert D. Tollison, and Gordon Tullock, eds., *Toward a Theory of the Rent-Seeking Society* (College Station: Texas A & M University, 1980).

5. It should be clear that not all economic analysis is ipso facto universal commodification. Actual thinkers are more complex than the archetype, although the archetype may coherently crystallize their premises. Moreover, many who practice economic analysis are sensitive to situations where complete commodification is troublesome. For example, Alan Schwartz finds previous economic analysis of the legal treatment of minority shareholders in corporate takeovers to be wanting in not recognizing that people may value corporations as communities in some non-market sense. See Alan Schwartz, "The Fairness of Tender Offer Prices in Utilitarian Theory," *Journal of Legal Studies* 17 (1988): 165.

6. See Posner, *Economic Analysis of Law*, 238–44.

7. Ibid., 139; Richard Posner, "The Regulation of the Market in Adoptions," *Boston University Law Review* 67 (1987): 59.

8. The prophylactic personhood argument is also thought of in connection with aspects of sexuality and reproduction. Examples are prostitution, surrogate motherhood, and release of infants for adoption. The argument is further criticized in Radin, "Market-Inalienability."

9. See Richard Titmuss, *The Gift Relationship: From Human Blood to Social Policy* (New York: Pantheon, 1971).

10. See Titmuss, *The Gift Relationship*, and the construal of Titmuss by Peter Singer, "Freedoms and Utilities in the Distribution of Health Care," in *Markets and Morals*, ed. Gordon Bermant, Peter Brown and Gerald Dworkin (Washington, D.C.: Hemisphere, 1977), chap. 9.

11. Allied to this argument about altruism is the claim that a nonmarket regime better preserves and expresses the sanctity of life than would

a market regime. In the market regime, recovering one's health depends upon ability to pay instead of merely one's desert or need as a person. See Michael Shapiro, "Regulation as a Language" (forthcoming).

12. Indeed, perhaps altruism, insofar as it connotes impersonal giving, is an artifact of liberal alienation. Thus I agree with Eric Mack ("Dominos and the Fear of Commodification," this volume) that my criticism of altruism in the context of sexuality should be generalized to include our conceptions of personhood and community.

13. For a somewhat more detailed discussion of baby-selling, see Radin, "Market-Inalienability."

14. See Hannah Arendt, *The Human Condition* (Chicago: University of Chicago Press, 1958). Arendt noted that many languages have two words corresponding to work and labor, and that only work can also be a noun. For her, labor meant the kind of activity necessary to sustain life. It is ephemeral and leaves no traces on the environment; and it does not distinguish human beings from animals, since they too must labor in this sense. Work, on the other hand, lives after us and changes the world in which live. (This seems to me similar to Marx's notion of "working up" our world.)

15. I do not believe, however, that the conception of work I am advocating here is Marxist. Marx argued for complete decommodification, whereas I am arguing for recognition of incomplete commodification. That is, I am proposing that market interactions can and do have a significant nonmarket aspect. This is an argument for "peaceful coexistence" that I think Marx would not have accepted; I believe he thought the logic of capitalism must perforce play out in practice as universal commodification (both in real life and in rhetoric), and that the only way to change this would be complete decommodification.

16. A balanced and thoughtful presentation of this concern is found in Dan W. Brock and Allen E. Buchanan, "The Profit Motive in Medicine," *The Journal of Medicine and Philosophy* 12 (1987): 1.

17. A well-known version of this critique is found in Roberto M. Unger, *Knowledge and Politics* (New York: The Free Press, 1975).

18. See, for example, Rawls's reference to "Hobbes's thesis" in his defense of the liberal ideal of the rule of the law, in John Rawls, *A Theory of Justice* (Cambridge: Harvard University Press, 1971), 240–41.

19. See, for example, Michael Sandel, *Liberalism and the Limits of Justice* (Cambridge: Cambridge University Press, 1982); but cf. C. Edwin Baker, "Sandel on Rawls," *University of Pennsylvania Law Review* 134 (1985): 895.

20. Michael Walzer, *Spheres of Justice* (New York: Basic Books, 1983). See also Walzer, "Liberalism and the Art of Separation," *Political Theory* 12 (1984): 315; criticized in Thomas Morawetz, "Tension in 'The Art of Separation,' " *Political Theory* 13 (1985): 599.

21. Although this is Walzer's theoretical assumption, in practice there would not be a very large free-market sphere left after all the various kinds of welfare regulation he recommends were implemented. Thus, in a sense, a theory of incomplete commodification would better have served Walzer's purposes than the spatial metaphor.

22. Walzer, *Spheres of Justice*, 120.

23. Ibid.

24. Although this boundary is described as a moral matter, and the market exceeding its bounds is—in a nice phrase—"moral irredentism," Walzer says that the issue of what things cannot be bought and sold, because we do not want certain values to be priced, is "an empirical matter." This is puzzling; surely this too is a moral matter since this too involves the containment of the market within its proper sphere, necessary for justice as complex equality. Walzer says as much when he says that these "blocked exchanges" "set limits on the dominance of wealth." See Walzer, *Spheres of Justice*, 100.

The puzzle is resolved to some extent when one takes into account that Walzer is at least sometimes a moral conventionalist. What *is* right is what the relevant social group *thinks* is right. Thus, if his list coincides with social practice, no further argument is needed to convince us of its moral rightness. Walzer's critics have taken him to task for his conventionalism. See, e.g., Brian Barry, review of *Spheres of Justice*, by Michael Walzer, *Columbia Law Review* 84 (1984): 806; James S. Fishkin, review of *Spheres of Justice*, by Michael Walzer, *Michigan Law Review* 82 (1984): 755. To be fair, however, I think that Walzer is only sometimes merely a conventionalist; sometimes he seems to be a pragmatist refusing to accept the positive/normative distinction (that is, the fact/value dichotomy). That position is capable of sophisticated defense, even though raising this position explicitly and creating that defense is not Walzer's project in this book.

25. The fourteen things are: human beings; political power and influence; criminal justice; freedom of speech, press, religion, assembly; marriage and procreation rights; emigration rights; exemptions from military service, jury duty, and "any other form of communally imposed work"; political offices and professional standing; the minimum level of "basic welfare services like police protection or primary and secondary schooling"; "desperate exchanges"; public and private prizes and honors; divine grace; love and friendship; and, "Finally, a long series of criminal sales are ruled out." See Walzer, *Spheres of Justice*, 100–103. In this list, all different kinds of inalienabilities are lumped together under a general ban on buying and selling. To speak only of sale when a particular inalienability is broader than that distorts its political and social significance, and reflects a tendency toward universal commodification, at least in rhetoric.

26. Walzer, *Spheres of Justice,* 100–103.

27. In Radin, "Market-Inalienability" I show how the traditional liberal idea of the wall between nonmarket and market realms is rendered unstable by the commitment to negative liberty, which is in tension with the commitment to substantive requirements of personhood. The instability results in a pull toward universal commodification as one way to resolve the inner tension.

28. To think of "market liberty" under these circumstances as "liberty" raises echoes of the Lochner era—but the opposition, market liberty "versus" personal liberty would not have made sense to them. Market liberty simply *was* liberty. See Gary Peller, "The Metaphysics of American Law," *California Law Review* 73 (1985): 1151, 1193–1219 ("The Liberty of Contract Era").

29. See Robert Nozick, *Anarchy, State, and Utopia* (New York: Basic Books, 1974).

30. See, for example, James M. Buchanan, *The Limits of Liberty* (Chicago: University of Chicago Press, 1975).

31. Rawls's ideal scheme "makes considerable use of market arrangements." Rawls says, "It is only in this way, I believe, that the problem of distribution can be handled as a case of pure procedural justice. Further, we also gain the advantages of efficiency and protect the important liberty of free choice of occupation." See Rawls, *A Theory of Justice,* 274. In his discussion of public goods, for example, Rawls relies on the Hobbesian model of politics (265–74). John Stick argues that Rawls's methodology readily leads to Nozickian results. See John Stick, "Turning Rawls into Nozick and Back Again," *Northwestern Law Review* 81 (Spring 1987): 363–416.

32. For example, T. M. Scanlon's influential essay, "Contractualism and Utilitarianism," in *Utilitarianism and Beyond,* ed. Amartya Sen and Bernard Williams (Cambridge: Cambridge University Press, 1981), cogently argues in favor of a moral methodology based on hypothetical uncoerced agreement. The market metaphor of contract is not a necessary part of this argument, and may in fact detract from its breadth and force.

33. See Margaret Jane Radin, "Property and Personhood," *Stanford Law Review* 34 (1982): 957; Margaret Jane Radin, "Residential Rent Control," *Philosophy and Public Affairs* 15 (Fall 1986): 350; and Margaret Jane Radin, "Rent Control and Incomplete Commodification: A Rejoinder," *Philosophy and Public Affairs* 17 (1988): 80.

34. See Walzer, *Spheres of Justice,* chap. 3.

35. See, e.g., Ronald R. Garet, "Community and Existence: The Rights of Groups," *Southern California Law Review* 56 (1983): 1001; Sandel, *Liberalism and the Limits of Justice.*

36. See Ludwig Wittgenstein, *Philosophical Investigations*, sect. 255 ("The philosopher's treatment of a question is like the treatment of an illness").

37. In the same vein, it should be noticed that arguments urging that commodification of something would set off a domino effect often involve things that would be commodities produced and/or controlled largely by women. There is a deep dilemma or double bind created if both commodification and noncommodification of certain things would, under the current surrounding social circumstances, be degrading or disempowering to women. The double bind should lead us to rethink the surrounding circumstances. The double bind is discussed further in Radin, "Market-Inalienability."

38. More of my nonideal views on these subjects will be found in my "Market-Inalienability."

39. See William Landes and Richard Posner, "The Independent Judiciary in an Interest Group Perspective," *Journal of Law and Economics* 18 (1975): 875.

40. Radin, "Market-Inalienability"; see note 2 above.

41. I am aware, of course, that the liberal proponent of free speech would see a powerful objection here: How can mere choice of rhetoric be wrong or unjust? I think that this objection cannot be so powerful for someone who already accepts certain important views of the antifoundationalist trend in philosophy, according to which it is impossible to maintain a bright-line distinction between discourse and the world, and discourse and value. If, in our terms of discourse, we are making choices for constructing our human world of facts and values, like it or not, we cannot maintain liberal neutrality on the good life for human beings. If it is true that the discourse in which human life is conceived and the nature of human life itself are not fully separable, it seems we must be able to say that there are better and worse discourses, just as there are better and worse views of what it is to be human.

To say that a discourse can create wrongs, and (ideally or under certain nonideal circumstances) injustice, is not—it should be clear—to argue that it would be right or just for the government to try to suppress it. To suppose that any conviction that something is unjust necessitates the conviction that the government should suppress it makes justice completely the province of government, a conflation I do not espouse.

7

DOMINOS AND THE FEAR
OF COMMODIFICATION

ERIC MACK

> But tho' this self-interested commerce of men begins to take place, and to predominate in society, it does not entirely abolish the more generous and noble intercourse of friendship and good offices.
>
> DAVID HUME, *A Treatise of Human Nature*

I. INTRODUCTION

The market order and the liberal individualism that order expresses and reinforces has, throughout its history, been subjected to a complex critique that has united traditionalist and revolutionary opponents of capitalism. This critique invokes a number of familiar themes: alienation from self; alienation from community; the loss of values and of a sense of rationality that transcends the instrumental; the corruption or narrowing of moral sensibility. Almost any malaise that is directly experienced or believed to be suffered by others in market societies has been laid at the doorstep of liberal individualism and the market. This psycho-philosophical critique often takes form around the notion of commodification. An object, or activity, or

This chapter was completed during the tenure of a summer research grant from the Murphy Institute for Political Economy of Tulane University. I am very much indebted to Mary Sirridge for her advice and counsel and for her suggestion of the term *The Exchangeable An Sich*.

skill, or character trait is commodified when its value is perceived to be determined by what that object, or performance of that activity, or the exercise of that skill, will bring through impersonal economic exchange.

The process of commodification leads an agent to produce objects, engage in activities, exercise or develop skills, not for the sake of the value that agent directly attaches to those objects, activities, etc., but rather for the sake of what the market offers in return. When what is offered in exchange is not itself a tangible object or service directly valued by the agent but, instead, a payment in money, the agent's productive activity further loses touch with, further loses the character of being expressive of, his own felt values.[1] The productive activity comes under the sway of external, alien, depersonalized forces. The agent learns that rationality consists in submission to these market forces and dismissal of his own pre-market evaluations of his activities, interests, and relations. The result is, under the best of circumstances, a wealth-maximizing zombie whose soul can be restored only by return to precapitalist, traditional, and intentional (e.g., feudal) economic relations or a transcendence to a post-capitalist economy by and for self-realized species-beings.

Margaret Radin's "Justice and the Market Domain" and "Market-Inalienability" represent a sophisticated and measured exploration of elements of the commodification critique so baldly presented here.[2] I shall pursue a number of the issues she introduces. Special attention will be paid to the domino theory and to universal commodification. The domino theory asserts that market evaluations of objects and activities are imperialistic, driving out other and better ways of perceiving or evaluating objects and activities. Once some individuals attach a price to a given object, relation, or activity, they and others tend to lose their capacity to perceive or evaluate that object, relation, or activity as anything but a commodity with a specific market price. Moreover, the theory asserts, once certain objects or activities are commodified, there is a tendency for other objects or activities of the same sort or even of other sorts also to be seen and evaluated merely in terms of their actual or potential market value.

For example, when a market in blood is allowed, a price is

attached to a pint of blood. The value of providing that blood
and the value of receiving it will then be reduced to the dollar
value at which it sells. Others with blood to provide or with a
need for blood will tend to see any provision and any receipt of
it as being on a par with the provision or receipt of an equiva-
lently priced bottle of toilet water. Moreover, the commodification of an otherwise "priceless" object or activity such as blood
creates or reinforces a tendency toward the commodification of
further otherwise "priceless" objects or activities, e.g., bodily
parts or acts of friendship. Commodification of blood will incline people to think of their healthy kidneys (or those of their
recently deceased loved ones) as alienable capital assets. These
bits of human capital will come to be perceived as mere commodities that should rationally be sold if the price is right. Or,
if their possessor should somehow still wish to donate these
kidneys, the donation will tend to be seen, by donor and recipient, as equivalent to a gift of their market price. Even charitable
acts become market surrogates. When commodification is complete, I experience my acts of friendship as transfers to my
"friends" of what they otherwise would have had to pay to
secure or as trades in which I barter my acts of "friendship" in
exchange for their supplying me with equally genuine acts of
"friendship."

Fears about increasing commodification can be divided roughly
into fears about loss of self (or personhood) and fears about the
loss of valuable personal interactions and relations (or community).[3] In the first case, the victim comes to see all of his attributes and possessions as fungible commodities. He comes to
experience himself or his life as a bundle of market values so
that his value is the sum cost of acquiring the items in that
bundle. In the second case, commodification is feared to undercut comradeship, familial ties, cooperative and mutually satisfying work, and so on. Here I will focus more on the second set
of fears, although the first set will be addressed indirectly in the
course of remarks about the strange doctrine of universal commodification.

Whereas the domino theory asserts the existence of domino
processes that radically transform the motivation of agents, universal commodification is a doctrine about what motivation
underlies all human action and/or all rational human action.
Universal commodification can be understood descriptively or

prescriptively. Descriptively, it is the claim that all agents are profit-maximizers.[4] Prescriptively, it is the claim that *rational* agents are profit-maximizers. Obviously, concern about domino processes requires disbelief in both versions of universal commodification. For, if all of us are profit maximizers, then domino processes will at most alter the specific details of our profit-seeking and will not radically transform our motivations. And, if to be rational we must be profit-maximizers, then domino processes are not to be feared but rather to be welcomed as leading us down the path of reason. Disbelief in universal commodification is, however, entirely consistent with concern about others' belief in or promulgation of this doctrine. Indeed, it is natural and fitting that someone fearful about domino processes also be concerned about ways in which belief in universal commodification sustains those processes or is an expression of their insidious strength.

In what follows I shall engage in the type of speculative moral sociology that characterizes all discussions of commodification. I seek to allay fears about rampant commodification, especially the sort of fears that inspire politically imposed limitations on the scope of the market. As the reader will soon discover, this chapter represents a series of observations and analyses and not a geometrical proof or refutation of some precisely defined philosophical thesis. In the next section, I try to identify more clearly the claims of the domino theory. Section 3 clarifies the doctrine of universal commodification and begins an inquiry into its plausibility and danger. In section 4, I attend, in a highly idiosyncratic fashion, to instances in which nonmarket activities and relations persist in a substantially market world. This persistence is accounted for in terms of a distinction between internally and instrumentally valued activities. This distinction also provides the basis for a further criticism of, and further doubts about the seductiveness of, universal commodification. The penultimate section reasserts the usefulness of the internal versus instrumental distinction as a prophylactic against domino processes. The final section speculates about what sort of a mix of internally and instrumentally valued activities and relations can reasonably be expected in an enviable life. The entire chapter travels through murky waters. Its goal is more to trace certain of the currents than to arrive at any particular bank.

II. THE DOMINO THEORY

According to Radin: "The domino theory implicitly makes two claims: first, as a background normative premise, that it is important for a nonmarket regime to exist; and second, as an empirical premise, that a nonmarket regime cannot co-exist with a market regime. The market drives out the nonmarket version, hence the market regime must be banned."[5] However, I shall identify the domino theory with the second, Greshamite, claim. It is helpful to decouple the domino theory proper (that is, the second claim formulated by Radin) from the normative assertion that "it is important that a nonmarket regime exist." This makes it clear that one may question the momentum of domino processes while still endorsing the imposition of limits on the market for the sake of a larger nonmarket regime than would exist in the absence of those limits. Similarly, one can be dubious about the force of domino processes while endorsing the imposition of limits on the market, if not for the sake of the value of a specific nonmarket preserve, for the sake of the general value of nonmarket, noncommodified dimensions in people's lives. This, I take it, is Radin's own position—one that she wants to contrast sharply with the "traditional liberal view" that a nonmarket *regime* is important and can exist if a sufficiently sturdy wall is built between it and "the market regime."[6] Finally, of course, one can be dubious about the domino theory proper and, for that reason, project a satisfactory *nonimposed* co-existence of market and nonmarket dimensions of our lives.

We should note that only an extreme version of the domino theory asserts categorically that the market drives out the nonmarket. We can distinguish between a number of more or less extensive domino theses. There is the thesis that any commodification of objects and activities, or at least any commodification beyond a certain threshold, creates significant pressure toward the commodification of all objects and activities, even or especially those objects and activities least appropriate for commodification. There is the thesis that the commodification of certain types of objects or activities—persumably those least appropriate for commodification, e.g., bodily parts or sexual interactions—creates a significant tendency for all objects and activities to be commodified. And there is the thesis that the commodification of certain types of objects or activities—again, presumably those least appropriate for commodification—creates a significant tendency for all objects or activities in those sensitive classes to be commodified.

The last of these theses, by most narrowly construing the range of domino processes, would seem to be the most modest version of the thesis. Yet it seems that this is the version about which Radin is most dubious. This is because Radin has two different sorts of objections. The first, which I share with her, is an objection to domino theses at large, that is, that people have at least some capacity to continue to appreciate the nonmonetarized aspects of their activities and relations even in a world that allows considerable monetarization. The other objection, however, is specifically against a presumption of the third domino thesis. The presumption is that there are distinctive classes of objects and activities that especially should not be commodified and that are especially vulnerable to commodification. Radin associates this presumption with the "traditional liberal view" that proposes protectively quarantining these classes of objects and activities from the market's infectious commodification. Her claim against this presumption and the traditional liberal proposal is simply that there are many more classes of objects, activities, and relations that ought not to be fully commodified and yet are in danger of full commodification in market society; that "the traditional view is wrong in granting too much ground to the market." This is why, in contrast to the liberal quarantine, Radin says, "The way to a less commodified society is to see and foster the nonmarket aspect of much of what we buy and sell, rather than to erect a wall to keep a certain few things completely off the market and abandon everything else to market rationality."[7] Since Radin's doubts about the domino theory are substantially doubts about its most restrictive version, they serve to discount the more modest traditional liberal response to concern about domino processes while, at the same time, to pave the way for more wide-ranging limitations on the market.

Finally, we should note that the domino theory is really one of a class of similar theories asserting some undesirable domino process. According to each of these theories, once some external result is employed as the standard for evaluating certain actions, relations, etc., there is a tendency for actions, relations, or personal conditions that should be valued for their own sake to come to be perceived in terms of and evaluated solely on the basis of the extent to which they promote that external result. Consider, for example, the hedonic domino theory, according to which, once pleasure motivates or is recognized as the standard for evaluating certain actions, policies, etc., other actions or relations, for example, acts of friendship and familial relations, which should be valued for their own sake come to be seen in terms of and evaluated on the basis of the pleasure that they promote. It is the pleasure principle rather than the profit motive that is corrupting and destructive. What we have been calling and will continue to call the domino theory is, more strictly speaking, the *monetary* domino theory. One knows a good deal about any social theorist when one knows what form his dominos take.

III. UNIVERSAL COMMODIFICATION

Belief in and concern about monetary domino processes requires disbelief in the doctrine of universal commodification, the expression of which is market rhetoric. If what one must disbelieve can also be pictured as the expression of and the cause of the commodifying processes that one disvalues, so much the better for the unity of one's worldview. What is false turns out also to be potently *bad*. According to Radin:

> universal commodification means that everything that people need or desire, either individually or in groups, is conceived of as a commodity. . . . Hence, under universal commodification, all social value is capable of being expressed in money terms. . . . [E]verything that is desired or valued is conceived of and spoken of as a "good." Everything that is desired or valued is an object that can be possessed, that can be thought of as equivalent to a sum of money, that can be alienated. The person is conceived of as the possessor and trader of these goods, and hence all human interactions are sales.[8]

Radin holds that in market rhetoric, everything can in principle be assigned a monetary equivalent; the individual good is to be sought in maximizing individual gains from trade. This is why, Radin thinks market rhetoric invites us to see the person as profit-maximizer.[9]

Even before we inquire about precisely what universal commodification amounts to, it is clear that it is a conveniently outrageous view. It is precisely what the critic of the market order might want to represent as the ideological expression of market social relations. We are to picture the victim's implicit acceptance of universal commodification as the source of his losing touch with valuable nonmonetizable aspects of life.[10] Furthermore, the explicit promulgation of universal commodification may also cause people to adopt this mode of thought and thereby injure their self-development.

When the market rhetorician invites us to see the person as profit-maximizer in all things, a stark and substantively valueless universe is conveyed to us. It is the universe of the senseless and unending pursuit of money—a pursuit that is no less senseless and barely more satisfying in the rare moments of success allowed to some of its alienated participants. The image evoked by this characterization of market ideology serves to reconfirm the dismal picture of the increasing and destructive commodification of life that proceeds in domino fashion from existing market relations. Universal commodification has a triple role to play in a view like Radin's. It must be clearly false so that the prospect of monetary domino processes can be both real and frightening. It must also be seductive enough to be guilty of contributing to those processes. Finally, it must be expressive of the underlying character of market society so that its falsity and its guilt reflect back upon the market. I shall suggest, however, that universal commodification is so clearly false that it cannot be very seductive and, further, that it is more of a parody than an expression of the underlying character of the market.

Presumably, the market rhetorician, whoever and wherever he is, is presenting a claim about the ultimate objective of action, or rational action, that is universalistic and of standard consequentialist form. That is, the rhetorician purports to reveal what goal underlies all action, or rational action, whether the action occurs in the market, in nonmarket aspects of market-oriented societies, or in thoroughly nonmarket societies. Descriptively, all the motivation for action derives from agents' interest in the specified goal. Prescriptively, all the motivation for rational action derives from the agents' interest in the specified goal. Universal commodification is, then, one member of a class of similar universally consequentialist theories. Each such theory identifies some state of affairs, for example, some type of experience or condition, as the ultimate goal of all action and/or rational action. Other states of affairs and, especially actions and relations, are pursued or are rationally pursued only on the basis of their contribution to attainment of that ultimate goal. Consider, for example, universal hedonism, according to which the ultimate objective of all action and, presumably, the only thing it makes sense to pursue for its own sake, is pleasure.[11] Other states of affairs, for example, an agent's being alive or being knowledgeable, and all actions and relations are pursued and/or are rationally worthy of pursuit only insofar as they contribute to pleasurable consequences. As always, hedonistic utilitarianism is the paradigm of standard consequentialism. Complex forms of consequentialism that attach intrinsic value of either an agent-neutral or an agent-relative sort to actions or relations fall outside the standard format.

Obviously, there are two basic types of objection to any given theory that has this consequentialist form. One can deny that it correctly identifies the ultimate goal (or basket of goals) of all action or of all rational action. Or, more fundamentally, one can deny that actions, practices, relations, etc., need be motivated and/or evaluated in terms of their ultimate consequences. The opponent of universal hedonism can insist that something other than pleasure is the ultimate motive for all action or the ultimate standard for all rational action, or the opponent can insist that certain actions, practices, or relations are or deserve to be engaged in for their own sake and not merely for the sake of any further consequence. This more fundamental objection can take the form of a more complex consequentialism that assigns intrinsic value to certain actions. Or it can take the form of a deontic doctrine that yields judgments about the rightness or wrongness of actions that are not based on prior judgments about the value or disvalue of states of affairs or actions. This section takes note only of the first basic type of objection to universal commodification. The second basic type of objection, in the form of a more complex consequentialism, appears in the next section in connection with the contrast between internally and instrumentally valued actions.

What does the commodificationist assert to be the ultimate objective of human action? It cannot be money per se. This would at least be manifestly false with regard to actions undertaken in societies employing little or no money. Yet the imperialistic economist seeks not only to explain apparently non-economic behavior in market societies, but all behavior in all societies. According to universal commodification, *all* things of value are described in money terms, can in principle be assigned a monetary equivalent, and *all* gains are monetarizable. Moreover, the monetary descriptions of all things of value, their monetary equivalents, are not epiphenomena that play no role in motivating or in evaluating action. Rather, it is the monetary equivalent of the object of any action that motivates that action and/or provides the basis for evaluating it. The money equivalent does the work. To say that I am a profit-maximizer in all things is to say that maximizing the sum of the monetary equivalents of the objects and states I possess explains my choices. But what precisely is it the maximization of the sum of which accounts for my decisions? What am I maximizing when, for example, I forego a certain amount of actual currency for the sake of leisure? It will not do to say that I am really increasing my income, as measured by that currency, because I would have paid more for that leisure than I have foregone to get it. For even if this is true, it neither explains or displays the rationality of my choice. Why would I have paid more of that currency for the leisure?[12] The only answer consistent with the profit-maximizing model is that there is some more primordial currency in terms of which the leisure is worth more to me than the mundane currency I have to forego to get that leisure.

The commodificationist is, it seems, committed to there being a sort of ur-currency (The Exchangeable *An Sich*) such that the implicit goal of every person's (or every rational person's) actions is the maximization of his holdings of it. So, besides presupposing the commensurability of the good things of life in terms of their respective monetary equivalents, universal commodification is committed to a bizarrely inverted picture of the world. All the good things of life are portrayed as being pursued and/or as being worthy of pursuit because their attainment maximizes the ur-currency payout. The value that resides in our having anything consists in its potential for exchange.

No doubt it is the anticipation of the progressive adoption of this view that inspires fears about loss of self. For this view does not contemplate persons, with their respective bodily constitutions, beliefs, desires, and commitments, for whom various conditions, objects, relations, and actions are valuable either as constitutive of their respective goods or instrumental to those ends. Rather, the view abstracts from the concrete person for whom these conditions, objects, etc., are valuable, sees their value as their impersonal market value, and attempts to reconstruct the value of the person or his life as the sum of those abstracted, impersonal values. This does leave us with the vision of persons as bundles of fungible goods. The person who has that vision of himself will significantly lack what we normally take to be a sense of self.[13]

If this is universal commodification, it surely is manifestly false. Descriptively, even if we allow that for the goal of any action there is a description in (ur)money terms that expresses the value the agent places on attaining that goal, at least in general it will be the agent's placing value on or seeing value in the goal that then allows the goal to be described in (ur)money terms. While there may be some plausibility to the psychological hedonist's claim that all outcomes are pursued because of their perceived hedonic fecundity, it is far more difficult to credit the intrinsic motivating force (much less the uniquely intrinsic force) of The Exchangeable *An Sich*.[14] And, prescriptively, even if we allow that for any valuable goal there is a description in (ur)money terms that corresponds to the value of the goal, there is no plausibility to the claim that the goal's value is due to its monetary equivalent. If this be universal commodification, it is so manifestly false that those who fear its insidious effects should encourage its explicit proclamation. Nothing else would so readily remind us that, for any goal, action, or relation that has a monetary equivalent, that monetary measure is not the source of the value attached to that goal, action, or relation.

It is not easy to specify the alleged feature of life within the market order of which universal commodification may be thought to be a revealing manifestation. My guess is that the alleged feature is the reduction of all motivation and practical rational-

ity to pointless instrumental motivation and rationality. I imagine the idea is that: (1) There is a strong tendency for each
individual in the market order to be motivated to engage in or
pursue and to believe himself to have reason to engage in or
pursue actions, relations, and states of affairs only insofar as
they are perceived to have monetary payoffs; while (2) monetary payoffs lack the substantive value they would have to have
in order to confer even genuine instrumental value upon the
means to those payoffs. The crucial and contentious claim is (1),
which is hardly subject to philosophical evaluation. Were (1)
true, however, one would expect a higher savings rate than
characterizes our market society and less consumer spending.
The response that by means of consumer spending, people
display their monetary success, is one which posits something
other than monetary payoff as the ultimate goal of people's
actions.

IV. Opting for the Non-Cash Nexus

The concern evoked by the monetary version of the domino
theory is, in fact, not about people being caught up in a conceptually bizarre maximization of The Exchangeable *An Sich.* Rather,
it is a concern that actions and relations that are not appropriately perceived and evaluated in monetary terms—ordinary
monetary terms—will come to be so perceived and evaluated.
The concern is with the psychological monetarization of these
activities and relations. In order to begin to get a purchase on
this fearful monetarization, consider a homey example. For
Christmas I bought my wife a nice wool sweater. I did not buy
her a gift certificate equal in cost to that sweater even though
doing so would have economized on my shopping time and
would have less constrained her consumer choice. Worse yet,
from the perspective of what is supposed to be market rationality, I did not hand her an envelope with the equivalent cash—
even though this was the alternative that would most fully have
economized on my shopping time while also most fully preserving her consumer sovereignty. The sources of my conduct are,
no doubt, many and varied. Perhaps as a victim of commodity
fetishism I enjoy shopping and, perhaps paternalistically, I prefer my taste in women's sweaters to my wife's. Yet I do not think

that factors of this sort explain why I prefer bestowing the sweater to conferring the cash-filled envelope. And I cannot satisfactorily account for my choosing to shop for and bestow the sweater rather than presenting a cash-filled envelope by citing my wife's preference for gift bestowal over cash conferral. This citation would just raise the question of why she has that noneconomic preference and why I wish to satisfy it.

Consider another, more complex case. A friend is in the hospital and has used a lot of blood. I go to the hospital and donate blood to his account. For every pint donated to his account he is not charged for a pint of blood he has used. However, my friend is not in dire financial straits; and—in these circumstances anyway—were the available alternative a cash donation sufficient to cover the charge for one pint of blood, I would not make that payment. If I had a choice between the two forms of donation, I would certainly opt for the in-kind donation. (In the real world circumstances it occurs to me that my friend's medical coverage probably picks up most of the charges for blood used. Yet this somehow does not seem relevant to my decision. It would seem more relevant if the only available form of donation was cash.)

I value giving a pint of my blood more highly than I value giving the $50 that would buy my friend a comparable pint of blood. Do I prefer donating the blood to donating the $50 because I value the money more highly than I value the blood? Apparently not. For I would not sell the pint of blood for this amount of money.[15] The cost to me of going through the process of giving blood were I to go through this process for the sake of a $50 payment exceeds the cost to me of foregoing that payment. Yet the value to me of giving blood for this friend clearly exceeds the $50 which I forego in sales revenue.

What these fascinating little stories bring out is that what one sometimes cares about is being engaged in a certain activity or relation. One wants to please a loved one, express one's affection in a way that especially exemplifies one's sense of another individual, or to stand by a friend in a personal way that directly responds to what he has undergone. Here we are two steps removed from any standard consequentialist account of the value of actions. We would be one step removed from that standard picture were we to ascribe value to some action, for example, the direct donation of blood, in virtue of what type of action it is and not simply in virtue of the value of the states of affairs the action produced. Here we are further removed by valuing, not the occurence of an action of a certain type, but rather one's own particular engagement. One does not abstractly value the performance of certain types of action, much less the type of condition produced by the action. Rather, one values one's doing this or that with respect to this special individual (or group of individuals).

My having the option of simply and directly saving my friend $50 by applying $50 to his hospital bill does not lead me to view my donating my blood as merely a matter of saving him $50. If it did, I would not donate the blood since I would not donate the $50 (given his financial condition) were that my only alternative. Indeed, my recognition upon reflection on the mechanics of the blood donation and insurance systems that at most he only benefits financially from my actual donation of the blood, does not deter me from giving the blood. For, despite this reflective knowledge, I continue to perceive my action as a precisely responsive and personal reaction to his having lost blood. And since this is what I value doing, this is what I do. Were my friend to learn of my blood donation, presumably he would not perceive this as equivalent to a cash donation to either himself or to his insurance company—although this would be the view of standard consequentialist eyes. Similarly, my having the option of presenting my wife with the cash equivalent does not lead me to view bestowal of the sweater as merely a matter of saving her the cost of securing that sweater. It does not lead her, I hope, to seeing my action as equivalent to saving her a certain outlay in cash and time.

These little stories, especially the blood donation story, suggest an account of how the domino theory can be false. It is simply that a given nonmarket interaction is not simply a fee-free version of its (closest) market counterpart. Providing someone with funds to cover the fee for needed blood does not accomplish what one accomplishes in donating blood. This discrepancy between what the market can deliver and what can be delivered in a nonmarket manner is especially clear in the area where the domino theory is manifestly empirically false: sex or sexual love. Why does a market in sexual services not drive out or undercut free-of-charge sex? Because we are talking about two radically different—albeit not absolutely different—forms of human interaction. What I have called, with intentional perversity, free-of-charge sex, is sex engaged in by the agent for the sake of the pleasure of that agent, the pleasure of the agent's partner, the pleasure in the pleasure of the partner, the pleasure of the partner in the pleasure of the agent's pleasure about being the agent of this partner's pleasure, etc., where "pleasure" of course is a misleadingly narrow term for all the valued sensations, emotions, relations, etc. involved. Qua agent in such a sexual exchange one correctly does not think of oneself as providing a service. And qua recipient in such a sexual exchange one correctly does not think of oneself as receiving a service.

This is not to say that marketed sex cannot ever have or be perceived as having the qualities of nonmarket sex or that nonmarket sex cannot at all be motivated by instrumental considerations. There is no readily observed limit to the complexity of our motivations, to our ability to combine incongruent motivations, and to our capacity to delude ourselves about what we are doing and why. But the potential for a complex intermeshing of sex engaged in purely for the sake of an external payoff and sex engaged in for the sake of the valued intrinsic features of that sexual relation does not negate the difference between these two or the capacity of the typical supplier or consumer to recognize this difference. This, again, is why the supplier of nonmarket sex will not see himself as merely saving his partner the price of a prostitute. Hence, even in a world in which commercial sex exists, he will still think that he can give effect to and fulfill his noninstrumental motives for giving sex.

Understanding even such simple and common nonmarket actions and relations and the discrepancy between them and their closest market counterparts requires abandonment of the standard consequentialist picture. It requires that actions (and perhaps other non-states of affairs) sometimes be valuable and undertaken for their own sake and not merely for the sake of their anticipated consequences. We should distinguish between internally valuable and motivated activities and (merely) instrumentally valuable and motivated activities.[16] The existence of internally motivated actions contradicts the descriptive side of standard consequentialism while the existence of internally valuable actions contradicts its prescriptive side. The existence of these actions is the basis for the second and more fundamental objection to any version of standard consequentialism, for example, to universal commodification, anticipated in section 3.

Internally motivated actions are undertaken by a person because of the value that person perceives in or attaches to his performance of that action, to the relations it places him in, or to the overall scheme or way of life that is partly constituted by his performance of that action. When value attaches to this person's action in virtue of the value that attaches to the relations or ways of life the action helps to constitute, there is a sense in which the value adheres to the action because of the value of the action's results. Yet in such a case there is a complex interplay between the value of the result and the value perceived in the action itself. One values another's being better off as a result of one's generosity. But it is at least partially that other person's being better off by means of one's act that one values and that feeds back into the value of one's generous act. In contrast, an action is instrumentally motivated insofar as it is performed for the sake of an outcome that is conceived of and valued entirely separately from one's performance. The value of the action entirely derives from the external value of its yield.

It seems clear that there are internally motivated activities; except to the dedicated moral skeptic or standard consequentialist, it seems plausible that some of these are internally valuable. Productive activity carried on for its own sake, the proverbial self-actualizing work, epitomizes internally motivated and valuable activity. Economic activity engaged in for the sake of payment, in cash or kind, the proverbial alienating labor, epitomizes instrumentally motivated and, at most, instrumentally valuable action. The monetary domino theory, requiring as it does disbelief in universal commodification, requires belief in internally motivated and valuable activities. These must exist so that monetary domino processes can threaten their extinction.

Yet, rather than heighten fears about monetary domino processes, I think that this distinction helps allay them in two ways. The first way, already mentioned and to be re-emphasized in the next section, is that the distinction reminds us of how readily people operating out there in the real world can identify and be motivated by the value of various activities and relations and thereby resist the pressure of domino processes. The second way is that the distinction between internally valuable and motivated actions and (merely) instrumentally valuable and motivated ones allows us to dispel a misleading contrast between the altruism of nonmarket activities and the selfishness of market activities. The association of nonmarket activities with altruism and market activities with selfishness falsely conveys a sense of mutually repelling polar opposition between nonmarket and market activities. But the distinction between altruism and selfishness does not in fact correspond to the distinction crucial to describing and anticipating the force of domino processes, that is, the distinction between internally and instrumentally motivated and valuable activities.

It is mistaken to think of all those internally valued activities as altruistic in the sense of having the purpose of serving others, especially at some perceived loss for oneself. And it is mistaken to think that the type of displacement of internal valuation by instrumental valuation that domino processes are supposed to threaten must occur through the invasion of a market rationality that is selfish in the sense of having the purpose of advancing one's interests fairly narrowly construed.

Radin herself recognizes that attention to nonmarket sex relations reminds us that not all nonmarket activities are altruistic. She writes, "Those who are against monetized sex are probably against altruistic sex also."[17] Nevertheless, she continually suggests a general association of nonmarket interactions with altruism and service to others. For example, workers who care about their work and not merely the money it brings are thereby declared to be givers. But this association of productive activity (or athletic or artistic activity) engaged in for its own sake or for the sake of valued productive cooperation with "altruism" is as forced as the tie between internally valued sexual activity and sacrificial service to others.

At what point does internally valued activity that is perceived as enhancing another's welfare become altruistic? The donation of blood to a friend is done for the value of one's standing in a certain special relation to that person, albeit the friend's need is a precondition of the relation's being possible and valuable. More distant and impersonal contributions, for example, the donation of cash for famine relief, also can be done nonaltruistically—out of generosity, sympathy, and sense of solidarity even with far-off people and for the sake of realizing those traits in oneself—albeit the need of those people is a precondition of one's valued action. It should be clear that these are no more egotistical accounts of internally valued actions than are the nonaltruistic accounts of the knowledge-seeker's or the stamp collector's internally valued actions. My point is simply to undercut the implied link between internally valued activities and altruism and the implied polar opposition between internally valued activities and (purportedly) selfish market activities.

Nor am I implying that no acts are really altruistic. But, ironically, the actions that are most plausibly described as altruistic are performed as instrumentally valued means toward standardly consequentialist ends. I am acting altruistically if, solely on the conviction that this will increase the balance of good over bad in the world, I take an intrinsically unrewarding second job in order to contribute the proceeds to famine relief. I act for the sake of that balance of good over bad without personal reward either in the results or the course of my activity. The irony is that a policy of acting in accord with such a standardly consequentialist view threatens precisely the more particularist values of personhood and community that anti-commodifiers cherish.

It is not only that the actions demanded by a standard consequentialism will compete with and morally outweigh the actions constitutive and expressive of one's personhood and personal relations. In addition, acceptance of such a morality commits one to evaluating all one's possessions, skills, hopes, personal ties, etc., in terms of their payoffs for and their costs in the universal maximizing program. A thoughtful person will inevitably come to see his more personal projects, his distinctive values and commitments, as costly, unjustified self-indulgences.[18] By pursuing intrinsically rewarding work, I rob others of the good I might have done for them either directly or through financial contribution. By donating blood for a friend, I rob others of the famine relief funds that I could have generated through the sale of my blood. Calculation for altruism, the potential demands of which are unending, can threaten the perceptions and evaluations needed for personhood and community as much, if not more, than calculation for individual financial enrichment.[19] Indeed, the particularist character of the values of personhood and community seem to be more threatened by the prescriptive call for universal hedonism or welfareism than by either the prescriptive call for the maximization of ordinary monetary holdings or the prescriptive call for the maximization of The Exchangeable *An Sich.* For, whatever their implausibilities, universal hedonism and welfarism at least avoid positing as ultimately valuable something that is obviously solely of instrumental value or something that is contentless.

V. The Persistence of Internally Valued Activities

There must be some difference between blood and sex—for there is some evidence that commodified blood does crowd out nonmarket blood—indeed, crowds out more nonmarket blood than commodification at standard prices draws forth. The sort of story told by Titmuss and Singer about how this crowding out occurs is not inherently implausible.[20] The speculation is that when blood has no market price potential donors are strongly motivated to give blood because they (correctly) perceive that only through such gifts will those needing blood receive it and that to give under such circumstances is to bestow an enormous benefit—life itself. This motivation is lost, it is suggested, when commercial blood enters the scene and more giving is discouraged than selling is encouraged.

Blood is a good while sex is an activity (or a service). The blood with which the patient is about to be transfused is much further detached from its donor and, therefore from the donor's motivation, than the sex that the partner is about to enjoy is detached from the sexual agent—especially since the sex depends upon an ongoing complicated interplay between agent and partner. For this reason it makes sense to say—there is a sense in which it is true—that purchased blood is as good as, *because it is the same thing as,* donated blood. (I leave aside contingent complications regarding both the quality of blood and the quality of sex.) The recipient is unable to distinguish between blood that has been given and blood that has been sold. In this respect there is no discrepancy between what the market can deliver and what can be delivered by gift. Focusing on this fact, the potential blood donor may think that the only thing that differentiates him from the blood seller is his willingness to forego the $50, his willingness that the blood recipient be spared a $50 charge.

This is less of a mistake than the lover's thinking that he is saving his partner the cost of a prostitute. But isn't it still a mistake? Whatever reasons we have for regretting the prospective discouraging of the blood donor (aside from worries about the overall supply of blood, which could be handled by offering a high enough price for blood) are reasons for the potential donor himself to distinguish between giving blood and (merely) saving the recipient the price of blood. Those reasons have to do with the values of acting out of friendship or fellow feeling in particular ways that, at least conventionally or symbolically, represent direct responses to another's condition, and the value to the recipient of being responded to in this way. The donor's action still achieves these values or, perhaps, especially achieves these values, in a world in which some blood moves in the market. It seems that all potential donors have to do in order to avoid making the lover's mistake is to remember that sometimes what is valuable is one's engagement in a particular action or relation. One need only remember that what is valuable for each of us is our living our lives in certain ways, not simply our being generators of or ready receptacles for good consequences.

Typically, one can know the price of something yet not identify the value of that something with its monetary price because the two somethings are not identical. Giving blood is not the same as giving cash to purchase blood. The friendship one receives free of charge is not the same as the friendship one would otherwise pay for. What is paid for when one "buys" a child is the opportunity to become parent to that child (the child it will become through one's parentage of it); one does not buy that developing child and one's relation to it. The costs incurred for such an opportunity can hardly be identified with the value (even the discounted value!) one enjoys in the child.

The value for oneself of what one has or does need not be identified with the market price one foregoes or the market price one pays. Neither should the value of what is done for one be identified with the market price which otherwise one might have paid for the closest market counterpart to what one has received. Yet the Titmuss/Singer account also focuses on how commercialization of blood is supposed to diminish the value to the recipient of receiving blood and on the fact that this diminution undercuts donation on the part of those who want to give something of great, indeed, unmeasured, value. Here, again, I want to suggest that insofar as this process actually occurs, it rests on a mistake on the part of the potential donor. It is simply not true that the value to the patient of the blood that is donated to him is what he would otherwise have to pay for it. Were the subjective value of commodities identical to their market price, no commodities would ever exchange (and there would be no market prices and no commodities). A system that provides the patient with blood for a $50 charge enormously benefits him. In this case, as in others, even the very object that has a market price (that is, the blood) can be pricelessly valuable. If you donate the blood or receive a donation, you are still directly and intentionally giving life or receiving it, even though it is also true that via commercialization people can get life at a bargain price. It remains true that the donor has saved somebody's life even if there was another Good Samaritan or paid rescuer waiting in the wings.

I have argued that commercialization should not stand in the way of one's realizing the value of responding in friendship, or empathy, or solidarity, to the needful condition of another. But commercialization does stand in the way of realizing a related, but more complex, desire. This is not the desire to respond in a certain way given the other's needful condition, but rather the desire that this response on one's part be needed. It is the desire that one's responsive act be indispensible to the relief of the other's needful condition. Even less attractively, it can be portrayed as the desire for the needful person to be utterly dependent upon one's going to his aid. (But not because one wants to threaten not to go to his aid.) It is not a desire merely for opportunities for altruism but rather for there being dependents upon (one's) altruism.

Commercialization frustrates this sort of desire by eliminating the needful one's dependency on those who value one's dependency on them. This speaks well for commercialization, for this sort of desire seems to me to be thoroughly worthy of frustration. Again, this is not to deny the value of acts of direct friendship, generosity, etc.—their value to those who perform them and the value of the knowledge that they have been performed to the recipients of those acts. To be shown friendship and noncalculating support in a time of need is a good that quite literally cannot be purchased at any price. It is because neither it nor any close substitute can be purchased that commercialization need not threaten the bestowal of this good or the good of bestowing it. The only good reason for desiring dependency on such acts is the proposition that, if dependency does not obtain, the value of the acts and reception of them will dissipate or be forgotten. Since I find this proposition dubious, the only remaining reasons I see for desiring dependency are the unwholesome desires to be depended upon and to be dependent.

VI. THE PERSISTENCE OF INSTRUMENTALLY VALUED ACTIVITIES

In seeking to cast doubt on the idea that, within the market order, monetarizing domino processes develop dangerously powerful momentum, I may seem to have endorsed implicitly the normative ideal that the best life is one in which all actions are internally motivated. On the contrary, however, such an ideal is at best silly. Imagine that we were miraculously freed from the need to engage in decisions and endeavors for the sake of their externally valued consequences. That is, imagine that we were finally and totally released from the realm of necessity. One's only choices would be about which of the available internally valued activities or relations one should pursue. Let us further assume that such choices would themselves be effortless either because the available alternatives would not conflict or because their respective intrinsic values would be readily commensurable. There would be no hard choices impinging upon the realm of freedom. Yet, under these circumstances, one's life would hover between the brutishness of immediate (albeit, perhaps, polymorphous) gratification and the godliness of post-revolutionary fulfillment. The tendency would, I think, be to settle on the former. The more elevated fulfillments would only be available to those individuals who had previously postponed gratification in order to prepare themselves for those highbrow evenings of literary criticism. Absent such instrumentally motivated preparation, there would not be much of a self to be gratified or fulfilled.

Moreover, it would be a mistake to forget the many less lovely forms of internally motivated actions. The individual acting out of malice, sadism, or power lust is also engaged in activity for its own sake, or for the sake of the relations of power or dominance it serves, and not for the sake of some entirely externally valued end. The sadist's actions as much involve the personal touch as the lover's. With respect to such cases, we may well long for an insidious domino process which, for example, by so focusing the sadist's mind on the financial opportunity costs of his leisure-time torture, leads him away from his meaningful personal relations into an alienating pursuit of Mammon.

This is not to deny the possibility of lives in which all or almost all major undertakings are significantly and attractively suffused with the agents' respective values. It is not crazy to aspire to a rewarding career, valued avocations, and warm, affirming, familial relations and friendships. But these and similar components of an enviable life all have their inescapable and deeply embedded necessities. These include the costs of opportunities foregone, the costs of developing the insights and skills and strength of will needed to choose well among opportunities, and to choose apt and mutually coherent routes to chosen ends. A tolerance for costs, either in the form of foregone ends or nonrewarding means, is crucial to life building, that is, crucial to personhood and community. A social system that does not free its members from all internally unrewarding necessities need not be an enemy of personhood and community.

Moreover, at least in socially complex and technologically advanced societies, the islands of self-realization that individuals do create are secured and supported by vast networks of nonintrusively instrumental ties. There are the commonly impersonal ties to one's employer, to the manufacturer of one's favorite camera, fishing equipment, or music albums, to one's real-estate agent or neighborhood drug dealer, to the trustee of one's annuity plan, and the impersonal ties of all of these people to yet others. It is precisely these networks that made possible the great variety of chosen arenas for self-fulfillment that characterize pluralistic liberal societies. These impersonal ties, which sustain a pluralist pursuit of personhood and community because they do not require uniformity of belief in substantive values, are constituted by market relations that are motivated largely by anticipated monetary payoffs.

It is certain, however, that observation of and participation in market relations does act as a solvent of traditional and habitually valued patterns of behavior and does encourage people to pursue or create alternative courses of action on the basis of the longer term and, hence, external payoffs of those courses of action. One of the great liberating features of the market order is the way it challenges existing social patterns. Consider the traditional housewife who, upon seeing many women from her neighborhood working outside the home and hiring household help, begins to wonder whether what she is doing is merely saving the household budget the cost of a housekeeper. Is this a hurtful commodification of her previously internally valued activity or a necessary ingredient in her more autonomously deciding what to do with her life? Another liberating feature of the market order is precisely its depersonalization and monetarization of otherwise oppressive and intrusive relations. One is freed from society as one big family. The alternative to the society of contract is the society of status. While the latter may provide its creatures with a sense of self and place, it is an assigned self and a confined place.

Life in a market order does encourage the instrumental rationality of projecting and choosing among complex plans that involve elaborate hierarchies of instrumentalities, and that may require the postponement, or even abandonment, of otherwise available forms of satisfaction. Of course, the special role of instrumental rationality and the postponement of gratification within the market order can be exaggerated. This exaggeration is natural in reaction to the false nostalgic picture of prior ages in which hearty yeomen and self-realized craftsmen could achieve their long-term goals of sustaining themselves, their families, and their lords and bishops by rewarding and joyful toil.

Yet, whether or not instrumental rationality is especially characteristic of market societies, it would be an error to picture the typical practitioner of instrumental rationality as radically separating instrumentally motivated activities and relations from the internally valued activities, relations, and other ends that they allow him to enjoy. As Radin notes with regard to occupational decisions, means to ends may be chosen partly on the basis of their own appeal. Activities and relations originally adopted purely for the sake of their external payoffs may come, perhaps through association with those payoffs and perhaps by tapping an unrecognized interest in those activities or relations, also to be valued in themselves. (Recall the previously noted capacity of people complexly to intermingle internal and instrumental sexual motivations.) People who join firms for the sake of the salaries and retirement benefits develop valued personal ties and institutional loyalties. Owners of car-repair shops may quite calculatingly set out to be friendly with and have a personal relation with their customers; their customers, in turn, may cunningly invest some time and effort in developing these personal relations. Yet that does not mean that some comfortably low-keyed bond of mutual recognition and confidence will not ensue.[21] I assume that Radin does not mean to deny this interpenetration of what is instrumentally and what is intrinsically valued when she writes that "Commercial friendship is a contradiction in terms."[22]

It is, of course, always possible to develop a disproportionate occupation with the means one employs toward one's further ends, be it with money, or vitamins, or the favor of those in authority. So, in a society in which money is a key means for achieving ends, fears about the commodification of activities and relations that should be valued for their own sake are not fantastic. There are features of our society that may dim people's perception of the values internal to certain ways of acting and relating to other people. There is a consequentialist mentality, strongly exemplified by but hardly the product of or confined to Chicago economics, that portrays the value of actions and relations as entirely derivative of their consequent, external payoffs. Given this perspective, actions performed in the market for the sake of their financial payoff may come to be seen as paradigmatic of all rational action. Dovetailing with this perception is the appeal of money as the best candidate—which is not to say that it is a good candidate—for a common standard by which most, if not all, of our endeavors can be measured against one another. The plausibility of money as the measure of all things—if there is to be a measure of all things—is further reinforced in monetarized market societies that emphasize a systematic connection between success, reward, and money. These are reasons for moralists to be concerned with portraying more adequate conceptions of human flourishing. But, in standardly liberal fashion, I presume that such projects of moral edification are to take place outside of the political realm and without employing the power of the state to supplement the persuasive powers of the moralists.

But rather than attempt to defend this general presumption, I return to my basic question for those who fearfully entertain the monetary domino theory. If nonmarket activities and relations are so much better, so much more valuable, than their market counterparts (if any), and if market activities and relations do not preclude these internally valuable activities and ties (and I have argued that commercialization only precludes the indispensibility of nonmarket activities and relations), then won't people in general continue their nonmarket, internally motivated, actions and relations—unless people in general be knaves or fools? And if the problem is that people are such knaves or fools that they cannot recognize or will not choose these components of human flourishing, then who is to be entrusted to design and enforce limitations on the market that will advance genuine personhood and community?

NOTES

1. Its advocates point out that production for exchange is crucial for a pluralist society because it allows cooperation among individuals who do not share substantive values. Production for monetary exchange allows this exchange to transcend the barriers of barter.

2. Margaret Jane Radin, "Justice and the Market Domain," in this volume, and "Market-Inalienability," *Harvard Law Review* 100 (June 1987): 1849–1937.

3. Margaret Jane Radin, "Property and Personhood," *Stanford Law Review* 34 (May 1982): 957–1015.

4. According to Radin: "Under universal commodification, market trading and its outcomes represent individual freedom and the ideal for individuals and society. Unrestricted choice about what goods to trade represents individual freedom, and maximizing individual gains from trade represents the individual's ideal. All social and political interactions

are conceived of as exchanges for monetizable gains" (Radin, "Market-Inalienability," 1861).

5. Radin, "Justice and the Market Domain," 173.

6. The peaceful co-existence that Radin calls for between market and nonmarket aspects of people's lives is akin to a policed quota system. Only so much commodification of this or that aspect of life will be allowed. Insofar as it is feasible, so much non-commodification of this or that aspect of life will be mandated.

7. Radin, "Justice and the Market Domain," 178.

8. Radin, "Market-Inalienability," 1850, 1859–60, 1861.

9. However, Radin points out in "Market-Inalienability" that "Universal commodification is an archetype, a caricature" (1862).

10. Radin speculates that "it may be that market rhetoric, the discourse of commodification . . . [t]o the extent the rhetoric is internalized . . . alienates us from our true selves as persons" ("Justice and the Market Domain," 190).

11. In a manner that parallels a focus on monetarization, the observer who is concerned about the force of hedonistic domino processes must disbelieve in universal hedonism. Yet that observer is likely to consider universal hedonism to be highly seductive and to perceive the belief in and promulgation of universal hedonism to be expressive of the underlying and increasing hedonism that he deplores.

12. If profit or income maximizing is not supposed to explain preferences among alternatives, but is only a different way of saying that people prefer what they do and do what they prefer, it loses all its imperial force.

13. Again, a hedonic parallel exists. If someone comes to believe that the good lies in the maximization of pleasure, in himself or across the collective, that person too may come to see all attributes, conditions, etc., as resources that are valuable only insofar as they can be converted into or traded for pleasure. Under these circumstances, we might observe the dissolution of self feared by the opponent of universal hedonism.

14. Recall that even frenzied pursuit of real mundane money is no more evidence of the pursuit of ur-currency for its own sake than is the pursuit of nonmonetary goals evidence against the universal motivating force of ur-currency. It's that sort of theory.

15. I assume no significant wealth effect. That is, the value to me of the $50 I would surrender through a cash donation is not significantly greater than the value to me of the $50 I would receive were I to sell my blood.

16. See the similar distinction between activities valued instrumentally and activities valued substantively spelled out especially on pp. 393–95 of C. Edwin Baker's "Counting Preferences in Collective Choice Situations," *UCLA Law Review* 25 (Feb. 1978): 381–418.

17. Radin, "Justice and the Market Domain."

18. The desire to preserve what I have called the "particularist" values of personhood and community against the onslaught of evaluative universalism reminds one of the strand of anticonsequentialist thought in recent moral literature that began, perhaps, with Bernard Williams's "A Critique of Utilitarianism," in J. J. C. Smart and Bernard Williams, *Utilitarianism For and Against* (Cambridge: Cambridge University Press, 1973). For a recent statement of this anticonsequentialism, see Loren Lomasky's *Persons, Rights and the Moral Community* (Oxford: Oxford University Press, 1987).

19. Radin thinks that the concept of altruism already presupposes more distance between people than we wish to countenance in our ideals of sexuality. I suggest a parallel, but more general, tension between altruism and the ideals of personhood and community.

20. Richard M. Titmuss, *The Gift Relationship: From Human Blood to Social Policy* (New York: Pantheon, 1971); Peter Singer, "Freedom and Utilities in the Distribution of Health Care," in *Markets and Morals*, ed. G. Dworkin, G. Bermant, and P. G. Brown (Washington, D.C.: Hemisphere, 1977), 149–73. An instructive and amusing response to Singer appears in Loren Lomasky, "Gift Relations, Sexual Relations and Freedom," *Philosophical Quarterly* 33 (July 1983): 250–58.

21. I hypothesize that here, as everywhere else, unintentionally beneficient invisible-hand forces are more at work than critics of the market realize. People pursue, usually without conscious design, an "optimal" mix of personal commitments and freedom from social bondage. And the market, which includes both for-profit and not-for-profit institutions, is always alert to the differing demands from potential customers for autonomy and for belonging.

22. Radin, "Justice and the Market Domain," 174.

8

MARKET CHOICE AND HUMAN CHOICE

ROBERT E. LANE

I. We Live in Systems

There are four major targets of criticism of the market: efficiency, distributive justice, personality, and quality of life. Market influences on any one of them also influence the other three; hence criticism of market influences on any one implies something about the others. Changing one market relation changes others. As the ecologists say, "you can't do just one thing." In the interest of brevity we will selectively combine the third and the fourth targets, personality and the quality of life.

Levels of efficiency and productivity affect justice. Most obviously: (1) distribution depends upon production, and (2) relief of poverty requires resources. Many justice theorists have recognized this. Gregory Vlastos once pointed out that any just custodian of goods must, as a condition of his fiduciary responsibilities, maximize the resources available to his wards;[1] as Rawls reminds us, even egalitarians must make provision for resource development unless they prize equality over well-being.[2] In quite a different sense, economic growth permits Pareto optimal increments to the poor. Finally, and less certainly, a curvilinear relation between economic growth and egalitarian distribution obtains such that at a late stage of industrial development some

I wish to express my thanks to the Institution for Social and Policy Studies, Yale University, and to Nuffield College, Oxford, for hospitality and logistical support.

intrinsic properties of market systems favor a (modestly) more egalitarian distribution of the product.[3] If efficiency and equality represent "the big tradeoff," one can choose to emphasize one over the other, but responsible moral theorists cannot choose to ignore the effects of the one upon the other.

Economic efficiency affects personality and quality of life. Everywhere poverty is the enemy of personality development and a decent quality of life. Scrambling for a living is preoccupying and, even without the culture of poverty (which is said to be a feature only of capitalist societies), the poor cannot reflect upon themselves to achieve self-knowledge; they cannot devote their meager resources to cultural enrichment or self-development. Across societies members of the more developed economies have higher levels of moral reasoning, or at least develop them earlier in adolescence; within the modern American society, the college-educated are overwhelmingly more likely than those without this education to develop standards of principled moral reasoning.[4] College costs money. Cognitive development, which is the foundation of moral reasoning and has many other desirable personality effects, is a function of resources given to education. Higher per capita GNP is certainly not a sufficient condition for personality development, but up to a point (perhaps one we have now reached) it is a necessary one.

Distributive justice affects efficiency, partly because it affects incentives—hence Rawls's difference principle. Carelessly applied, the distribution of money (but not of work) based on principles of need seems to undermine initiative and enterprise. Although in both the British and American economies most people believe that they get about what they deserve,[5] some strikes, labor turnover, and withdrawal of initiative stem from a sense of injustice and do have efficiency costs.

Justice affects personality and some aspects of life quality, although it affects these less than does efficiency. This is because poverty has a much greater effect on personality than does inequality. For example, above the level of decent subsistence, that primary good, self-esteem, is only minimally related to level of income.[6] On these narrow grounds, and taking due care not to create feelings of dependency, the justice of need seems better devised to protect personality than the justice of equality (where these two kinds of justice may be distinguished).

Personality affects efficiency in all the obvious senses: work ethic, entrepreneurial spirit, sense of responsibility, ability to delay gratification, self-reliance are all related to economic development. About one sixth of the American productivity increases in the 1929–1969 period were attributable to the development of human capital.[7]

Personality affects justice in a variety of ways: variations in belief in a "just world" create variation in tendencies to justify injustices;[8] most people show a strong tendency to desire that one person's (often the self's) ratio of input (cost or effort or sacrifice) to outcome (pay or status or power) is the same as any other's similar ratio, but people differ in their responses to unbalanced ratios;[9] the level of moral reasoning mentioned above, especially the capacity to rise above conventional reasoning based on consensus or law and order to levels of principled reasoning, is a personality trait; so is the sense of responsibility for the fate of others that must precede prosocial or altruistic acts[10] —all these qualities, while often situationally influenced, are differentially distributed in the population, that is, they reflect dispositions of personality.

We live in social systems where any one of the properties mentioned above affects the others—and the effects are reflexive. For example, the market's efficiency effects on personality in turn affect the market's efficiency. For this reason those market critics who desire to alter one relation must think of the second-order effects of that alteration on the relation criticized and on the values that the criticism is designed to advance. The unintended consequences of any one policy, whether it is the current policy or a proposed reform, are substantial and often self-defeating.[11]

That society is a social system where alterations in one element affect others is obvious enough, but its realization is inhibited by a general feature of our analytical world and by a special feature of some ethical thought. The general feature is the division of labor among analysts: economists devote their attention to efficiency, ethicists to justice, psychologists and psychiatrists to personality, and everyone, it seems, to observations on, if not the study of, the quality of life. In order to promote rigor, each discipline believes it must treat the others as ceteris paribus. It is a rigor bought at a high price in understanding system qualities and in the consequences of policies based on that understanding. The special impediments to systematic thought are of two kinds: one is the narrow deontological claims to the priority of duty over other considerations, such as efficiency and mental health. The other is the proposition that rights are absolute. It is the virtue of some rights theorists, like Dworkin,[12] to recognize the limits to absolute claims. Emphasis on good will, rigorous performance of duty, and absolute rights in a world of poverty is heroic but empirically improbable.

Recognition of the interrelatedness of things is sometimes reflected in efforts to protect or wall off one cherished value from contamination by the other elements of the system. Since it is impossible to perform an efficiency act without consequences to justice or personality, or to be virtuous without affecting both justice and efficiency, this solution by spheres and walls and boundaries and tiers offers problems that we shall have to examine below. Suffice it to say here that systems do not require unimpeded influence of every system element on every other. Institutional arrangements can fruitfully insulate one sphere from another for the very purpose of protecting the system, as the injunction (in spite of Posner)[13] to the courts to ignore efficiency considerations in rendering justice illustrates. The interrelation of things does not imply their confabulation.

II. Criteria for Judging Market Effects

Our primary concern is with criticisms of the market falling under the third category above: personality, although the relations between personality and the fourth element mentioned, quality of life, are especially close. The two are different as the quality of person and the quality of experience are different. A fine person can have a miserable life, and an objectively secure and prosperous life, enriched by all the advantages, can be lived by a person of low moral character and obtuse sensibilities. In discussing personality, however, we necessarily touch on quality of life.

Criticism of the market's effects on personality (or human flourishing or human development) employs two visible terms, "personality" and "market," and one invisible term: the standards employed.

Personality. The conceptualization and evaluation of personality development offers many difficulties, difficulties familiar to psychiatrists and social psychologists as well as to philosophers. We will not pause here to explore these concepts, but rather refer to one source of standards by means of which to evaluate market effects on the human personality. Two, of many, definitions of mental health by psychiatrists suggest both the common and variant themes that enter these definitions:

> Let us define mental health as the adjustment of human beings to the world and to each other with a maximum effectiveness and happiness. . . . It is the ability to maintain an even temper, an alert intelligence, socially considerate behavior, and a happy disposition.[14]

> In very simple terms, a mature and mentally healthy person is one who (1) respects and has confidence in himself and, because he knows his true worth, wastes no time in proving it to himself and others; (2) accepts, works with, and to a large extent enjoys other people; (3) carries on his work, play, and his family and social life with confidence and enthusiasm and with a minimum of conflict, fear, and hostility.[15]

The ethicist will notice the minimal role of moral qualities in these accounts. Possibly this omission is due to the fact that the psychiatrist knows that a person's mental illness is more hurtful than ethical deficiences to that person's associates and to society more generally. But let us add virtue and a sense of justice to the criteria by which market influences are to be judged.

Markets. The ordinary person is deeply engaged in only two markets, the labor market and the consumer market; almost never in interfirm markets and only glancingly, when he or she saves, in the capital market. Success in the labor market establishes one's place in the economy and to a large extent one's status in the community; it gives one the means for entry into the consumer market. Although on the average a person enters the labor market only about twelve times during his life, the fact that one *sells* one's labor, talents, and devotion can be expected to influence one's thought and perhaps one's personality throughout life. A person's economic anxieties, sense of independence or dependency, alienation (in all of the Marxian senses), self-respect, self-reliance will depend more on the labor than the consumer market.

The consumer market is another matter. In 1965 for the American population the average time spent marketing and shopping was 31 minutes a day, an increase of 40 percent over the preceding 30 years. Women spend more time shopping than men, the French and West Germans spend more time shopping than Americans.[16] The figures do not include market experiences such as eating in restaurants and exposure to advertising, the latter greatly increasing children's exposure to market norms. The critics' argument is that a person's exchange orientation, "commodification" of friendship (see below), pricing of the intrinsic, and so forth is learned from and reinforced by these experiences in the consumer market.

Attitudes toward money, tendencies toward instrumental, cost/benefit thinking (as contrasted to reflection and appreciation), and materialistic values might be expected to flow from both of these experiences, probably interactively as well as cumulatively. But since it is possible independently to vary the marketization of labor recruitment and assignment, on the one hand, and the distributions of goods and services, on the other, reforms flowing from the criticisms of the market depend for their effectiveness upon a more careful specification of the particular market that shapes the pernicious learning experience.

The common lack of specification has a rationale: a *market culture* permeates all institutions and practices in market societies—literature, religion, politics, family. Given what is thought to be the primacy of economic institutions, this assumption has some initial plausibility, but it must be examined in the light of the many theories of the autonomy of art, the family, religion, and even politics, the autonomy of the last of these illustrated by such recent titles as *The Autonomy of the Democratic State*, by Eric A. Nordlinger (Cambridge, Mass.: Harvard University Press, 1981), and *Bringing the State Back In*, edited by Peter Evans, Dietrich Rueschmeyer, and Theda Skocpol (Cambridge: Cambridge University Press, 1985). The latter title is largely addressed to earlier Marxist theories of the state as a dependent servant of the ruling economic class.

The importance of the market in shaping our consciousnesses has a direct and an indirect aspect. Only a modest element of our daily consciousness is focused directly on market-related things. A much larger portion is occupied by work (which is quite different from the labor market), family, friendship, un-commercialized leisure, education, worship, musing/reflecting/wool-gathering—whatever people do when they are unoccu-pied and alone—eating and drinking, sleeping, health care and health worry, growing up, gardening, walking down the street. Allowing seven hours for sleeping (which is about the United States average), what people think about in the 16 hours and 29 minutes wakeful time when they are not shopping and in the 58 years of their allotted 70 in which they are, on the average, not looking for a job has little to do with money and markets. Those who doubt this perspective might reflect upon how much of their conscious life is devoted to thinking about market-related things in their own lives. Nor is the unconscious much more occupied with such things: for example, in one analysis of the dreams of 1,000 men and women only 43 dreams had to do with money, compared to 149 dealing with automobiles (adven-ture and symbol more than price), 125 with "rooms" (of which more were with living rooms than bedrooms!), 118 with "home," 62 with water, 49 with hands, and 46 with faces.[17]

But the indirect effect of the market on the way we think is substantial. We assume without thought that goods are ex-changed for precise money amounts and not given in the man-ner of gift-exchange economies. We think of goods as individ-ually and not collectively owned and that their usufruct pertains to their individual owners. We accept that we must earn our living in the labor market, that it is shameful to be dependent on kin, that the money in our pockets is exchangeable for com-modities, and so forth. If we do not think *about* market related things what we do think about often (but certainly not always) reflects what we have learned from the market.

Standards. Most market criticisms are ambiguous regarding the standards employed, that is, they do not specify whether "the market" (undifferentiated) fails to meet some ideal stan-dard or whether it fails to do as well in the specified respects as traditional economies or command economies, or as some known or imagined mixed economies. Nor is it clear whether the observed market fails to do as well as another, superior kind of market (such as market socialism) might do, or whether, instead, the defects are inherent in any market economy. If the market fails to develop ideal people, even the most enthusiastic market supporter must agree. But that would be true of all known economies and it cannot be that the critics propose to do away with the production and distribution of goods entirely. If we are to deal with the body of criticism as it presents itself, we must accept this ambiguity and take it to mean that, compared to some other form of economic organization, the market has more of the specified defects.

The implicit model. The critics' basic theoretical model, then, assumes the following form. Compared to some other economic system, ideal or historical: (1) certain qualities of materialism, individualistic selfishness, competitiveness, exchange orientation, instrumentalist thinking, single-dimensional (price-conscious) evaluation, and appetite-enhancing characteristics of market experiences, are (2) learned both from experience and market culture, (3) rewarded by status and power and wealth, and (4) taught to children as conditions of success; what is learned, then, (5) both governs the domain of life covered by the market *and* generalizes to the larger nonmarket life domains, where it (6) influences behavior and (7) becomes internalized as socially functional features of personality.

III. THE COMMODIFICATION OF HUMAN RELATIONS

Of the many criticisms of market effects on personality suggested above, we will choose only one for illustrative, if sketchy, treatment: the commodification of human relations. Our purpose is to suggest a way of thinking about the complex problems that all the criticisms—and a parallel set of defenses—raise; it is not a defense of the market but a defense of scholarship in an area saturated with ideology.

The criticism of market effects on human relations has a long lineage: Montesquieu commented on "the monetization of all human relations"; Carlyle's phrase on the reduction of human relations to "cash payment" is, of course, echoed in Marx and Engel's "cash nexus"; like others, the authors of the *Communist Manifesto* refer to the conversion of human value into "exchange

value." Both Simmel and Lukacs speak of the way human relations in a market economy are cold and anonymous; Fromm
gives this interpersonal orientation a name: "The character orientation which is rooted in the experience of oneself as a commodity and of one's value as exchange value I call the marketing
orientation . . . [which] has been growing rapidly."[18] Many of
these critics allege that warmth has gone out of human relations
in market societies with the consequence that people become, as
Simmel said, "intellectually calculating egoisms . . . [who] need
not fear any deflection because of the imponderables of personal relationships."[19]

What is to be explained, then, seems clear enough. But the
evidence for the increase in these unfavorable qualities parallel-
ing the rise of the market economy is not offered; perhaps there
is nothing of this sort to be explained, or, miraculously, what
must be explained is the *decline* in cold, stiff, formal qualities.
The allegations certainly seem dissonant with the alleged dominance of "other-directedness," that exaggerated concern for
what others think of the self. Only after some estimate of the
truth of the allegations will it be worth while trying to assess
whether it is the market economy, or urbanization, or the division of labor, or the market's effects on these mediating forces,
or something else that accounts for whatever changed human
relations has taken place.

Observations on the character of human relations are easily
made, hard to prove or disprove. Impressionistic observers of
the American character, for example, differ on how to characterize the way we treat each other: Tocqueville says "the temper
of the Americans is vindictive," while Bryce says the Americans
typically take a "charitable view of wrongdoers." Max Lerner,
like Laski, speaks of the "friendliness" of the Americans, but
Tocqueville noticed a certain "coolness" and anxiety in their
mutual relations. Are the observers wrong, or between Tocqueville and Bryce or Lerner and Laski have the Americans become
less vindictive, warmer and more friendly? Those who characterize the temper of the times, or of Western market civilization
more generally, also differ from each other: like Simmel, Lewis
Mumford characterizes the human relations of modern man as
"cold" while Allen Wheelis, a psychiatrist, says: "the key words
for our time are 'flexibility,' 'adjustment,' and *'warmth.'* "[20] If

observations are ambiguous in one way, statements of "felt need" are ambiguous in another. The psychologist, Seymour Sarason, speaks of the widespread, deeply felt, contemporary American need for closer personal ties, "the sense that one was part of a readily available, mutually supportive network of relationships upon which one could depend."[21] But, is this because of our isolated, atomized lives (more isolated and atomized than a farm household in Nebraska in the 1880s?) or because we have developed a higher standard of human relations than we had before? Or a lower standard? The psychologist, Abraham Maslow, says that *needing* others, as contrasted to wanting them, is a sign of incomplete personality development.[22]

Systematic studies with controlled observations and better conceptualization do not tell us of the effect of markets but do give a clue as to what it is that must be explained. A detailed study of people's beliefs about themselves, their social roles and life concerns, shows a shift between 1957 and 1976 toward a greater attention to and a higher evaluation of personal intimacy and more concern with personal relations, as contrasted to an emphasis on relatively impersonal status and role relations earlier.[23] Another American national study using 1957 and 1978 survey material reports that, "most [but not all] people in this country are surrounded by a network of relatives and friends whom they see frequently and who provide for them feelings of satisfaction with family and friendships which we know to be important to the individual's sense of well-being."[24] For our purposes, the important point is that those lacking this supporting friendship network are not those most exposed to the market but marginal people who have failed in the market, a fact suggesting an explanatory theory very different from the ones mentioned above. Therefore it is reasonable to doubt the range and depth of the phenomena alleged to be characteristic of modern market societies.

The causal sequence that might bring about the commodification of human relations, wherever it may be found, cannot be elaborated here, but we might take a few tentative excursions in that direction. One follows the critics' argument mentioned above: we learn human relations in the market (not the home, where *Gemeinschaft* still prevails); the materialistic values that inform the market come also to inform our relations in such a way that other people become primarily instruments for enhancing our wealth; and treating others as human beings or ends in themselves or primarily as persons whose company we enjoy impedes our single-minded pursuit of economic goals. While initially plausible, this argument does not square with: (1) what we know about people's value systems ("a prosperous life" ranks [1971] 13th out of 18 "terminal values," far below "peace," "equality," and "self-respect");[25] (2) findings on the sources of people's happiness (number of friends is a much better predictor of life satisfaction in this market society than is family income),[26] or even (3) what people value in their work, where congenial workmates ranks only a little below pay, which itself generally ranks below challenge.

The second causal exploration deals with the effect of changing role relations. Assume that Parsons is right and that human relations in modern market societies are characterized by more role-specific behavior and that, by way of contrast, in *Gemeinschaft* people are known to each other in their several capacities or roles: a person is not just "the postman" but also a neighbor and father of one's children's friends. Because the market (but also the command economy) does seem to facilitate the division of labor where role specificity might flourish, an indirect causal relation would be established and these relatively more anonymous relations might be interpreted as cold and exchange-oriented. If that were true, then we would still have a choice: on the one hand, Godfrey and Monica Wilson suggest a displacement effect: the number of interpersonal contacts times the depths of these relations equals a constant.[27] On the other hand, Lyn H. Lofland suggests an additive relation: "The cosmopolitan did not lose the capacity for knowing others personally, but he gained the capacity for knowing others only categorically."[28] Studies of friendship networks in cities suggest that the Wilsons' theory may be marginally true for the working class, while Lofland's observation is more valid for the middle class.

A third line of exploration follows the idea that the market effect on human relations is not a product of exchange orientation, but rather of the market's encouragement to geographical mobility: going where the jobs are. We did not grow up with our neighbors; we are all transient strangers to each other. The plausibility of this hypothesis is partially undermined by the research findings that (1) after five years a person has as many friends in the place to which he has migrated as he did in the old place,[29] and (2) there seems to be no difference in willingness to share confidences, to lend and borrow, and to experience intimacy with relatively new friends compared to old ones.[30] Not wholly irrelevant to the issue of human relations is another set of findings: people who migrate do better economically and professionally than comparable others who stayed in the same place, whether that is the place of destination or the place of departure.[31]

Then, too, we have problems of evaluation of mixed results. One of these, of course, is mentioned at the beginning of this discussion: how much prosperity we should sacrifice (if that is necessary) for a marginal gain in the kind of human relations embraced by community solidarity. A second evaluative problem is suggested by the findings that looser social networks are associated with decreased sex discrimination and an increase in the activities married couples do together.[32] A third is indicated by the title of Richard Sennett's book, *The Tyranny of Intimacy,* and presents the dilemma posed above by the Wilsons. Intimacy, says Sennett, impedes sociability, a wider but looser set of relations.[33] Finally, in this abbreviated, illustrative list, is the problem of a tradeoff between cognitive development and intimate human relations. If it were the case that the market's stimulative effects and thrust toward self-reliance increased alertness and learning capacities (as new playthings do for monkeys and rats) but also that the market destroyed the easy bonding of neighbors, by what criteria of mental health or ethical prescriptions should we choose among these goods?

Holding ideology and anger in suspension as best we can, it is along such lines that we might investigate the allegations of the market critics that markets commodify human relations—and the proud boasts of market defenders that the market releases people to make their own friends wherever they choose.

IV. GLOBAL EVIDENCE ON ECONOMIC SYSTEMS

If the complex and multifaceted criticisms of market effects on personality have validity, we would expect market societies to reveal more of the personality damages than either household (peasant) economies or command (communist) economies. So much is going on (especially cultural variation) in these comparisons that any finding would be inconclusive, but it would be suggestive and might alter the confident tone of both critics and defenders of the market system. Obviously, we cannot rehearse the evidence here, but let me illustrate the kind of evidence that leads one to doubt at least the sweeping character of the criticisms. On the matter we have just reviewed, human relations, two studies on command economies suggest caution in attributing to market economies a primary modern source of coldness: one, entitled "From Friendship to Comradeship," points out that intimacy and trust among friends in communist China has been eroded by fear of disclosure to the authorities of casual heterodoxy by one partner. The second study reports the use of informants by the Soviet Union and the communist regimes of Eastern Europe as a means of controlling the population and vesting prosecutorial powers in the public; the result was that each person held the fate of his friends in his hands. In both cases suspicion took the place of intimate human relations.[34] Of course, socialism, as originally conceived, is not indicted, but those command economies speaking in the name of socialism are; it is a question whether concentrated, centralized economic power does not risk such results.

The apparently widespread use in command economies of under-the-table payments for officially free or government subsidized goods (a hospital bed, housing) also suggest an exchange orientation that must infect friendship in such a way as to cause a person to consider the extrinsic payoffs of friendship—even in a society of historically warm relations. On the other hand, recent reports of the rise of market relations in Hungary suggest exactly the kind of changes market critics would anticipate: conspicuous consumption and consumer competition. "Father Kuklay [the local priest] said competitive acquisitiveness now dominated life in Korom [a small city some distance from Budapest]. Devotion to work [he said] used to bring the highest prestige. Now it comes from prosperity and property and knowing how to get them. . . . The priest lay the blame for the decline in selfless values on a headlong rush of competitive materialism unleashed by the 1968 economic changes."[35] The point is not that market societies are worse or better in their human relations but that no presumption exists that they are worse and reasons do to believe that exchanges protect human relations in a way not true of unilateral commands (see below).

Following Karl Polanyi, Marshall Sahlins, Stanley Diamond, Marcel Mauss, and other anthropologists (and the industrial psychologist Fritz Roethlisberger), we would conclude that primitive societies, and to some extent also peasant societies, have warmer and less exchange-oriented relations, less materialistic values, less competitiveness and more cooperation, and more secure identities. Following Oscar Lewis (on Tepoztlán), Margaret Mead (on the Manus), R.F. Fortune (on the Dobus), Cora Dubois (on Alor) A.I. Hallowell (on the Ojibwa) we would doubt at least the allegations about warm, trusting, and cooperative relations. More cogently, examining the codified reports in the Human Relations Area Files on relations, values, property rights, and entrepreneurship in hundreds of societies we are led, with better evidence, to doubt Polanyi's categorical statements.[36] Robert Redfield studied and restudied a society (Chan Kom) that went from subsistence agriculture to cash crops; he reports that their internal relations were equally trusting after the change and their treatment of strangers was much more hospitable.[37] The ethnography on the Canadian Eskimos, encountering "civilization" in the persons, not of priests and soldiers but of traders employed by the Hudson Bay Company, reveals a benign change from precarious existence to secure existence without identity problems or social disintegration, although with increased individuation and materialistic values.[38] On the single, troublesome theme of materialism, the evidence from many studies suggests that it is a function of opportunity; people only want what there is some possibility of their having —whether the context is the market or a colonial power or the red army or whatever.

The evidence from both command economies and primitive and peasant economies certainly does not give much confidence in the validity of the market critics' indictments, but neither does it wholly refute them.

One other set of comparisons: are soldiers and priests and academics less competitive, less materialistic, less exchange-oriented, and less selfish than businessmen? In some ways, yes. But fellow academics, do look around you.

V. ALL CHOICES ARE PRICED

When a father chooses to read the newspaper instead of playing with his daughter he "prices" the value of the newspaper higher and the cost lower than playing with his daughter. Every good that is chosen has an *opportunity cost* measured by the values of the goods not chosen. To choose something is to "exchange" it for something you might have had if you had chosen something else. Thus, the pricing of goods in the market and the exchange orientation involved in market transactions are merely extensions of nonmarket acts, extensions to situations where the pricing and the exchanging are made more conscious. They are not different in kind. Compared to household economies, markets merely externalize and give names to actions that occur every day under other names within the household.

Market exchanges have the social advantage over other kinds of choices in the constraints imposed on each choosing person: each must be willing or the transaction will not take place. Critics rightly observe that in market exchanges the asymmetry of power and of alternatives available often invite exploitation. What they fail to note is that choices where the implicit exchange is only the opportunity cost of the chooser may have even fewer constraints, that is, they may be tyrannical. The common comparisons of market exchanges with gift giving or altruism give moral advantages to noncommercial choices, but comparisons with "tyranny" would often give the market exchange moral advantages. For example, compared to selling blood, giving blood may offer moral advantages to the giver and solidarity advantages to his or her society, but selling blood is advantageous compared to being ordered to "give" blood. In the example given above, the father, with more discretion and power, is behaving tyrannically toward his daughter.

Market exchanges may or may not be more materialistic than other kinds of choices. If we take materialism to mean the nature of the goods chosen or exchanged, contrasting them, for example, with love and knowledge, I am as materialistic when I choose a chisel instead of a screwdriver as when I sell my chisel (now nicked) for money. If we take materialism to mean evaluating wealth over, for example, wisdom or friendship, I am as materialistic when I can my fruit to save money, instead of talking to friends, as when I sell my canned fruit in the farmers' market.

Market exchanges may or may not be more selfish or self-interested than other kinds of choices. Depending on the poor father's and nagging daughter's circumstances, the father may seem selfish in reading the newspaper, just as selfish and self-interested as when he bargains with the butcher, the brewer, and the baker over the price of his dinner.

So what is all the fuss over marketization and exchange orientation and price-consciousness about? We suggest three aspects of exchange that differentiate it from nonmarket choices: (1) Making conscious and manifest what was unconscious and latent does have consequences. While it may be true that all gift-giving follows the norm of reciprocity, the act of giving is perceived differently from the act of selling by both the giver and the receiver. Giving, even at Christmas time when gifts are exchanged, is more of an expression of sentiments, often genuine, of respect, affection, and solidarity that is clearly not true of selling or exchanging exact equivalences. In some ways, the stipulated exactness of the equivalence in a market transaction is what undermines the solidarity, for in comparison with the inexactness of reciprocal gifts, it expresses a conventionalized distrust in the partner. And, in spite of the doctrines of social exchange theory, there are many acts of generosity where the relevant return is not gratitude and deference,[39] but a private pleasure in the welfare of another. Anonymous philanthropy is just such a case. The idea of an extended ego, where what happens to another who is linked by some tie to the self, however remote that tie may be (as in the cases of common ethnicity or nationality) makes altruism a selfish pleasure that does not rely upon the returns stipulated by social exchange theory. For such reasons as these altruistic choices are different from exchanges in market transactions.

(2) Normally choices are made on the basis of multiple criteria: the intrinsic pleasures of friendship, curiosity, achievement motivation, revenge. The kinds of evidence by which we judge the success or failure of these choices are also multiple; they are, in addition, often subtle, hidden in the small signs we get from others or from ourselves. Market transactions, however,

are made under circumstances where there are public indicators that all may read: price, cost, comparative economic value. One should not make the mistake of believing that price and economic value are the sole or even the principle criteria employed in consumer purchases, for repeated inquiries into consumer behavior reveal that in the "satisficing" process employed, some performance criterion or life-style or image advantage turns out to be the first of the several desiderata to be satisfied.[40] Nevertheless, following a variety of known cognitive heuristics, people tend to use the most visible, cognitively available information they have—and that is often price. Furthermore, since price is a dimension permitting comparisons of many choices—its a great advantage over qualitative criteria running over several dimensions—price is used as a surrogate measure of subjective profit in the absence of others. The very advantage of economic choices over the other kinds of choices we mentioned, their comparability, tends to twist evaluations, and indeed values, along the price dimension. Even the opportunity costs of leisure, as Linder has pointed out,[41] tend to be priced.

Price is often a surrogate for other information. Just as a more expensive good is thought to be better than a less expensive one, so a richer person is thought to be better than a poorer person. Given information on a person's wealth and nothing more, people tend to infer a host of favorable personality qualities for a hypothetical prosperous and unfavorable qualities for a hypothetical poor man. This is wholly spurious, that is, poor men taking the same personality test that was used for the hypothetical evaluations by the subjects of the study, had personality profiles much more favorable than those assigned to the hypothetical poor man.[42] In this more limited sense, human relations *are* affected by the money-consciousness taught by market economies. (Whether this same stereotypical behavior would be seen if knights and dukes were compared to yeoman and peasants in feudal society, or section chiefs and clerks in a bureaucracy, or party members and nonparty members in the Soviet Union remains to be seen; the halo effect is probably universal.)

(3) Forced and coerced choices are always unfortunate; it is the circumstances of the choice and not whether or not money changes hands that should affect our judgment of the choice or

exchange. The concepts of forced and coerced choices may be explicated as follows:[43]

   i. All choices are constrained by nature, human possibility, and so forth. Choices constrained only by these factors are not coerced; they are choices among *limited alternatives*.

  ii. Where there are universal social constraints applying to all individuals within a society and we know that customs and institutions could be different, the choices are *forced* but not coerced.

 iii. Where an individual, John Doe, has choices P and Q, but P involves serious and punitive consequences, then Q is *coerced* if:

    a. we know that there are feasible choices R, W, etc. that are not ruled out by nature or universal social practices, and;

    b. there are others who are like Doe in relevant respects but unlike him in the respect that robs Doe of choices R, W, etc., and;

    c. this respect is by some standard wrong, and;

    d. Doe knows of these alternatives. (If Doe does *not* know of these alternatives and could choose them if he knew them, the choice is not coerced, but Doe is *deprived*.)

Not market exchange, but forced and coerced choices are the enemy of human choice. As Walzer says, "there is nothing degrading about buying and selling—nothing degrading in wanting to own that shirt (to wear it, to be seen in it). . . . If the sphere of money and commodities is properly bounded" there is no great harm in trying to sell more. What is degrading is a "desperate exchange,"[44] such as one requiring long hours of unremunerative work from a person with no alternatives, or prostitution, perhaps at any time (or perhaps not if one is a popular courtesan), but certainly under duress. Although many choices quite outside the market are degrading (ingratiation toward a tyrannical father, supplication for grace from an intolerant priest), the most common site for forced exchanges is in that area where a livelihood is to be gained: in a market economy, the market. (As a parenthetical remark, we might note that in our opinion the sale of one's blood and organs is rather like the sale of one's labor, although probably less degrading because less intimately tied to self-esteem, for one's blood and organs are rarely matters of pride or so vulnerable to criticism as one's work. Selling either one's labor or one's blood and organs in a desperate exchange or under threat of starvation are equally degrading.)

Because of their opportunity costs nonmarket choices generally reflect most of the characteristics of market exchanges: their implicit pricing, their materialism, and their selfishness. But the market's explicit pricing, its invitation to use a single, readily available, easily comparable money dimension for judging everything, and its more frequent incidence of desperate exchanges make market choices different from others. It should be apparent, however, that the main problem for the development of the human personality is the character of the choices made and not the exchange of goods and services for money in the market.

VI. Walls and Systems

How can it be that in a system where each element affects others, we could ever hope to erect a wall between the market and certain protected kinds of practices? This is a particularly cogent question if we accept Churchman's idea that in any system the system goal determines the goals of all its subsystems.[45] Would it not be the case that the subsystems behind any wall designed to reduce the power of money and "to make money harmless"[46] might serve purposes quite uncongenial to the purposes of the overall system, and worse, feeling protected by walls, people would come to believe that everything else is by some magical, perhaps invisible, hand serving a valuable social purpose?

Walls may do two things: they may insulate the subsystem from pollution by the system goal, and/or they may insulate the subsystem from pollution by other subsystem goals, protecting the integrity of the subsystems. (To avoid such infelicities of expression we hereafter refer to subsystems as institutions or practices and the overall social system as society.) Walzer's *Spheres of Justice* offers a useful scheme for the second of these purposes: protecting such institutions as criminal justice and such practices as merit awards from contamination by the institutions and practices of the market. The purpose is to keep separate the power of money from other kinds of power and the criteria of wealth from other kinds of criteria.[47] This kind of insulation has many other guises: in the interest of personality development we prohibit child labor, thus insulating children from demands for direct and immediate contributions to productivity; to promote productivity we protect factories (even socialist factories) from demands based on the justices of need and equality; an elaborate system of rights protects certain acts from trespass by the government; Rawls's "lexical ordering" of freedom is a form of boundary creation. Like our theories, our social system is full of walls and boundaries, isolating, protecting, and bounding the institutions and practices considered vital for our society.

The criteria employed to justify boundaries and walls are devised to protect one set of institutions and practices against invasion by another; they are not devised to serve an overall societal goal—because there is no agreed-upon overall societal goal. We have, therefore, no means of assessing whether the walls and boundaries serve such a goal. Many such goals have been suggested: W. D. Ross proposes four: (1) "virtuous disposition and action," (2) merited pleasure, (3) justice, and, more ambiguously, (4) knowledge.[48] Following Kant, we might consider such a goal to be human dignity; following the utilitarians, we would say happiness; in this volume Radin suggests "human flourishing," which is very like William Galston's "developed existence."[49] Radin suggests further that the wall metaphor fails because it seems to protect only some aspects of human flourishing, leaving practices outside the wall free to trespass on such flourishing. Her concept of the overriding societal goal is attractive and congenial to our point of view, but unless it can be reconciled with other concepts of the good it represents only one more vague formulation of a supreme good. We cannot yet follow Churchman's precept and ask of each proposal to insulate one set of practices whether it both protects that set from other institutions and practices *and* serves the overall purposes of society.

But we can do something more modest. Proposed legislation must defend itself against charges that it will unfavorably impact the environment. In the same way, we may ask of every criticism and every defense of the market not only whether it would serve the short-run, institutionally defined purposes for which it is established or proposed, but also how it does or would affect other social purposes, specifically, economic efficiency, justice, personality development, and the quality of life. For example, we cannot defend rent control because it protects the rights of tenants to circumstances favorable to their quality of life without also asking how it affects the production of housing and therefore the interests of the homeless. Nor can we propose that all jobs be devised to develop human capital without also asking how this affects labor costs and therefore unemployment—bearing in mind that our Taiwanese competitors whose jobs might be protected by an expensive job-enrichment program in the United States are also people with moral claims.

Ethically informed proposals to promote justice and virtue must, like economic proposals to promote efficiency and like psychological proposals to promote mental health (or human flourishing), ask these kinds of questions about system effects and weight the answers with care. If they do not, in each case they not only risk jeopardizing the values they have ignored, but also, because of systematic interconnections, risk defeating their own purposes.

NOTES

1. Gregory Vlastos, "Justice and Equality," in *Social Justice,* ed. Richard B. Brandt (Englewood Cliffs, N.J.: Prentice-Hall, 1962).

2. John Rawls, *A Theory of Justice* (Cambridge: Harvard University Press, 1971).

3. Simon Kuznets, "Economic Growth and Income Inequality," *American Economic Review* 45 (1955): 1–28.

4. Lawrence Kohlberg and R. Kramer, "Continuities and Discontinuities in Childhood and Adult Moral Development," *Human Development* 12 (1969): 93–120.

5. Wesley H. Perkins and Wendell Bell, "Alienation and Social Justice in England and the United States: The Polity and the Economy," in

Comparative Social Research, vol. 3, ed. Richard F. Tomasson (Greenwich, Conn.: JAI Press, 1980).

6. Angus Campbell, *The Sense of Well-Being in America* (New York: McGraw-Hill, 1981), 216–17.

7. Edward F. Denison, *Accounting for United States Economic Growth 1929–1969* (Washington, D.C.: Brookings Institution, 1974).

8. Melvin J. Lerner, *The Belief in a Just World: A Fundamental Delusion* (New York: Plenum, 1980).

9. Elaine Walster, Ellen Berscheid, and G. William Walster, "New Directions in Equity Research," *Journal of Personality and Social Psychology* 25 (1973): 141–76.

10. Shalom H. Schwartz, "Moral Decision Making and Behavior," in *Altruism and Helping Behavior,* ed. J. Macaulay and L. Berkowitz (New York: Academic, 1970).

11. The social system, of course, is much larger than the economic system, with families, communities, religious institutions, and so forth all sharing in the system effects, but there is enough to do in the above analysis without complicating it further.

12. Ronald Dworkin, *Taking Rights Seriously* (Cambridge: Harvard University Press, 1977).

13. See Richard A. Posner, *The Economics of Justice* (Cambridge: Harvard University Press, 1983).

14. Karl Menninger, quoted in W.A. Scott, "Conceptions of Normality," in *Handbook of Personality Theory and Research,* ed. E.F. Borgatta and W.W. Lambert (Chicago: Rand McNally, 1968), 974.

15. T.A.C. Rennie and L.E. Woodward, *Mental Health in Modern Society* (New York: The Commonwealth Fund, 1948), 334.

16. Alexander Szalai, *The Use of Time* (The Hague: Mouton, 1972), 578.

17. Calvin S. Hall and Robert L. van de Castle, *The Content Analysis of Dreams* (New York: Appleton-Century-Crofts, 1966), 243–72. Studies of the content of daydreams reveal more economic content, but in that area it is work and not pay, buying, selling, money, or exchange that people turn to in their musings.

18. Erich Fromm, *Man for Himself* (New York: Holt, Rinehart and Winston, 1947), 76.

19. George Simmel, "The Metropolis and Mental Life," in *The Sociology of George Simmel,* transl. and ed., Kurt H. Wolff (Glencoe, Ill.: Free Press, 1950), 154.

20. Allen Wheelis, *The Quest for Identity* (New York: Norton, 1958), 85.

21. Seymour Sarason, *The Psychological Sense of Community* (San Francisco: Jossey-Bass, 1974), 1.

22. Abraham H. Maslow, *Toward a Psychology of Being,* 2d ed. (Princeton, N.J.: Van Nostrand, 1968), 26, 401–42.

23. Joseph Veroff, Elizabeth Douvan, and Richard A. Kulka, *The Inner Americans: A Self-Portrait from 1957 to 1976* (New York: Basic Books, 1981), 530–31, 537.

24. Campbell, *The Sense of Well-Being in America* 110. Not all research reports are so favorable to the idea of warm contemporary human relations. Richard Christie and Florence L. Geis report the rise of a manipulative attitude toward people that would seem to support one theme among the critics. See their *Studies in Machiavellianism* (New York: Academic, 1970).

25. Milton Rokeach, "Change and Stability in American Value Systems, 1968–1971," *Public Opinion Quarterly* 38 (1974): 222–38.

26. Angus Campbell, Philip E. Converse, and Willard L. Rodgers, *The Quality of American Life* (New York: Russell Sage, 1976), 368.

27. Godfrey and Monica Wilson, *The Analysis of Social Change* (Cambridge: Cambridge University Press, 1945).

28. Lyn H. Lofland, *A World of Strangers* (New York: Basic Books, 1973), 177.

29. John B. Lansing and Eva Mueller, *The Geographic Mobility of Labor* (Ann Arbor, Mich.: Institute for Social Research, 1967).

30. Nicholas Babchuk and Alan P. Bates, "The Primary Relations of Middle-Class Couples: A Study of Male Dominance," *American Sociological Review* 28 (1963): 377–84.

31. Peter M. Blau and Otis D. Duncan, *American Occupational Structure* (New York: Free Press, 1978).

32. Elizabeth Bott, *Family and Social Networks* (New York: Free Press, 1971).

33. Richard Sennett, *The Tyranny of Intimacy* (New York: Knopf, 1976).

34. Ezra F. Vogel, "From Friendship to Comradeship: The Change in Personal Relations in Communist Societies," *China Quarterly* 21 (1965): 46–70; Jan T. Gross, "A Note on the Nature of Soviet Totalitarianism," *Soviet Studies* (1982): 367–76.

35. *New York Times*, March 12, 1987.

36. See Robert B. Textor, *A Cross-Cultural Summary* (New Haven: HRAF Press, 1967).

37. Robert Redfield, *A Village that Chose Progress: Chan Kom Revisited* (Chicago: University of Chicago Press, 1950).

38. Nelson H. H. Graburn, "Traditional Economic Institutions and the Acculturation of the Canadian Eskimos," in *Studies in Economic Anthropology*, ed. George Dalton (Washington, D.C.: American Anthropological Association, 1971).

39. See Peter M. Blau, *Exchange and Power in Social Life* (New York: Wiley, 1964).

40. See, for example, James R. Engel, Roger Blackwell, and David T. Kollat, *Consumer Behavior* (Hinsdale, Ill.: Dryden, 1978).

41. Steffan B. Linder, *The Harried Leisure Class* (New York: Columbia University Press, 1970).

42. Joseph Luft, "Monetary Value and the Perception of Persons," *Journal of Social Psychology* 46 (1957): 245–51.

43. The following explication has been greatly assisted by comments by Ian Shapiro and others in a discussion of the Yale Political Science Department Political Theory seminar. See also Ian Shapiro, *The Evolution of Rights in Liberal Theory* (New York: Cambridge University Press, 1986), 180–85 and 290–99.

44. Walzer, *Spheres of Justice*, 109–10, 102.

45. C. West Churchman, *Challenge to Reason* (New York: McGraw-Hill, 1968).

46. Walzer, *Spheres of Justice*, 107.

47. Robert E. Goodin proposes to insulate ethical decisions from materialistic ones on the grounds that "material incentives destroy rather than supplement moral incentives" (113). This formulation ignores the system properties of societies, as outlined above, and also runs into the difficulty that few ethical decisions are free of material consequences and few material decisions can be divorced from ethical considerations. See his *Political Theory and Public Policy* (Chicago: University of Chicago Press, 1982), chap. 6.

48. W.D. Ross, *The Right and the Good* (Oxford: Clarendon Press, 1930), 134–40.

49. William A. Galston, *Justice and the Human Good* (Chicago: University of Chicago Press, 1980).

9

THE JUSTICE OF THE MARKET: COMMENTS ON GRAY AND RADIN

JAN NARVESON

INTRODUCTION

Is the free market a just institution? I will support an affirmative answer here, mainly by way of discussing two chapters in this volume, those of John Gray and Margaret Jane Radin. They deal with very different aspects of this question, but my remarks present a unified view that benefits from reflection on each of these interesting and well-argued essays. To a degree, my view will be developed independently as well.

What we have in contemporary developed nations are partial market societies, where markets operate with a substantial overlay of public-sector activity. This presents a problem. The many who wish to condemn market society on the basis of perceived shortcomings in our general socioeconomic fabric need to show that the problems are due to the market portion rather than the rest. In turn, defenders of the market argue that those shortcomings are due to the public sector rather than to the market, and that the cure for what is wrong consists in extending market methods beyond their current rather constricted limits. I incline toward the latter view. The question is how far it can be reasonably taken. Some aspects of this large issue will be addressed here, though it will not, of course, be resolved.

1. GRAY ON MARKET SOCIALISM

Gray is instructive in his treatment of "market socialism," wherein enterprises are worker-owned and worker-managed, but compete freely with each other for the consumer dollar. When the worker's connection with the firm is via an inalienable share in its capital and a vote in its management, shortcomings ensue, familiar from the case of family-owned enterprises in free-market economies: the firm is reluctant to take on new employees who will dilute existing shares of profits, and it tends to be risk-averse and consequently slow to innovate. But these, as he says, are of secondary importance. The more fundamental problem of market socialism lies in its socialism, which now takes the form of state control of investment. This creates an institutional problem of substantial magnitude: "All our knowledge of bu-reaucracies suggests that the permanent officials of the state bank would be conservative and risk averse in the extreme and would shy away from investment strategies involving substantial speculative risks even if these were dictated by accepted princi-ples of justice. . . . Large existing enterprises with political clout will be favored over small and struggling ones . . . malin-vestments would be unlikely to be eliminated, but instead would be concealed by further inputs of capital."[1] And so on. Gray observes that the "upshot of the calculation debate . . . is that calculational chaos—waste, malinvestment, and discoordination in the economy—can be avoided, or at least minimized, only if decision-making is decentralized to the level of the individual through the institution of private or several property."[2]

With all of this I agree entirely, and would only add some further reflections on the whole idea of market socialism. As Gray observes, the calculational debate took place between pro-ponents of the free market and socialist theorists who were aware of the advantages of the pricing mechanism and hoped to retain most of those advantages in their versions of socialism without what they took to be the disadvantages of capitalism. The Austrians in effect argued that they could not succeed in this, and Gray summarizes that case. Meanwhile, we should raise the prior question of what the market socialists think they are up to. Why be a market socialist?

The standard answer provided by these theorists—almost all of them academics—is that the socialistic aspect of market so-cialism provides the "democracy" supposedly lacking in an un-varnished market system, while the market aspect supplies, as it were, the efficiency. Gray gives good reasons for doubting that efficiency will in fact be achieved in such a system. What about the alleged democracy? Does it even provide that? Further reflection, I suggest, will show the answer to be in the negative.

The argument is that worker's democracy is called for by the principles of democracy in general, when applied to the workplace in particular. Is this so? It is not. The usual arguments for industrial democracy are fallacious.

Let us use the latter term in its conventional sense, that is, to refer to a system in which the workers in a given enterprise have a right to share in its management, a right that is strong in the sense of not requiring the owners, if any, to agree voluntarily to such sharing. This, of course, means that the owners are not really owners. But a free enterprise system already allows worker-owned enterprises, and it also allows owners for whatever reason to give their employees substantial managerial independence; in those cases, worker control obviously obtains, and industrial democracy in the sense defined is unnecessary. Thus those who advocate industrial democracy as an alternative to free enterprise must mean by this a system in which private ownership of productive property is prohibited; this fits it in with the classic Marxian idea. Given these assumptions and this definition, do we have an argument for industrial democracy based on democratic political theory? No.

Let us see why. Political democracy is more general than industrial democracy. Industrial democracy is an analogue of political democracy: it is democracy in the particular case of a productive facility involving the efforts of many people. But the case for political democracy, insofar as it holds at all, holds for an involuntary group, namely society. Supposing that we have a case for government at all (anarchists won't grant this, of course), then we can make a strong case for democracy, at least in reasonably favorable social circumstances. Democracy consists in an equal distribution (roughly equal, in actual practice) of ultimate political power. Such power is the power to govern or, in the cases (all the interesting ones) where direct employment of it is impracticable, to determine who will govern. But it is also, and for the same reason, the power to determine what sort of economic system we shall have.

Whether democracy even includes this power is, it should be noted, disputable. Democratic rights are limited, on any reasonable view. For example, democracy does not include the right arbitrarily to abrogate the right to vote, nor to revoke by majority vote any of the other basic rights we have come to accept as essential to any decent polity. Majority rule, in short, is limited by a set of rights. But libertarians insist that one of those very rights is the right to hold property, and they would therefore insist that this gives capitalism a fundamental status that cannot properly be modified by political procedures no matter how democratic they are.

However, for the sake of argument we will not adopt this view here. We assume, then, that the choice of economic system is available for democratic decision. But if it is, then one of the choices facing the voters is whether to go for industrial democracy. They might so choose, but they might not. The right to help manage any enterprise one works in simply is not entailed by political democracy. Voters could decide, all entirely within the spirit of democracy, that any form of public ownership *or* of entrenched workers' rights to manage is a bad idea. They could even, in their wisdom, so decide for some of the very reasons Gray has so acutely identified. And indeed, that seems to be the way voters in the capitalist democracies *have* decided. Does this show that those countries are not really democracies? No. It simply shows that industrial democracy isn't essential to political democracy.

Of course, some voters would disagree with the majority on this point. But the existence of disagreement cannot be of fundamental consequence to any serious advocate of democracy, for to accept democracy is ipso facto to deny the necessity of unanimity on political matters, except, perhaps, on the matter of whether to have a democracy or not. A contractarian, for instance, might hold that democracy is the best bet for all rational persons for resolving various conflicts of interest: In those areas, we should all go along with the majority, even when we disagree with the majority's view of what is best. The value of having that mechanism, so the argument would go, exceeds the value of getting our way on particular issues.

If a majority were to vote for industrial democracy, it would deprive everyone, to begin with, of the right of free enterprise, that is, the right to start up a business on one's own, raising capital from whomever is willing to provide it, and taking the risks this may entail. It would limit the freedom of workers to determine the degree to which they are to participate in the operation of any business in which they happen to be employed. This is something with which a reasonable person might well not want to bother. Some people choose to live in housing cooperatives because of the opportunities for political participation this affords. But others choose *not* to live in them for that very reason. The many workers who would likely prefer not to bother with such things, leaving them instead to those who have the most direct interest in running things efficiently (namely the owners, when there are any), would not have this option in a society determined to impose industrial democracy on all. Moreover, as Gray points out, it would probably severely limit their mobility for employment purposes. Since free enterprise permits cooperative enterprises to be formed and run on the basis of as much industrial democracy as one likes, how could a rational voter prefer imposed industrial democracy to it, qua system at any rate?

In short, we may argue either that democracy, being self-rule, implies the freedom to choose one's own employment situation insofar as that is possible, or that it at least implies the right to vote on what sort of economic system to have. It does not, therefore, imply that the vote must, if democratic, go one way rather than another.

2. HOBBESIAN JUSTICE

The argument thus far supplements Gray's important insight that "Any economic system which imposes on all a productive ideal which not all share must be condemned as unjust from the standpoint of contractarian method."[3] Gray reaches this conclusion, properly in my view, by a broadly Hobbesian construal of contractarian theory, one which does not proceed, as does Rawls's, via the incorporation of any particular ideal of the person. It assumes only that we are all agents, concerned to pursue a variety of purposes and not, for example, that we are members of any particular moral community devoted only to the purposes it decrees. "We theorize the person . . . as an unsituated individual, defined not by communal attachments but by prudential interests."[4]

Two important conclusions, he thinks, derive from this construction. One is that "there can be no question of pure redistribution emerging as a policy."[5] Moral equality does not imply an ideal of equality in economic well-being. On the other hand, however, "because the Hobbesian construction does not contain proprietary rights at a foundational level, nothing is exempt from redistribution, either."[6] Indeed, because of the same egalitarian element, "it is not to be supposed that the Hobbesian contract could yield an outcome in which . . . there were some without assets or resources of any kind. Rather, it is reasonable to suppose that the Hobbesian contract would guarantee to each an initial capital endowment which would be his to dispose of."[7]

Is this plausible? Gray does not develop the details, yet those details are crucial if that conclusion is to be reached. Consider the previous issue of choice of a productive system. In the absence of any sort of ideal of the person we cannot argue as might, for example, a Nietzschean, an Aristotelian, a Protestant, or even an early Marxist. Any of those theorists might insist on the importance to personality of production, which might lead to our putting special emphasis on the ability to determine with what sort of productive system one is to live and work. Productive systems and the choice thereof are strictly a means to an end, in the absence of such ideals. If so, however, why should we accept so strong a conclusion as the one Gray arrives at? What if it is argued that Gray's second point, that each should be guaranteed a certain capital endowment, is of such importance that it could allow the imposition of one or another kind of productive system in order to secure it? Mightn't one have to choose between freedom of production and guaranteed freedom from want? If so, would the former have priority over the latter?

It seems to me, on the contrary, that the sort of assumptions Gray proposes to work with will endorse the first conclusion at the expense of the second. If we are endowed only with prudence and a variety of goals, we will not accept as a basic feature of the social system any requirement that we all see to each other's minimal good any more than that we all join hands in a socialist productive cooperative. The reason for this lies in the independence and prudential orientation of the parties, plus the fundamental feature of contractarian method that it re-

quires *unanimity* on the choice of the fundamental principles
that are to govern us as social beings. Given unanimity, no one
will be able to coerce any particular outcome from others. The
productively weak, therefore, will not be able to coerce the
productively strong into guaranteeing that social minimum they
no doubt may want but which there seems to be no reason to
concede. The social agreement must instead be that people may
utilize their productive powers as they judge best. If they judge
that some of their output should go, gratis, to the otherwise
poor, so be it. If not, it is difficult to see what recourse those
otherwise poor could have, at the very least *unless* we allow
coercion.

Suppose that we do permit coercion at the outset. That is the
defining feature of Hobbes's State of Nature: Since there are no
rules, literally nothing is forbidden, and therefore coercion in
particular is not. As Hobbes conceives it, it is the permissibility
of coercion that causes the problems inherent in that condition.
Everybody loses—both the weak *and* the strong—because human powers are sufficiently equally distributed that no one can
gain an advantage if all are able to use their powers without
restraint.

Gray's proposal would call for measures to be taken to see to
it that everyone has a minimal stock of capital over and above
the stock of "capital" inherent in one's person by virtue of being
a (more or less normal) human being, that is, one's inherent
repertoire of capabilities. But how are these measures to be
conceived? There would seem only two options: either they are
voluntary, or they are exacted coercively. The former resolves,
in turn, into two possibilities: either such a social guarantee is
held to be literally in the interest of each individual, or it is
conceived as stemming from such things as sympathy or possibly an innate moral sense that one should share. Now, the latter
conjectures are dicey if the claim is that all humans have the
necessary measure of sympathy or benevolence toward all others. It is surely far more plausible to restrict the likely operation of any innate sympathy to narrower classes of persons
such as parents and kin—and even there, as we have witnessed
throughout history, cases typified by that of Cain and Abel crop
up along with all the cases more favorable to the hypothesis. If
the moral version is taken, then one has simply dissented from

the contractarian idea—and also, of course, one is back to the empirically insoluble problem of showing that all humans do have an innate moral sense of the requisite kind.

Absent either of these hopeless maneuvers, what about mutual self-interest? The problem here is that we are now using what amounts to an insurance argument. The idea is that it is worth our while to be assured some minimal share of capital, or the equivalent, at the cost of some loss of economic liberty. But surely temperaments, proclivities, and plausible estimates of situations will differ far too much to make the conjectured universality plausible. Moreover, there is this obvious objection to any enforced system along this line: if people think this is a good idea, they can arrange insurance systems or mutual aid arrangements with whatever individuals are willing to go along. That way, the levels of minimal capital are at least determined by the interests of the parties concerned and not by some social theorist's view of what they should want. Unless we are to indulge in a degree of paternalism plainly unwarranted by the rejection of ideals of the person, this option is therefore extremely dubious.

Thus it appears that an imposed solution would be necesary if any such social minimum is to be achieved. But how can we suppose, in view of the points just made, that individuals operating under no prior constraints and in response only to their own sense of what is prudent or, in any sense in which this may be allowable in contractarian theory, of what is moral, would *unanimously* agree to this system? Far more plausible, surely, would be to argue that we will adopt a basic constraint of the type proposed by Gauthier, which he introduces as a variant of the "Lockean proviso on acquisition." His form of the proviso prohibits acquiring by taking advantage of others. The baseline for interaction is that in which we have nothing to do with each other. No fundamental duties to supply each other with anything are assumed or forthcoming. The only rational restriction is that our acquisition is not to be at others' expense: utilizing the other person's efforts to promote one's own good is forbidden.[8] Obviously, this means that one may not use coercion for that purpose: All acquisitions must be by cooperation rather than force. In the absence of some extremely conjectural argument, this also rules out Gray's idea as a fundamental one for this purpose. The social minimum is simply noninterference.

Gray, to be sure, does not explore the baseline issue. But his suggestion about initial capital endowments came, as we have seen, from the thought that "because the Hobbesian construction does not contain proprietary rights at a foundational level, nothing is exempt from redistribution, either. From the standpoint of a Hobbesian variant of contractarian method, all assets pass from civil society back into a circumstance of no-ownership (not collective ownership) when initial endowments are to be allocated."[9] But how would this initial allocation work? For one thing, they would surely be variable from one social group to the next. More importantly, if they are genuinely initial, made all at a given time, then what happens to later generations? It is not to be expected that every family would retain its capital intact, and it is to be expected that many would have children numerous enough to require reduction of the shares they could hand on. Within a very few generations, the effect of these initial endowments would therefore be dissipated, even obliterated. So would Gray call for a continuous readjustment, along the lines of the welfare state? One supposes not. And if one does so suppose, then how is that idea to be reconciled with the claim that we are presupposing only prudence and no ideals of the person, no morality, at the outset?

3. THE CASE FOR LIBERTY

In the course of his development of a Hobbes-like contractarianism, Gray claims that it "contains nothing which might guarantee the priority of liberty over other political goods. . . . The basic liberties themselves will not in the Hobbesian account be immune from trade-off with other values (such as peace and security)."[10] Should we be content with this rather negative conclusion? I think not. There is, I suggest, a deep reason, arising from the method itself, for expecting certain general results of this type. Trying to specify civil liberties for all and forever may be futile, but the basis for a general right of liberty, a right that does carry priorities over "other values," is at hand by the very terms of a contractarian dispensation for fundamental political principles. In fact, it is misleading to put it this way, for in a sense there are no "other values" in the Hobbesian perspective. There are your values and mine and other people's, but the only way they can appear in the contractarian argument is *as* yours and mine and so on; and when we contend, what is in contention is whose values are going to prevail, if anyone's, and how. The answer is that nobody's are going to literally prevail; rather, we must find ways of enabling each to enjoy his or her realizations of value without any imposition of one on another.

This is reflected in the contractarian's employment of the agent's presumptively considered preferences. In major clashes of values we assume that those preferences have been considered and that the consideration has done nothing to change the contending parties' minds. Then each must ask whether there is anything to gain from interaction with the other party, and if so, whether the price—forgoing such gains—is worth paying. Where it is not, we have the basis for agreement despite disagreement: namely, agreement that each will allow the other to go his own way, so far as possible. The absence of an overlapping moral consensus need not in principle prevent this result. If anything, indeed, the presence of such a consensus is likely to generate tyrannies of its own; for this consensus will surely not be unanimous in any case, and if we think that its presence is what founds political morality, then the content of the near-consensus there would at best ever be available for bringing any dissenters to heel.

Whether a case for general liberties is possible depends, I would suggest, on how basic the liberties in question are, and also on just which versions of which liberties we are considering. For example, I accept that there is indeed little reason to assume agreement on what constitutes "primary goods," and thus on the principles regarding their distribution. To take another example of great interest to today's liberals, consider the supposed right of nondiscrimination.[11] I do not see how we could get unanimity on such a right either. There is no reason, given absence of any ideals of the person, why someone should not prefer to expend resources in a discriminatory manner: for example, should prefer hiring women to men even if it entails a cost in efficiency and excludes some who are better qualified for the job. Since many contemporary theorists understand the basic liberties to include such things as nondiscrimination, however, it is clear that Gray is right, unless we considerably reduce the scope of the supposed liberties.

To take another important example: Is abortion, as Gray

suggests, "radically undecidable"? Not as a public issue in a pluralistic society. The "conservative" position requires a contentious assumption, either normative or metaphysical, which the position of the "liberals" does not: either (ethical) that it is part of the point of morality to protect organisms (that is, fetuses) wholly lacking in occurrent rationality; or (metaphysical) that, despite the evidence, such organisms do have rationality of the appropriate kind ("souls," perhaps). Fetuses are potentially rational, of course, but there is no logical basis for extending the rights we all accept for occurrently rational beings to occurrently nonrational ones. Lacking agreement on the contentious claims required by the conservative view, liberalism is driven toward accepting as the social compromise an agreement to disagree among the citizens: Those who accept the contentious positions in question may practice what they preach, but others who do not are also free to practice what they think to be right, which in the case in question is abortion on demand.[12] The right to do what we think right when our actions do not force others to act against their own values is inherent in liberalism.

On the other hand, extension of this purely negative right to abortions to such measures as public payment for the abortions in question is, of course, quite another matter. Agreement to that level of liberties is not readily forthcoming.

From a Hobbesian perspective, the liberal hypothesis may be stated as follows: that in the medium-to-long run, cooperation will always be the best bet for each party concerned. Gains from noncooperation in the short run will always be more than offset by longer-run losses. If we can identify each party concerned with a set of personal powers, then the immediate output of this procedure applied globally is a simple prohibition of violence as a way of pursuing one's ends. Is this hypothesis plausible?

It is by this time unnecessary, in view of the publication of Gauthier's *Morals by Agreement,* to review the decision-theoretic facts about prisoner's dilemma games or coordination games. It is, however, necessary to say a few words about their significance, which has been the subject of much and heated discussion. The more important case is that of prisoner's dilemma. Here we have a partial conflict of interest. The way that this is usually characterized is that each party to a prisoner's dilemma finds that if he chooses the "noncooperative" strategy, he "does better no matter what the other person does." In a narrow sense of the term does, this may be true. If you defect and I don't, I come out worse than if I had defected also; if you cooperate and I do, I come out better than in the foregoing eventuality; but if I don't, I come out still better, namely with the maximum utility by hypothesis available in the situation. But the fact that if we both play this allegedly most rational strategy, then we will end up in a position inferior for both to what we could have had by cooperating really ought to be taken as some indication that the bald claim that rational players will defect has something dubious about it. Gauthier argues that rational players will abandon any interpretation of maximization that would lead to universal defection; instead, they will adopt the disposition to cooperate with others willing to do so.[13] It is important to see that this is a higher-level strategic principle that can be adopted unilaterally by anybody, though it will only pay off when dealing with others who have adopted it. The important point, however, is that it *will* pay off when so dealing. I now find Gauthier's argument wholly convincing.

What prisoner's dilemma most directly shows is that social reinforcement should rationally be directed at cooperation. It shows that individuals ought, insofar as they can do so without incurring great costs, to stimulate the social reinforcement of cooperation, for example, by distributing appropriate epithets to the so-and-sos who insist on defection. It is rational for everyone to attempt to get cooperation adopted as the standard strategy in prisoner's dilemma situations—and an astonishingly large number of situations turn out to be such. Most importantly, for present purposes, the standard situation of agreements is itself one, as Hobbes pointed out. Suppose that A and B make an agreement: A will do x, yielding payoff i to B, provided that B does y, yielding payoff j to A. By hypothesis, i is preferred by B to what he would have without the agreement, call it k, and j preferred by A to what A would have without agreement, call it m. However, also by hypothesis, i + k is preferred to either i or k alone by B, and j + m preferred to either j or m alone by A. Thus both have a temptation to break the agreement in the case where the other person acts first, since at that point, one has one's cake and can eat it too: if A acts first, then B has both i and k. But as Hobbes also pointed out, if both players know these facts in advance and have no trust in the other, then neither will ever make an agreement.[14] Both will then be worse off so long as any potential gains from cooperation exist.

And this, in the case of virtually any two humans, they assuredly do, especially if one takes the Hobbesian point of view about the State of Nature. Dispensing with Hobbes's particular political views, let us define a "moral state of nature" as one in which there are no *moral* rules—no one is responsive to any moral considerations. In such a situation, absolutely nothing is thought to be wrong, by anyone. In that case we can expect, at least for a very wide range of human temperaments, the result depicted by Hobbes. And so refraining from violence in the pursuit of our ends is an instance of cooperation. Each agrees to refrain from violence provided the other does. This is certainly cooperation in the standard decision-theoretic sense of the term, once we renounce the usual philosophical strategy of presupposing a moral framework already in existence (or of benign philosophical temperaments such as grace the gentle reader and myself). That it is fruitful cooperation is obvious once we see that it *is* cooperation, in the somewhat special sense of decision theory, for it enables each of us to reap the fruits of his labor without incurring the losses that would be entailed by efforts to ward off predation by fellow rational animals.

If this is accepted, then I think we should reject Gray's assertion that the Hobbesian account contains nothing that might guarantee the priority of liberty over other political goods. It is difficult to see how he can say both that the enforcement of any particular system of production or, among mutually agreeing persons, distribution, would be unjust if it were also true that liberty has no special claim on our attention. It is not only quite unnecessary but also entirely unacceptable to derive liberalism from any "ideal of the person." Let the ideals of a person be what they may; that that person is to deal with others different from himself, yet also possessed of reason and the usual repertoire of human powers—notably the power to inflict death and other substantial disutilities—determines the proper character of those relations. That proper character clearly must include acknowledgement of what amounts to the general right to liberty.

If it is a mistake to try to construct liberalism on the basis of an "ideal of the person," so too is it to suppose that we need a "conception of the person." We do not, for example, need to adopt the Spinozian idea suggested by Gray, that what defines an individual is "the disposition to assert his power and freedom in the world."[15] Many actual people will have little disposition to do that, whatever it is supposed to be. They have all sorts of interests, some of which some of them assert and about others of which they are quite unassertive. Only if the idea is watered down to the point where our unassertive individuals are nevertheless reckoned to be "asserting" something will we capture everyone in its net. The assertion consists in nothing more than the having of interests that motivate action, in particular those actions that require adjustment in response to the actions of others.

We have seen that if any moral consensus can emerge among very diverse persons whose diversity encompasses strongly held religious views and the like, it can be only the consensus of liberalism: that each has the right to live according to her various beliefs, provided only that she not force them on those with whom she interacts. Let there be no mistake that this is a genuine moral outlook, and not a mere avoiding of the issue or somehow a value-free, utterly impartial, and supposedly scientific or objective attitude. It is a condition of entrance into the liberal community that one become liberal in that sense: that is, that one renounce any intention of enshrining by force one's own particular values, whatever they may be, as the normative regimen for the community as a whole or indeed for any other person or persons. We have only too persuasive evidence of what happens when this attitude is not taken, in such phenomena as the Thirty Years' War and the current situation in the Middle East. Gray is to be commended for pointing out that the same holds for productive systems. A socialism that would impose cooperation on all is as inimical to this general liberty as would be a capitalism that would break up voluntary socialist communities by force. The liberal commandment is: Thou Shalt Respect! It is, to be sure, the *only* liberal commandment, but that it is a commandment—if a uniquely rational one—rather than merely one incidental recommendation among others, must be perfectly clear.

4. Liberalism and the Free Market

We may turn now to the subject of the free market. A market is free when its agents have private property rights. Those rights tell us whom we have to see if we wish to acquire this, that, or the other, or make this or that change in the configuration of goods and services. Given such rights, it follows that transfers in the ownership of goods and services will proceed only by agreement of the parties whose goods and services they are. Insofar as there are property rights, there is a market. If everything is owned by individuals or voluntary associations of individuals, then we have full market society.

What the terms of reference are for defending the justice of the market is not entirely clear. To defend some market activity is surely trivial; to defend full market society is another matter. I shall select a version that puts the predominant portion of economic activity in the market sector, but will not here attempt to go the whole way. The proposition to be defended, then, is that whatever *can* be on the market normally *should* be. In my comments on Margaret Radin's chapter I shall agree that some things cannot be so. By implication, however, we are left with most things being properly so.

David Gauthier does the market philosophy a slight disservice when he entitles his otherwise admirable chapter on this subject "The Market: Freedom from Morality."[16] His reason for doing so is understandable, for what he there calls the market is defined in terms of the abstractions of neoclassical economics. Gauthier's market is devoid of externalities; all of the goods and services produced and consumed, and all of the factors of production, are the property of individuals without remainder; technology is known and fixed; information about products and prices is complete and costless to each actor, who is also indifferent regarding the origin of the products (for example, the consumer cares only about its utility qua product, not qua manifestation of a certain ideology); and there is perfect competition in the sense that no one producer can significantly influence prices on his own. In such a situation, each agent simply aims to maximize her utility from her own production and exchange activities, and the result will be terrific for everybody: the invisible hand lives!

The theoretical demonstration of optimality under these conditions is of real interest. Its practical importance is obviously a function of the degree to which these conditions are realized or realizable in the real world, and it is here that morality must enter the picture. Morality consists of recognition and respect for private property rights, starting with such rights in one's own person (this being the fundamental "factor of production"), and of the obligation to live up to one's agreements.

Gauthier insists that "the idea of morals by agreement may mislead, if it is supposed that rights must be the product or outcome of agreement. . . . the emergence of either co-operative or market interaction, demands an initial definition of the actors in terms of their factor endowments, and we have identified individual rights with these endowments. Rights provide the starting point for, and not the outcome of, agreement. . . . Market and co-operative practices presuppose individual rights. . . . And the rights so grounded prove to be the familiar ones of our tradition—rights to person and to property."[17] That these are the rights we need is clear enough. Most libertarians, I believe, would agree with Gauthier about the nonconventional character of these rights. If we are going to insist that the rights that frame the market must themselves be founded on a prior agreement, then Gauthier's view must be rejected, and we must take up a more radical stance, holding that there is what Jules Coleman calls a "pre-market agreement" to set up the market. This is equivalent to an agreement on property rights, as he also says.[18]

My position on this matter is that such rights fall straight out of the initial agreement to turn away from the Hobbesian premoral condition. Ownership of one's natural endowment is implicit in any fully social agreement, for it is impossible not to want these things respected if one wants anything at all. In turn, regarding external property: If the problem is that individuals want various things, and need the security to pursue them, then what other form can the Hobbesian social contract have than a general recognition of the rights of these various individuals to those things, provided they have been obtained without force and fraud? Agreeing not to molest Jones in his activities of cultivating, building, creating, and consuming is agreement that the ground he cultivates, the buildings he builds, the works he creates, and the consumables he consumes are in truth his to do these things with. That's what property rights are: they are rights to do things with things. Which acts may we perform vis à vis things? Any that do not require force or fraud. The market is simply the subset of activities in which we trade rights to do these various things with the various objects involved in those activities. The fundamental right of liberty is, I suggest, all we need. The market is not a separate institution in the free society. It simply *is* the free society.

5. Radin on "Commodification"

Margaret Radin, in "Justice and the Market Domain," argues that "the traditional view," according to which the market "appropriately encompasses most desired transactions between people," is "wrong in granting too much ground to the market," and indeed that it "wrongly suggests that a laissez-faire market regime is prima facie just."[19] She objects also to the idea that there is a sort of wall between the market and nonmarket realms, suggesting that "the battle-lines prevent us from appreciating the nonmarket aspects of many of our market relations."[20] Since the traditional view as she states it is certainly something I would wish to maintain, we must take a careful look at her objections. With her objection to the wall idea, on the other hand, I was at first sympathetic, and wondered whether we can combine approval of the market with this perception, that certain nonmarket aspects of what is on the market need to be protected in some way from its ravages. I have instead found to the contrary, as will be seen. We start with the charge of commodification.

Radin is concerned that the market may lead to "universal commodification," the attitude that "all things can and should be separable from persons and exchanged through the free market, whenever some people are willing to sell and others are willing to buy. All human attributes are conceived of as possessions bearing a value characterizable in money terms, and all human interactions are conceived of as exchanges understandable in terms of gains from trade."[21] Radin objects to this in terms, broadly, of respect for persons and the fostering of community: to think of everything in terms of monetary value is to depersonalize in a potentially disturbing way. Consider the adopted child. People sometimes give up their children to others "in hope that they will have a better life elsewhere. There is at least some human glory in being able to do this. Perhaps it disappears if the child bears a market value. If money is paid, it would contaminate the experience of the adoptive parents as well as that of the natural parents, since they will be aware that they valued the child as much as a car, perhaps, but not as much as a house. The adopted child herself . . . may always wonder whether a higher asking price would have left her without parents. Even if the natural parent doesn't accept the money . . . perhaps knowledge of the price could contaminate the experience, making it seem as though the natural parent is giving the adopting parent $10,000 out of pocket. . . . We will all know how much we cost our parents. We will all conceive of ourselves as objects bearing monetary value."[22]

How narrowly are we to construe the notion of a commodity here? Commodities as Radin says, "are usually pictured as objects separate from the self and social relationships. Hence, universal commodification is a form of objectification. It assimilates personal attributes, relationships, and desired states of affairs to the realm of objects."[23] However, this doesn't really help as much as one might think, because the term "object" is likewise subject to narrower and broader construal. When a logician expresses part of the form of an English sentence in partially quantified terms, for example, (x) (x is an aunt → x is female), the variable x ranges over everything, all "objects." But of course some of those objects are people, rather than inert, material objects, and philosophers debate over the status of lots of other possible referents, such as properties and space-time points. It would be absurd to reject the use of quantificational logic, when the things quantified are persons, on the ground that "you can't quantify persons, since persons are not objects." Nevertheless, there is a deal of difference between a person and an inert object, or for that matter a person and, say, a deerfly, and in some contexts the difference will matter a great deal. We must ask, then, whether viewing things as having exchange value is *eo ipso* to regard them as "separable from the self and social relationships." And this is to ask also just what a market society is—what we are conceiving when we conceive such a society.

To begin with, not everything available on a market is an

object in the narrow sense of that term. Economists speak of goods and services, goods referring to objects, services not. When I buy someone's services, then, I am not usually buying something separable from his self. Perhaps if the service is one that can also be done by a robot, we might say this. But what about those that cannot be done? Suppose I am a movie director and I wish to purchase the acting services of Robert Redford. Are these separable from Robert Redford? They may not be. It may be, for instance, that nobody else has the unique personality of Redford, who is just right for this part.

Now suppose the service I buy from person A is one that I could indeed get from a machine or a robot, but that I deliberately choose the personal one instead—I *prefer* A to a robot. Or suppose you are evaluating two applicants for some quite routine job—checkout person at your supermarket, for instance. You note that one of the applicants has a lively, outgoing personality that comes through when she says "Thank you for shopping at XMart!" while the other seems quite hollow—"just doing her job," as we say. In the case of this job, though, the one who is just doing the job isn't doing the job very well. Personality may count for quite a lot. (There may be little else to go by; other talents required may be modest.) Well, these things *make a difference*. In fact, they make a difference that can sometimes be translated into dollars and cents. But how can this be so, if market relations mean commodification which means depersonalization?

Now, consider free exchange. Suppose I befriend you because I like your style, because I find what you have to say interesting, because I know I can count on you when the going gets tough, and can rely on your word. You have a similar evaluation of me. We get on famously. But if you were to cease doing and saying things that interest me, or were to become extremely vague and hopelessly unreliable, to show no interest in me, and so on, the relationship would likely wither. Your company is no longer worthwhile from my point of view, or mine from yours. Aren't personal relationships—as the term is not far from implying on the face of it—in fact exchanges? And isn't that the way it should be?

But this doesn't imply that they could be "commodified" in the particular sense of being maintainable through monetary means. Suppose that next time you tell a particularly good joke, at which I laugh fit to be tied, you continue by saying, "That will be $55.90, please!" Likely I would suppose this was a further part of the joke . . . but if it were not? This too would obviously alter our relationship for the worse. But that is not because our relationship is one in which exchange is not even an applicable concept; rather, it is because it's one in which monetary payment is simply the wrong kind of currency. Money isn't what we're after. In short, the market in friends cannot be carried on in dollars and cents—yet for all that, it is an exchange system: nobody is *required* to provide friendship to anyone else, and each will select friends, from the available possibilities, on the basis of who will offer the highest "return" on his or her "investment" in terms of time and energy (including emotional energy).

Now it may be said that if I were sticking to my last, I would be defending a society in which money was the only thing anyone was after. Isn't that what is involved in saying that everything is on the market? Let us see.

If the market is framed by the rule that people own things and in consequence may do as they please with them, including giving them to others, either as a gift or in exchange for other things, then is it true that the market involves universal commodification? In exchanges each person acquires things he values more, giving in return things he values less but which the partner to the exchange values more. Will everything I have become a commodity? Commodity is a quite narrow concept, it seems to me: to be a commodity is to be quite literally for sale; if the monetary price is right, it will be sold, or bought. If that is right, that commodification implies attaching specifically monetary values to everything that is within the power of anyone to alienate to others, then the free market, conceived as that institution in which people may do whatever they wish with what is theirs, does not and cannot have precisely that implication: universal commodification is a nonstarter.

For one, lesser thing, market society obviously does not imply the sense of everything's actually being for sale: I may be perfectly happy with some of my things, and there may be others that no one would give me enough for to make it worth my while to part with them. If I just don't want to sell x, then by virtue of x being mine, I do not need to. If I may do what I want with x, then one of those things could be, simply, to keep it, resisting any offers to buy. People in fact do this all the time, even though they usually are under no legal or moral necessity to do so. "That's not for sale!" is a familiar remark among economic agents. In this respect, then, the commodification charge is far too sweeping.

But let us turn to the more fundamental question: whether there is any conceptual limit to commodification. There would be if for each person, A, there is something A values so much that it would be in principle impossible for A to prefer anything else. Can we trade in ourselves, for example? To be sure, it is not entirely clear what doing that would consist in—selling oneself into slavery, perhaps? This presents an evident problem, since one would thereafter be unable to do anything with the money. Since the whole point of money, though, is that it represents an exchangeable right to perform various activities, namely those one can do with the things one gets, the reasoning of those who would sell themselves into slavery seems to be defective.

People have sacrificed their lives for the sake of friends, loved ones, ideals, country. None of these would seem to qualify as an exchange in any sense that would permit speaking of commodities. Indeed, it seems on further reflection that if commodification is supposed to imply capacity to enter a market in which things are literally bought and sold, for the medium of money, then it is very plausible indeed to think that selves will not be among the things available for purchase. Money is purchasing power, command over goods and services. Wherever the command in question would in principle be useless or impossible, the item in question ceases to be commodifiable. Slavery is a departure from the market, not an extension of it. It requires that some agents not be treated or regarded as agents.

Money is a means, and that for which it is exchanged is an end. The ends in question can be converted into further means, but eventually we arrive at that for the sake of which everything else is done; and if we do, then that cannot possibly be further exchanged. Personhood, as Radin suggests, may indeed be "essentially unmonetized and not fungible." But whatever these ultimate values may be, it is worth pointing out that the very existence of the market is contingent on their existence. On a market, we trade that which we value less for that which we value more. By definition, that which we value above all cannot be rationally traded. Yet we cannot always be increasing values by trades, for that would imply, as Aristotle in effect says, that we don't really value anything at all. The entailment is strict. To have a market is to have a situation in which many things are not for sale.

A word about market value is in order here. When things are said to be worth such-and-such a number of dollars, what does this mean concerning their real value to their possessors? In a great many cases, it means essentially nothing. The use-value to me of an item that has a market value of $X is characteristically more than $X, which is why I bought it. A charming photograph of a much-loved child will have cost me, perhaps 50 cents. But that sum doesn't express its value to me, since it may well be irreplaceable, nor, very likely, to anyone else, for strangers would be unlikely to offer even the 50 cents it cost me to get it in the first place. Yet these features of exchanges are, I suggest, typical. It is radically mistaken to think that markets imply commodification in Radin's sense.

Parents will, in extreme circumstances, sell their children, either in fact or in effect. In nonextremities, why won't they? Suppose you are the parent of B, of whom you are very fond; and suppose that you see that C, who is extremely fond of B, would no doubt make B a wonderful parent, and is a person of means who would enable B to flourish in ways that you, a person of normal means, cannot. C makes a generous offer, in dollars. Should you sell? Most of us will think of selling one's child as rather like selling a part of oneself. We will suppose that no other persons could offer the child the personal affection that you can, and that this affection is virtually irreplaceable, in the sense that whatever the child did under the care of anyone else, the absence of you in particular will make his life less good than it would otherwise be. This personal factor will indeed put children, for most of us, beyond the reach of the market.

Well, what if someone doesn't care that much for her children, knows that she makes a poor parent, and reasonably believes that another could not only provide better care but would genuinely make the child happier? (Or—difficult case—someone who has good evidence that her beliefs of the aforementioned kind are false?) It is still hard to see, though, that a monetary offer would be appropriate, and the quality of that person's affective life would be very much in question were she willing to consider one.

Even so—as Radin seems to agree[24]—it is not clear that this is a sufficient reason for not permitting such exchanges. If you knew that your parents were willing to sell you to just anyone, provided only that the price was right, you'd probably be inclined to run away from home. You would be less inclined to love them, and less inclined to think that they loved you. Since the value of a loving domestic environment is familiar to all, it is difficult to see that permitting the buying and selling of children would bring it about that very many children came to be for sale. What one would expect is that altering current laws so as to permit the buying and selling of children would lead to a very tiny amount of activity in that market, except perhaps in the case of infants, who do not have personhood in sufficient degree to make these considerations quite as potent. (Similarly, we have the problem of orphans, to whom some of the foregoing considerations cannot apply.)

Do we treat children unjustly by buying and selling them? The attitudes most of us quite naturally have toward children are such that those aren't the terms we would be inclined to use. One who would sell her own child shows herself to be inhuman, deficient in a major area of human affection—and yet were she to go ahead and sell that child to someone who would also make the child a better parent, the transaction might well be to that child's benefit. (The hitch is that we might also think less of one who was willing to acquire a child by purchase. We might, but if that was the only way a loving adoptive parent could get the child, wouldn't that be forgivable?)

Fundamental to any consideration of what to do regarding children, surely, is the fact that they grow up to become adults, with the usual range of competences and powers for good or ill. There is plainly a community interest in how they will use those powers when they reach adulthood. That these particular commodities are loaded with potential for third-party effects is obvious, and that involuntary third-party effects are cause for the imposition of requirements and limitations is, therefore, also obvious. At the very least, young humans are potentially dangerous substances. Just as the defender of the market need not object in principle to restricting the sale of nitroglycerin or automatic rifles, so he need not object to restrictions on the sale of children.

A further point about this subject is more fundamental, if it is not actually another way of saying the same thing: namely, that the defender of the market may also take the line that children cannot be owned. Certainly the marketer thinks that adult humans are not ownable: slavery is fundamentally objectionable, in his view. Since slavery is a relation of domination in the literal and uncontroversial sense of that term in which it involves the exercise of force over one person by another, it is ruled out. At what point children become rational agents who therefore have the rights of agents on the market instead of commodities on it is no doubt difficult to decide in any satisfactory manner. Some, though not I, would hold that children simply are by nature not commodities. But even if we reject this latter, in my judgment obscurantist position, the considerations adduced in the foregoing paragraphs may have the same effect. It may be that we do best simply to declare that children are not to be for sale, and that is that.

This doesn't leave Radin answered entirely satisfactorily, I agree. But I hope at least to have shown that the specter of "universal commodification" is not one we need fear in market society.

6. RADIN ON "INCOMPLETE" COMMODIFICATION

Let us turn in conclusion, to Radin's theses concerning incomplete commodification. The suggestion is that we develop a theory of justice alternative to that in which there are, on the one hand, agents with their inviolable personal rights and, on the other, things owned or ownable by them that are available for exchange. In this alternative theory, "who should get what things of value depends upon the appropriate relationship between persons and things, and between persons and other people."[25] But that is not a helpful statement, since every theory of justice is statable in such a form. The underlying theory of the market, for example, is the theory that the appropriate relation between people and other people is that each should respect the rights of each other, including that other's rights in external property and personal capacity to render services.

But in Radin's version, various departures from this fairly simple principle are recommended. For example, she suggests that there is a connection between housing and personality. Housing is to be "incompletely commodified in recognition of its connection with personhood."[26] But why does that call for incomplete commodification? Consider, for example, the right of eminent domain, which is eminently claimed by all American community governments. If housing is so intimately connected with personhood, wouldn't that be best expressed by allowing individuals actual rights over their housing, instead of a set of watered-down rights, subject to the whims of the local government? What if Mrs. Jones doesn't want to part with her long-loved dwelling in order that a new school or expressway can go through? What if she will not accept any proferred price for it? Full property rights would protect Mrs. Jones, but I imagine that what Radin has in mind would do nothing of the sort.

Take, for example, Radin's disaffection for economic inequality, which she wishes to associate, as do so many, with economic injustice.[27] This is a very large issue, to be sure, but a couple of remarks are in order. One is that the vast majority of mankind over the ages have been very much worse off than the poorest of Americans, at least in material terms. Is it to be supposed that a malaise of injustice hung over all these ages? Or that people lacked personality or personhood prior to, roughly, the late twentieth century? If not, then is the objection to inequality an objection to poverty, as she implies, or is it something else? And if something else, then what possible connection does it have to personality? How does it promote personality and personhood to be foisting vast arrays of regulations and other incursions on what an individual can control? For that matter, how is genuine community fostered by such impositions?

The market idea divides the world into persons and nonpersons; it says that the nonpersonal is available for ownership by persons, who in turn must relate to each other by respecting their rights, including their rights to nonpersonal things. It reminds us that what we call sales are, after all, trades—money is a medium of exchange—and that all trades are trades between persons, persons who employ their own judgment on the matter of what to do with and to and about the material portion of the world. Radin is entirely right to say that "People engaged in market interactions are not just acquiring things, they are relating to each other."[28] It is difficult to see how we could have a better program for respecting personhood than this. One suspects that in Radin's proposal, we will find community often taking precedence over personhood. That can hardly be what she wanted: One supposes that a good community would be one that is enthusiastically and voluntarily supported by those who live in it, rather than an ideal crammed down the throats of its unwilling citizens by philosopher kings. And so on. In general, therefore, I am unmoved by her criticisms of the market, and emerge more, rather than less, impressed with its virtues.

NOTES

1. John Gray, "Contractarian Method, Private Property, and the Market Economy," in this volume, 32–33.

2. Ibid., 34–35.

3. Ibid., 40.

4. Ibid., 39.

5. Ibid., 42.

6. Ibid.

7. Ibid.

8. David Gauthier, *Morals by Agreement* (New York: Oxford University Press, 1986), chap. 7, esp. 200–221.

9. Gray, "Contractarian Method," 42.

10. Ibid., 44.

11. I have developed this point in "Is There a Right of Non-Discrimination?" in *Business Ethics in Canada*, ed. Deborah Poff and Wilfrid Waluchow (Englewood Cliffs, N.J.: Prentice-Hall, 1987).

12. A contractarian case for this position is argued more fully in Jan Narveson, "A Contractarian Defense of the Liberal View on Abortion and the Wrongness of Infanticide," in *Values and Moral Standing*, ed. Wayne Sumner, Donald Callen, and Thomas Attig, Bowling Green Studies in Applied Philosophy, (Bowling Green, Ohio: Dept. of Philosophy, Bowling Green State University, 1986), 8:76–89.

13. Argued in Gauthier, *Morals by Agreement*, chap. 6. Many have expressed doubts about Gauthier's view here, including myself in "Reason

in Ethics—or Reason vs. Ethics?" in *Morality, Reason and Truth,* ed. D. Copp and D. Zimmerman (Totawa, N.J.: Rowman and Allanheld, 1985), 228–50. But I now think Gauthier is entirely right. My agreement with him is amplified in *The Libertarian Idea* (Philadelphia: Temple University Press, 1988).

14. The point about promising was noted by Hobbes in *Leviathan,* chap. 15.

15. Gray, "Contractarian Method," 39.

16. Gauthier, *Morals by Agreement,* chap. 4.

17. Ibid., 222.

18. Jules Coleman, "Market Contractarianism and the Unanimity Rule," in *Ethics and Economics,* ed. E. Paul, F. Miller, and J. Paul (Oxford: Basil Blackwell, 1985), 69–114.

19. Margaret Jane Radin, "Justice and the Market Domain," in this volume, 165–66.

20. Ibid., 167.

21. Ibid.

22. Ibid., 171–72.

23. Ibid., 167.

24. Ibid., 175.

25. Ibid., 184.

26. Ibid.

27. Ibid., 183. She does not, however, flatly identify justice with equality.

28. Ibid., 184.

PART IV

ON THE FRONTIER

10

DISRUPTING VOLUNTARY TRANSACTIONS

CASS R. SUNSTEIN

The conventional market transaction takes many forms. One person sells a commodity to another who is willing to pay for it; the commodity may be a job, a part of the body, an artistic work, or an opportunity to advertise on television. Disruption of arrangements of this sort is the exception in most Western legal systems, and it is usually described as "paternalism," a term that serves as a pejorative. But the rise of modern regulation, especially since the New Deal, offers numerous illustrations of legal rules that ban voluntary transactions. Even in circumstances in which the legal system permits such arrangements to go forward, people sometimes invoke notions of justice in order to doubt that they should.

The purpose of this essay is to set out and evaluate various reasons for prohibitions on voluntary transactions even when there is no harm to others. The discussion is schematic, tentative, and exploratory, categorizing various arguments rather than deciding particular cases. I suggest that there is good reason for a presumption of respect for voluntary transactions, but that in certain identifiable cases, that presumption can be rebutted. Those cases are sufficiently numerous to allow considerable scope for collective intervention. A position of this sort is superior, I contend, to its two principal rivals. The first, built on the "revealed preference" tradition, treats harm to others as the only legitimate basis for governmental intervention. The second disregards existing preferences altogether—for reasons, for example, of "false consciousness" or of what might be called the social construction of preferences—and affords no presumption in favor of voluntary transactions. The more differentiated approach set out here is preferable to these approaches, whether the evaluation is based on welfare, autonomy, or some other ground.

I. WHY RESPECT VOLUNTARY AGREEMENTS?

Approaches to law that grow out of social contract theory tend to treat voluntary transactions as the starting point for both private and public ordering. Individual actors, autononous and independent of social ties, are the foundation for discussion. But no obvious reason supports this starting point. It would be equally natural to take collective action as the norm, or to start from a premise of mutual responsibility and care. In either case, protection of voluntary transactions would be thought to be an exception, permitted where adequate justification could be found.

An approach that treated voluntary transactions as the exception to be justified rather than the starting point might also appear sensible from the standpoint of explaining current practice in most Western countries, let alone political systems in which voluntary transactions are given only occasional protection. But in spite of the large territory captured by collective control, most democracies appear to begin with a presumption of respect for voluntary transactions. Without biasing the discussion in any particular direction, or accepting such a presumption without argument, we might start by untangling the reasons for respecting voluntary transactions. Later we will return to the question of foundations.

The argument for respecting voluntary transactions appears to be rooted in three distinct intuitions. The first is a belief in rights; the second refers to utilitarian or welfarist concerns; the third invokes, somewhat loosely, fears of self-interest and factionalism in governmental processes.

A belief in individual autonomy often underlies respect for voluntary agreements on the theory that without harm to others, government ought to respect divergent conceptions of the good life. Respect of this sort is sometimes described as government "neutrality," which is seen as an important guarantor of liberty. In this view, there is simply no predicate for collective intervention if the relevant actors are content. The position of course can be associated both with Mill's conception of liberty and with understandings arising out of the contractarian tradition.

A related but distinct argument for respecting voluntary transactions is based on utilitarian concerns. Claims from autonomy are considered quite secondary. The basic position is that people know what is in their own best interests and that respect for preferences, as expressed in market transactions, is the best way to promote aggregate social welfare. As a general rule, this argument is quite strong because voluntary agreements by hypothesis make both parties better off. Such agreements, almost by definition, lead to Pareto-superior positions. Mutually advantageous relations cannot, it is said, be disrupted without some kind of welfare loss.

Moreover, disruptions of such relations will, in this view, tend to prove futile. The preferences whose expression is suppressed by regulation are likely to manifest themselves in other, more destructive forms. Consider the claim that regulation of the landlord-tenant relation in the form of minimum conditions of habitability, has served to hurt tenants, because landlords simply raise rents in response; or the idea that the minimum wage has increased unemployment. The central claim is that interference with voluntary transactions will both produce welfare losses and, in the end, hurt the very people that intervention is intended to help.

A final argument for respecting voluntary transactions is somewhat loose, but it serves to account for some of the remaining intuitions behind the idea that government should not disrupt relations deemed mutually advantageous. The concern is that government interference in such situations presents a grave danger of distortion. This is because the government's own incentives may be parochial or perverse. Government decisions may be infected by factional pressures from narrow groups or by the self-interest, venality, or confusion of public officials. Consider, for example, the possibility that if government is permitted to regulate the consumption of sugar, salt, or alcohol, interest groups will influence regulatory decisions in such a way as to undermine whatever gains the system of regulation might provide if it were operating optimally. This position is buttressed by social choice theory, which has revealed that majoritarian processes have a high degree of arbitrariness built into them and that they are highly imperfect mechanisms for aggregating preferences.[1] In this view, the best approach is a bright-line rule prohibiting collective intervention into voluntary transactions unless there is harm to others.

In the aggregate, considerations of this sort provide plausible reasons for a general rule that government should respect voluntary transactions if there are no adverse effects on third parties. But the argument for that general rule is far from invulnerable. An initial set of responses would point to the possibility that both autonomy and welfare might be promoted, not undermined, by collective intervention.

The argument would begin by suggesting that the satisfaction of private preferences, whatever their content, does not respond to a persuasive conception of autonomy. The notion of autonomy might refer instead to decisions reached with a full and vivid awareness of available opportunities, or with all relevant information. When decisions are not so informed, they might be described as nonautonomous. Consider, for example, a decision to purchase cigarettes by someone unaware of the health risks. One goal of a legal system is to ensure autonomy not merely by allowing satisfaction of preferences, but also and more fundamentally in the processes of preference formation. This understanding responds to a prominent strand in liberal thought and is associated with Kant; freedom is seen in the free formation rather than the implementation of preferences. For the moment it is not clear how much in the way of interference with voluntary transactions such an argument will justify. At a minimum, it will furnish cause for occasional intervention.

A more dramatic set of responses to the argument counselling respect for voluntary transactions would be critical of the notion of autonomy itself. Preferences, it is claimed, are socially (or biologically) constructed; they are never autonomous. In this view, the social construction of preferences makes it chimerical to rely on neo-Kantian conceptions of autonomy as a basis for evaluating government intervention into mutually advantageous arrangements. Those conceptions are based on myths. I take up this view below.

With respect to welfare, the response to the case for respecting voluntary agreements would begin by observing that preferences are not static and fixed, but shifting. In particular they are endogenous rather than exogenous—endogenous to, or a function of, consumption patterns, legal rules, and social pressures most generally. If preferences are endogenous, legal rules that treat them as fixed will lose important opportunities for welfare gains.

Consider, for example, the possibility that legal rules prohibiting or discouraging behavior that is potentially addictive may produce significant advantages in terms of welfare. Regulation of such substances as heroin—at least if the regulation can be made effective—might well increase aggregate social welfare. Consider too the possibility that government regulation of broadcasting—encouraging or requiring, for example, nonentertainment broadcasting or high-quality programs—may in the end generate new preferences, providing increased satisfaction and in the end producing considerable welfare gains. Here too it is unclear how much in the way of collective intervention is desirable, but it is possible that the amount will be quite substantial.

That preferences are endogenous also weakens the objection that legal disruption of voluntary transactions will be futile. If the preference is itself a function of the legal rule, or of consumption patterns, legal barriers will not be circumvented, for the preference in question will be diminished or eliminated. Thus, for example, a law preventing sexual harassment is designed to, and may in fact, reduce the willingness of employers and teachers to harass employees and students. If so, the law will not be evaded by contracting parties. Similar points apply to laws prohibiting discrimination on various grounds.

The argument from factional intrigue and self-interested representation also depends on empirical judgments and contingencies that are highly speculative. It is both true and important that government action may be distorted by irrelevant or impermissible considerations and that it may make things worse rather than better. Considerations of this sort suggest that the possibility of identifying welfarist and nonwelfarist reasons for disruption of voluntary agreements creates only a prima facie case. Just as government action might not be on balance justifiable to correct a market failure—because of the risk that such action may make the situation even worse than the status quo—the existence of deficiencies in voluntary agreements may be on balance an insufficient reason for collective control. But the risk that intervention will make things worse rather than better is far too crude a reason for an across-the-board prohibition on interference with voluntary agreements. In some circumstances, interference may produce significant benefits and may have minimal costs. But it is time to explore the problem in more particular settings.

II. Disrupting Agreements: A Catalogue

The purpose of this section is to catalogue, with some particularity, a set of arguments for disrupting voluntary transactions. In the cases to be discussed, considerations of justice argue against rather than in favor of market ordering. Many of the examples might also be thought to involve harm to others; for present purposes, however, that possibility will be put to one side, and the cases will be explored as if others were unaffected. Moreover, I need not, for present purposes, make a choice between arguments from welfare and arguments from autonomy. Even competitors to those arguments—stressing virtue or certain forms of community—fit congenially with the various suggestions put forth below. The basic goal is to set out a range of reasons for disrupting voluntary transactions, even if such transactions deserve prima facie respect.

Collective action problems and the prisoners' dilemma. It is a familiar point that voluntary transactions that are individually rational will sometimes produce collective irrationality. A conventional example involves the decision whether to pollute the environment. In individual cases, pollution may be entirely reasonable in light of the subjective costs and subjective benefits, but collective action—in the form of legal proscriptions or private organization—may increase social welfare. Government intervention may be necessary to disrupt voluntary agreements when there is some such problem. Many areas of legal regulation may be thus understood. This ground for disruption of voluntary transactions is of course well established in both theory and practice, and it is not necessary to dwell on it in detail here.[2]

Preferences about preferences. People do not simply have preferences; they also have preferences about preferences. Some people may, for example, want nonentertainment broadcasting on public television, even though their own consumption patterns favor situation comedies; they may seek stringent environmental laws even though they do not use the public parks; they may approve of laws calling for social security and welfare even though they do not save or give to the poor. In all of these settings, the notion that voluntary agreements should be respected is complicated by the fact that people sometimes do or would decide to foreclose their own voluntary choices.

If the ultimate goal is autonomy, regarded in a Kantian fashion, there are powerful reasons to respect second-order over first-order preferences. Second-order preferences fit comfortably with understandings that see autonomy in the selection rather than mere implementation of ends. The second-order preference is of course a self-conscious selection of ends. One might therefore favor laws or private arrangements vindicating second-order preferences against voluntary behavior involving environmental harms, racist and sexist behavior, or consumption choices in the broadcasting area. In such cases, there is a good reason to reject voluntary transactions.

The notion that individual freedom might consist in self-determination through individual preferences about preferences is naturally, though not inevitably, allied with the idea that political freedom consists in collective self-determination, embodied in social decisions about what courses to pursue. This idea, reflected in republican theories of politics,[3] places a high premium on citizen selection of laws that decide on values rather than simply implement preferences.[4] On one view, the role of government might be limited to the provision of education, a range of information, and many available opportunities. But such an approach would forbid the public from enacting its own second-order preferences through legislation, and that prohibition is not simple to justify.

In some circumstances, however, the notion that collective second-order preferences should be vindicated seems weak. Consider, for example, the fact that some second-order preferences are objectionable. An example is a desire not to prefer to marry someone of another race, reflected in a miscegenation law; or a desire not to want to allow women to act on a plane of equality with men. Such examples suggest that it would be a large mistake to claim that all second-order preferences should be respected simply because of their status as such. Sometimes the vindication of second-order preferences will itself be troublesome on independent substantive grounds.

Moreover, second-order preferences, when enacted into law, coerce a minority whose members want to vindicate their own first-order preferences. Consider a law prohibiting the purchase of alcohol, adopted by a group some of whose members seek the coercive force of the law to vindicate their second-order preferences. Such a law necessarily affects a minority that would prefer to have alcohol freely available. In general, the coercion of a minority is not a sufficient reason to rule such measures off-limits. Majority rule is the ordinary governing principle, and in the absence of special considerations it ought to control here. But measures that are least restrictive of the desires of the minority are preferable if they are possible, and the vindication of second-order preferences through law may remove desirable incentives for self-control.

Finally, the notion that second-order should be preferred to first-order preferences might be criticized on the ground that it is unduly Kantian, depending on controversial distinctions between "reason" and "passion" and favoring the former over the latter. The presumption in favor of second-order preferences is associated with a doubtful tradition that understands some desires to reflect disembodied reason, and others to be based on mere drives. Moreover, the possibility of third- and n-order preferences complicates the inquiry considerably.

The existence of second-order preferences also makes it much more problematic to decide when and whether respect for voluntary agreements will promote welfare. It is unclear how the process of aggregation of preferences can occur in the face of second-, third-, and n-order preferences about preferences.[5] From one point of view, however, respect for second-order preferences might produce significant welfare gains. Such preferences exist; they are sometimes quite intense; the failure to vindicate them will yield welfare losses.

The basic point is that sometimes laws that forbid voluntary transactions might plausibly be understood as reflections of collective second-order preferences. It will be difficult to be certain whether this understanding is accurate in particular cases. In many contexts, regulation that is defensible in terms of second-order preferences might in fact reflect simple paternalism or distaste on the part of the majority. The movement for prohibition is an example. But when second-order preferences are at work, disruption of voluntary transactions will generally be justified.

Adaptive preferences. Sometimes preferences are a product of the absence of available opportunities.[6] Consider, for example, the possibility that the preference of some women for traditional sex roles is an adaptation to a system in which other opportunities have been unavailable. In order to reduce cognitive dissonance—the constant and irremediable frustration of attempting to change a seemingly intractable status quo—people adapt their preferences and beliefs to current options. Other examples are easy to find. Some of the newly freed slaves were ambivalent about their freedom;[7] workers may not seek self-government because it has traditionally been unavailable;[8] adjustment to widespread differentials in wealth might reflect efforts to reduce cognitive dissonance. The central point is this: When preferences are a product of the existing legal rule or an existing social practice, the legal rule or existing practice cannot, without circularity, be justified by reference to the preferences.[9]

It is important to acknowledge that all preferences are in some respect a function of the current regime, and that regime includes legal rules. A claim that voluntary transactions should be disrupted whenever preferences are not truly autonomous would therefore be a likely license for tyranny. The argument from adaptive preferences is restricted to desires that are the product of the absence of available opportunities. At least in certain cases, it is possible to identify that phenomenon with some precision. Moreover, the idea of adaptive preferences may carry with it a misleadingly quantitative connotation. In the cases under discussion, the problem is not simply that there are fewer opportunities than there should be simply in terms of numbers, but that preferences have been influenced by unjust background institutions. It is therefore important to understand that the categorys of adaptive preferences, and the assessment of available opportunities, have large normative dimensions.

The phenomenon of adaptive preferences is related to but distinct from that of preference change as a result of learning.[10] Sometimes preferences will be altered because new information has come from engaging in a new activity. In practice it will be hard to distinguish the phenomenon of adaptation of preferences to available opportunities and that of preferences uninformed by experience, though they are analytically separate. For purposes of deciding whether collective frustration of voluntary transactions is desirable, it is usually unnecessary to struggle to separate the two.

There is a strong prima facie case for disruption of voluntary transactions that are based on adaptive preferences. (Indeed, the problem of adaptive preferences may help identify the cases in which second-order preferences should not be respected.) The case for disruption may be based alternatively on considerations of welfare or autonomy. It should not be difficult to see that the disruption of adaptive preferences may in the end produce substantial welfare gains. Consider, for example, self-government in an industry in Seattle, Washington, where initially skeptical workers eventually came to consider self-government an important value.[11]

If the goal is autonomy rather than welfare, disruption of choices deriving from adaptive preferences may be highly desirable. A plausible understanding of autonomy would have it that people should not only be allowed to do what they choose, but should also be allowed to have their preferences formed in a system in which a wide variety of options is available.[12] In short, not only the free satisfaction of preferences but also their free formation is a legitimate social goal. Preferences that derive from the absence of available opportunities are hardly autonomous. Legal rules that disrupt those preferences might be thought in this sense to promote autonomy.

It is not clear what follows from the fact of adaptive preferences. The first problem here is that it is possible to identify a parallel problem: some people will want things precisely because they are unavailable. The grass is always greener phenomenon parallels the story of the fox and the sour grapes.[13] A second problem is that it is quite difficult to tell when a preference results from the perceived unavailability of an opportunity. If the fact of adaptive preferences is to be used as a basis for collective intervention, it is important to be sure that the phenomenon is actually occurring.

Moreover, the appropriate collective response to adaptive preferences is hardly clear. Perhaps the best and certainly the least intrusive response is to make the devalued option available rather than to require people to select it. Thus government might attempt to ensure that women can participate in the workplace or that self-government is available in some firms. Once the option is available, preferences will not be distorted by the absence of opportunities, and in time it will be possible to discover whether people are engaging or refraining from engaging in a practice because they genuinely want to do so. But sometimes mere availability is an insufficient remedy, since the governing preference structure is in place, and people may not take advantage of an opportunity that because of previous deprivation, they do not value.

The more intrusive remedy is not merely to make the opportunity available but also to encourage or force people to sample it. One might understand some of American labor and civil rights law on this ground.[14] But in view of its intrusiveness and the possibility of mistake, this remedy should be used quite sparingly.

The fact of adaptive or endogenous preferences is dealt with only rarely in current academic writing, even that on the intersection of political theory and economics, where one would expect it to be usefully treated.[15] This is an area in which significant advances should be expected in the future. But in any case, collective action in the face of preferences that have adapted to the absence of available opportunities will often be justified.

Intrapersonal collective action problems: addictions, myopia, and others. Many legal rules disrupt voluntary agreements when preferences are endogenous, not to legal rules, but to acts of consumption. It is a familiar phenomenon that consumption itself affects the taste for certain goods. The phenomenon occurs for an exceptionally wide range of commodities, including, for example, classical music, sports events, and literature. Standing by itself, this phenomenon offers no sufficient justification for legal intervention. But in some circumstances, the phenomenon of preferences endogenous to consumption may have distinctive characteristics that strengthen the case.

Consider, for example, the typical pattern with what is usually denominated an addiction: sharply increasing costs from non-consumption and decreasing benefits from consumption.[16] If this pattern is present, government might well intervene on grounds of welfare or autonomy. The welfare losses from behavior that fits this pattern are sometimes enormous. If the goal is autonomy, collective action might also be desirable. The pattern suggests, though it does not compel, the conclusion that the person would not choose to become involved with the good in question at all, were the person perfectly informed. Absence of information is of course a conventional basis for disruption of voluntary transactions.

But the category of addictions does not form a discrete class. It is simply a special case of what might be called intrapersonal collective action problems. The central problem here is that for some activities, the short-term costs are high relative to the short-term gains, but the long-term gains dominate the long-term costs. Consider efforts to break certain habits. Habitual behavior may produce long-term welfare losses for the relevant person, but the short-term costs of breaking habits may be quite high. Or consider myopic behavior, which reflects an undue concentration on the short-run. A related case is that of akrasia, or weakness of will. Here people choose certain options even though in a sense they know that their choices make them worse off.

Some of these cases are taken care of in most legal systems, which control a wide range of possible distortions in individual consumption patterns. Regulation of addictive substances is the most familiar example. Similarly, mandatory use of seatbelts might be justified in part on the ground that the subjective costs of buckling up decrease dramatically once people are in the habit of doing so; those costs are shifting rather than fixed, and people may be enthusiastic about regulation once they are in the habit.

The case for intervention here cannot, however, depend solely on habituation to the regulatory regime. Such an approach would be a license for tyranny—a point confirmed by the earlier discussion of adaptive preferences. The case for intervention will be most forceful if there are asymmetries, those subject to an intrapersonal collective action problem might well be able to take care of themselves. Their willingness to engage in a process in which their tastes will change might be regarded as a reason for praise—as "character planning"—rather than public interference. Consider the decision to purchase classical music records, with full knowledge that the (subjective) value of the records will increase over time as appreciation increases, with the ultimate consequence of significant expenditures. If the purchaser knows what she is getting into—in particular, if she is aware that the preference may change as a result of consumption, and proceeds happily regardless—the argument for government action is weaker.

These considerations suggest that government action may be justified to disrupt voluntary transactions when preferences are endogenous to consumption; when information is asymmetrical; and when the benefits of consumption decrease over time, as the costs of nonconsumption increase.

Absence of information. When those who participate in voluntary transactions lack relevant information, collective action is justified on grounds of both welfare and autonomy. It is no violation of autonomy to bar a person from doing something that she would not do were she armed with perfect information; and if the costs of government action are sufficiently low, intervention will be justified on welfare grounds. That intervention may take one of two forms. The first and less intrusive would be a disclosure requirement. This is the most direct remedy for an absence of information, and it is imposed in many contexts, most notably in cigarette advertising. Sometimes, however, public provision of information may be costly or ineffective. Here the best remedy is a flat ban on the conduct in question.

Such an approach has risks. Government may have less information than affected citizens, and its own incentives may distort the regulatory process. There is always a risk of factional intrigue and self-dealing on the part of governmental actors. But such risks hardly justify an across-the-board rule against either provision of information or prohibition of certain transactions in cases of lack of information.

The largest question for practical politics has to do with the size of the category of cases in which an absence of information justifies government action. Recent evidence suggests that the category is larger than has been suspected thus far. For example, people tend to have severe difficulty in assessing low-probability events.[17] Sometimes they act as if a low probability is in fact zero. Such mistakes may account for such phenomena as the failure to buckle seatbelts, continued smoking of cigarettes, and the failure to exercise. (Such phenomena are also examples of intrapersonal collective action problems.) On the other hand, sometimes the risks from low probability events are dramatically overstated. People tend, in short, to rely on heuristics that can produce serious mistakes.

There are characteristic dangers in grounding governmental action on this concern. What appears to be an irrational evaluation of a danger may in fact be a subjective attraction to risk, and it is not clear that government should interfere with the latter. The line between an irrational discount and attraction to risk can be drawn sharply in theory, but it will be hard to do so in practice. If, however, it is clear that irrational discounting is occurring, government intervention may well be justified.

Inalienable goods. In some circumstances, goods should not be treated as commodities; they should not be marketable at all. A conclusion of this sort represents a rejection of the notion that private preferences, as expressed in markets, should be even the starting point for analysis. Possible examples, derived from current practice, are easy to provide, though the underlying rationale is not always clear. Consider trading of the vote; of body parts; of the physical capacities needed to produce children; of sexual services; of children themselves.

The prohibition of purchase and sale of these items depends on a range of concerns.[18] We may group them in three categories: (A) Sometimes the fear is that if a good is made into a commodity, the result will be to diminish the amount of altruism and of donation in society, to the detriment of those who are least well-off or of the activity in question. Suppose, for example, that blood could be purchased and sold on markets.[19] The donation of blood might be decreased as a result; blood would have a price when it had previously been provided gratuitously; poor people might find it harder to obtain blood, and public subsidies would be necessary. But claims of this sort depend on highly contestable empirical judgments. It is hardly clear that a decision to turn something into a commodity will significantly decrease the amount of donation. Moreover, as a general matter a market system accompanied by government subsidies to the poor is probably superior to one in which goods may be either donated or not transferred at all.

(B) Resistance to purchase and sale of certain goods sometimes depends on the view that if such goods could be purchased and sold, people would have a different and inferior conception of themselves and of other people.[20] Perhaps the most dramatic example comes from the controversy over whether to allow for markets in babies.[21] One objection to such a step would be that to put a price tag on babies would alter, for the worse, parents' conception of their relation to their children. To think of a child as something that might be bought and sold is to change one's attitude toward it. If babies were freely tradeable on markets, parents would have to regard their children as transferrable and as sources of potential profit. The practice of purchase and sale would thus transform attitude and beliefs, and possibly in highly undesirable directions.

To some degree this objection is based on the possible adverse effects on children. But part of the instinct underlying prohibitions of this sort comes from a desire to ensure that people think of certain items as essentially priceless and nontradeable. Ideas of this kind underlie the notion to allow trade in certain items is to diminish and degrade them. Social attitudes toward sexuality and the right to vote, for example, would be significantly altered if prostitution and vote-trading were legalized.

This point suggests that the claim that prohibitions on sale are paternalistic is wide of the mark.[22] The choice to allow sale is itself a decision, and it might be objectionable on one of two grounds. First, that choice will intrude on those who would prefer that certain items not be subject to purchase and sale. Many people might find their own attitudes toward those items changed in undesirable ways if purchase and sale were available. A decision not to allow alienation of such items might be understood as a form of explicit or implicit second-order preference.

Moreover, the best substantive theory might hold that the items in question should not be alienable, quite apart from the subjective views of the citizenry. The rejection of efforts to turn certain items into commodities would depend on a conclusion that such items are diminished if they are traded on markets. To spell out such a substantive theory is a large task, but the examples given above might serve as a starting point.

(C) Sometimes goods are not made into commodities because

of the external and systemic effects that purchase and sale might produce. Thus the prohibition of sale of the right to vote might be based on the risk that purchase and sale would place political power in the hands of a wealthy minority or increase corruption.[23] Quite apart from its possibly degrading effects on sexuality, the institution of prostitution is likely to affect how men perceive women and how women perceive themselves. Social stigmatization of the sale of sexual services might therefore be justified on antidiscrimination grounds.[24] A system in which the ability to bear children is subject to purchase and sale might have a similar systemic effect on poor women or on women in general—and such effects are not sufficiently taken account of by the individual seller. The institution of trading may therefore contribute to the social subordination of a particular group. Slavery is the most obvious example here, but the principle is potentially quite broad.

III. QUESTIONS AND QUALIFICATIONS

The various categories of prohibition discussed thus far suggest that in a wide range of cases voluntary transactions should be disrupted. The market outcome is distinct from the outcome justice requires. This conclusion is likely to hold regardless of whether one's ultimate aim is autonomy, welfare, or something else. Governmental or private arrangements that disrupt such transactions might be justifiable even if there is no harm to others. But serious questions remain, and in order to generate a complete theory, such questions would have to be answered. I outline some of the relevant issues here.

The conundrum of autonomy. The first, and one of the largest, has to do with the status of arguments from autonomy. Here the problem stems from the fact that a positive definition of autonomy is exceptionally difficult to provide—especially in light of the social and biological construction of preferences.[25] The notion that people might genuinely select their preferences, during a process of self-creation, is absurd. There must always be some foundation from which to proceed, and that foundation cannot itself be created by the human actor.[26] Numerous modern criticisms of Kantian approaches proceed from perceptions of this sort. They suggest that the notion of autonomy, in its strongest and most rationalistic senses, should be abandoned altogether.[27]

In deciding whether and when to disrupt voluntary transactions, it would be a large mistake to believe that there is a pre- or post-social standard of autonomy that might be used as the basis for political criticism. Thus notions of adaptive preferences, or preferences about preferences, must not pretend to depend on a regulative ideal of pure self-creation or of acontextual selection of preferences. A positive definition of autonomy is likely to prove chimerical.[28]

But it would be an equally large mistake to abandon the idea of autonomy altogether.[29] There is a substantial difference between a preference that results from the absence of available opportunities, or a lack of information about alternatives, and a preference that is formed in the face of numerous opportunities and all relevant information. The examples of women and sexual equality and workers and self-government may be helpful here, although the latter is a controversial case. The notion of autonomy is probably the best term available for describing this difference, even if its most strongly Kantian forms are implausible.

The proposition holds at both the individual and collective levels. Deliberation about appropriate ends by individuals may be accompanied by collective deliberation by both small and large groups. Rational agreement on the good life is, to be sure, unlikely to be achieved in a pluralistic society. But examples of measures that involve collective decisions about desirable ends are not difficult to find. Consider laws prohibiting discrimination on the basis of race and gender or those protecting the environment. Such laws need not reflect exogenous interests on the part of the electorate, but may instead be an attempt to select values through a process of deliberation.

The relation between autonomy and welfare. All of the justifications for intervention described thus far can be made out in terms of both welfare and autonomy. But in some circumstances there will be a conflict between the two, at least in the short run. Adaptive preferences, for example, promote welfare even as they reduce autonomy. To make one's preferences conform to the available opportunities is a sensible and important way of reducing the frustration associated with rebellion against a seemingly intractable status quo. Efforts to disrupt preferences that have already adapted to the status quo may produce substantial welfare losses, at least in the immediate future, and possibly longer. Efforts to eliminate slavery[30] and sex discrimination[31] may produce short-term losses of this sort.

Respect for second-order at the expense of first-order preferences may also, on a certain view, be undesirable from the standpoint of welfare even if it is defensible on grounds of autonomy. Preferences bottled up by second-order rules may simply express themselves elsewhere, and in particularly destructive forms. Consider, for example, the possibility that laws substituting nonentertainment for entertainment programming on television will be counteracted by people who listen to the radio and go to movies.

For present purposes it is unnecessary to choose between welfarist and nonwelfarist approaches to regulation of voluntary transactions. But it is important to understand that the various reasons for disrupting voluntary transactions operate along quite different tracks.

Beyond autonomy: neutrality and substantive conceptions of the good life. To some, the notion that one ought to attempt to promote autonomous preferences is a mistake in light of the chimerical character of the idea of autonomy itself. That preferences are socially or biologically constructed means that the goal of legal policy ought not to be to promote autonomy, but instead to develop and implement substantive conceptions of the good life. In this view, one should not create a presumption in favor of private preferences, or attempt to make a wide variety of options available. Instead, the goal ought to be to generate a substantive theory of good preferences, perhaps based on a notion of what preferences would emerge under ideal conditions.

Such an effort might seem the natural conclusion of some of the arguments spelled out above. Judgments about collective intervention might be based, not on formal ideas of autonomy, but instead on substantive theories about what sorts of preferences will promote what is sometimes described as human flourishing. Under this view, the goal of neutrality is impossible to achieve. Since preferences are a function of the social structure, including the legal regime, a system of prima facie respect for private preferences combined with selective intervention will hardly be neutral. Consider, for example, the area of television broadcasting: A decision to allow a free market, or even to make a variety of options available, will create a regulatory system with its own effects on formation of preferences. Such a system might be thought inferior to a system that worked out an appropriate substantive theory and implemented it through regulation mandating a certain form of broadcasting.

The difficulty with such approaches lies of course in the problem of identifying what a substantive conception of the good life might entail. The problem is both theoretical and institutional. The theoretical task is to generate an antiliberal theory of the good life that is to be imposed in the face of plural and conflicting conceptions on the part of private citizens. Even if that problem could be solved, the institutional problem remains: To what institution might we give the power to implement decisions of this sort? This problem is no less important for its familiarity. In these circumstances the best strategy, as a general rule, is to create a presumption in favor of private choices and to allow rebuttal in a distinct class of cases. In a pluralistic society, it is better to struggle with the difficulties in the concepts of autonomy and welfare than to permit imposition of unitary understandings of what a good life entails.

The limits of inalienability. The discussion of alienability thus far has left a number of gaps. In particular, it does not identify those items that ought not to be traded on markets. Such decisions are likely to have a measure of relativity over time and across groups and cultures; generalizations will therefore be hazardous here. But we may suggest that the argument from social subordination will be most powerful in cases in which an item to be made alienable is associated with a particular social group. Thus decisions to allow the purchase and sale of reproductive capacities or of sex raise serious issues of equality, since they might perpetuate the social subordination of women.

The problem here is that at least for some women, a decision to allow purchase and sale of (for example) reproductive capacities might be regarded as liberating, at least in comparison with the alternatives. That subjective belief is quite powerful in many instances, and the counterargument—that the practice is question contributes to social subordination—is hard to measure in particular cases. It is therefore necessary to be precise in showing how a decision to allow a certain item to be made alienable will increase inequality, in the face of the gains of a sort to the people sought to be protected.

There is also a severe problem of enforcement. A decision to criminalize prostitution may be even worse than a decision to legalize it, because of the harms to women who will be prostitutes even in a world in which prostitution is unlawful—and the point holds even though the best world would eliminate prostitution altogether.[32] Moreover, some goods may be commodities already, and to bring their quality as such into the open may be desirable.[33] The central point, however, remains: A system that treats reproductive rights and sexuality as commodities will tend to entrench traditional gender hierarchies.

The argument that certain items should not be made into commodities because to do so is to degrade them also requires considerable elaboration. We have seen that this argument might depend either on subjective beliefs of the citizenry or on an independent substantive theory. If subjective beliefs are central, the problem is a variation on that of preferences about preferences. There is by hypothesis a collective decision to prevent certain items from being traded and sold on markets. But the mere fact that there is a collective decision to that effect cannot dispose of the problem, for that decision may be objectionable on separate grounds. Consider the view that certain books ought not to be subject to purchase and sale (a measure favored by those hostile to the books in question) or that a purchase of margarine should be outlawed (a measure sought by butter producers). Perhaps the best conclusion here—a vague one—is that a collective antipathy to the purchase and sale of certain goods should be permitted to control only (1) when the antipathy is based on reasons of the sort outlined earlier, (2) when it is not objectionable on independent substantive grounds, and (3) when it does not merely reflect an interest-group deal.

If subjective collective preferences are put to one side, the case for a refusal to treat certain items as commodities must be based on some separate theory. It is possible to begin the process with some current intuitions—consider the sale of body parts, the ban of prostitution, the problem of vote-trading—but the task is a large one that cannot be carried out here.[34]

Other foundations. The discussion thus far has been cast largely in terms of social efforts to increase welfare or to promote individual and collective autonomy. But other foundations are of course possible. For example, the social goal might be the inculcation of virtue,[35] the creation of certain forms of community,[36] or expression of an ethics of care and responsibility rather than justice.[37] Systems founded on such goals would provide different foundations from which to decide when government should disrupt voluntary transactions. All of them would be likely to be skeptical of the assumptions that underlie the presumptive respect for voluntary agreements. In particular, the beliefs in rights and welfare that underlie that respect would be substantially revised. These alternative foundations tend to stress the social construction of both preferences and personality; rights and welfare, at least if defended in the preceding terms, are foreign concepts. It is possible that the resulting regime would be fundamentally different.

We may suggest, however, that even if such alternative foundations were used, the resulting regime would ultimately not be far from that suggested here. The point can hardly be proved in this brief space. But the various cases of disruption of voluntary transactions suggested above are apt to be quite similar to those that would be described under different starting points. A system based on virtue, for example, would also place a premium on second-order preferences and at the same time express concern about adaptive preferences. An ethics of care and responsibility would also be troubled by the risks of turning certain items into commodities. There would of course be significant problems of translation, but it would be unsurprising if systems based on the more familiar goals of autonomy and welfare were to reach results broadly in accord with those based on other foundations.

IV. CONCLUSION

One way to approach the relation between markets and justice is to explore settings in which voluntary transactions should be disrupted even if there is no harm to others. We have seen that it is possible to identify a number of such settings. Sometimes transactions will be individually rational and collectively irrational; sometimes people will seek to vindicate second-order preferences by banning voluntary transactions; sometimes an absence of information will call for regulation; sometimes transactions are based on preferences that have adapted to the absence of available opportunities; sometimes legal regulation can counteract intrapersonal collective action problems, found in preferences endogenous to consumption. For various reasons, moreover, some items should not be treated as commodities at all.

It is important to acknowledge that government action may make things worse rather than better. The case for intervention is therefore only presumptive. But the catalogue offered here suggests that there will be severe problems in a system that permits all voluntary transactions to go forward when there is no harm to others. Such a system is likely to permit considerable injustice, and it will fail to take advantage of opportunities for collective improvements, whether they are measured in terms of welfare, individual or collective autonomy, or on some other ground.

NOTES

1. See generally Brian Barry and Russell Hardin, *Rational Man and Irrational Society?* (Chicago: University of Chicago Press, 1983).

2. For a detailed elaboration, see David Gauthier, *Morals by Agreement* (Oxford: Clarendon Press, 1986).

3. See generally Frank Michelman, "Traces of Self-Government," *Harvard Law Review* 100 (1986): 4–77; and Cass R. Sunstein, "Interest Groups in American Public Law," *Stanford Law Review* 38 (1986): 29–76.

4. For discussion of such a conception of politics, see Hannah Arendt, *On Revolution* (New York: Penguin Books, 1967).

5. For general discussion of second-order preferences, see Jon Elster, *Ulysses and the Sirens* (Cambridge: Cambridge University Press, 1979).

6. Jon Elster, *Sour Grapes* (Cambridge: Cambridge University Press, 1983).

7. Leon Litwack, *Been in the Storm So Long* (New York: Knopf, 1979).

8. Edward Greenberg, *Workplace Democracy* (Ithaca: Cornell University Press, 1986).

9. Elster, *Sour Grapes.*

10. Ibid.

11. Greenberg, *Workplace Democracy.*

12. Michael McPherson, "Want Formation, Morality, and Some Interpretive Aspects of Economic Inquiry" in *Social Science as Moral Inquiry*, ed. N. Haan, R. Bellah, P. Rabinow, and W. Sullican (New York: Columbia University Press, 1983).

13. Elster, *Sour Grapes*.

14. Paul Gewirtz, "Choice in the Transition: School Desegregation and the Corrective Ideal," *Columbia Law Review* 86 (1986): 728–98; and Richard Epstein, "A Common Law for Labor Relations," *Yale Law Journal* 92 (1983): 1357–1414.

15. Elster, *Sour Grapes*.

16. Richard L. Solomon and John D. Corbitt, "An Opponent Process Theory of Motivation," *Psychological Review* 81 (1974): 119–45.

17. See generally David Kahneman, Paul Slovic, and Amos Tversky, *Judgment under Uncertainty* (Cambridge: Cambridge University Press, 1982).

18. See generally Margaret Jane Radin, "Market-Inalienability," *Harvard Law Review* 100 (1987): 1849–1937.

19. Richard Titmuss, *The Gift Relationship: From Human Blood to Social Policy* (New York: Pantheon, 1963).

20. Radin, "Market-Inalienability."

21. Richard Posner, "The Regulation of the Market in Adoptions," *Boston University Law Review* 67 (1987): 59–72.

22. Radin, "Market-Inalienability."

23. Richard Epstein, "Why Restrain Alienation?" *Columbia Law Review* 85 (1985): 970–90.

24. Carole Pateman, "Defending Prostitution: Charges Against Ericsson," *Ethics* 93 (1982/1983): 561–65.

25. See, for general discussion, Elster, *Sour Grapes;* Thomas Nagel, *The View from Nowhere* (New York: Oxford University Press, 1986); Mark Johnson, *The Body in the Mind* (Chicago: University of Chicago Press, 1987).

26. Martha Nussbaum, *The Fragility of Goodness* (Cambridge: Cambridge University Press, 1986).

27. Brian Fay, *Critical Social Sciences* (Ithaca: Cornell University Press, 1987).

28. Elster, *Sour Grapes*.

29. Gauthier, *Morals by Agreement*.

30. Litwack, *Been in the Storm So Long*.

31. Jane Mansbridge, *Why We Lost the ERA* (Chicago: University of Chicago Press, 1986).

32. Carole Pateman, "Defending Prostitution: Charges Against Ericsson," *Ethics* 93 (1982/1983): 561–65.

33. Posner, "The Regulation of the Market in Adoptions."

34. Michael Walzer, *Spheres of Justice* (New York: Basic Books, 1983); Radin, "Market-Inalienability."

35. Michael Sandel, *Liberalism and the Limits of Justice* (Cambridge: Cambridge University Press, 1982).

36. Martha Minow, "Foreword: Justice Engendered," *Harvard Law Review* 101 (1987): 10–95.

37. Carol Gilligan, *In a Different Voice* (Cambridge: Harvard University Press, 1982).

11

MARKETS AND JUSTICE: AN ECONOMIST'S PERSPECTIVE

BERNARD SAFFRAN

INTRODUCTION

The interaction between moral philosophy and economics has a long history; many have worked in both fields and welfare economics is to a large extent an applied branch of moral philosophy. For a number of years this interaction lay dormant as economists unselfconsciously accepted Pareto optimality in their rigorous work (with a nod in the direction of a social welfare function) and relied on a rough-and-ready version of utilitarianism (cost-benefit analysis) in their applied work. Historically, the primary reason for this reliance on Pareto optimality was that it appeared to be the residual ethical assumption available to those economists who wished to keep their roots in utilitarianism but also had accepted the program of the positivists with its insistence that cardinal utility and interpersonal comparisons be outlawed.[1]

With the revival of a strong public and policy interest in issues of poverty and redistribution in the 1960s, economists began to search for theoretical frameworks in which to discuss them. The work of Mirlees and Rawls further spurred the interest of economists in issues of justice: Mirlees's seminal paper explored the optimal income tax in hopes of defending progressive taxation even while taking incentive questions explicitly into account;[2] Rawls's book *A Theory of Justice* used categories and modes of analysis that economists found congenial. Also, the renewed interest of philosophers in public policy issues has brought an increase in their conversation with economists. These days we see a new journal, *Economics and Philosophy,* alongside *Philosophy and Public Affairs.* The economics profession has certainly rewarded those who have done substantive work on justice and markets, as is shown by the awarding of Nobel Prizes to Samuelson, Arrow, Hayek, Friedman and Buchanan.[3]

Most of the discussion in economics continues to draw on the two classic theorems of welfare economics. First, what is now regarded as the Adam Smith theorem, that a perfectly competitive equilibrium is Pareto optimal (sometimes called Pareto efficient); and second, that any Pareto-optimal outcome can be achieved by lump-sum taxes and transfers (that is, their payment or receipt does not depend on the individual's behavior) and the use of markets to achieve a competitive equilibrium.

The applicability of the first theorem has been the subject of much debate. Discussion has centered on those conditions when a competitive equilibrium fails to develop (for example, economies of scale) or when a competitive equilibrium might still not be Pareto optimal (possibly, because of externalities). While the first theorem guarantees that competitive markets will lead to an efficient outcome, this outcome need not be a just one. Many economists would argue that it depends on the ownership of the initial endowments: If the initial distribution of inputs is fair, then the results of the market are fair.[4]

It is the second theorem that has formed much of the basis of the discussion of distributive justice and markets. A just allocation that maximizes a Bergson-Samuelson individualistic social welfare function can be achieved by the use of lump-sum taxes and transfers, then relying on the market to reach a competitive equilibrium. This theorem has provided a justification for separating distributional and efficiency issues as well as the theoretical justification for market socialism. While its purpose is to convince economists, this is hardly the sort of result that will lead anyone to the barricades.

Recently, work on incentives and information has dominated economic theory. This work has had important implications on how we view the possibility of using markets to achieve justice and so we shall devote a good part of this chapter to its analysis.

Even though the interest of economists in discussions of justice is growing, I believe that Baumol is correct when he argues that most economists do not want to get involved in this matter because they are uncomfortable with having uniquely to define justice, are afraid of imposing their own values, and have had difficulty finding an appropriate analytical mechanism.[5] This has become less true. Economists were able to avoid these issues earlier partly because they eschewed discussions of distributional issues. In the 1960s and 1970s, when questions of income distribution became paramount in both policy and academic discussion, it became clear that answering many of the important questions of income distribution and taxation required some criteria of justice.

It is difficult even to summarize the vast amount of work that has been done in this field. It has yielded important new insights and added a new subtlety to the debate. I make no claim for comprehensiveness; the issues discussed are those that I am interested in and that I believe may not be well known to legal and political philosophers—in particular, I have omitted any substantive discussion of the works of Hayek and Buchanan.[6]

The first section of the chapter will review the standard work on the two theorems of welfare economics and then look at the optimal tax literature's exploration of the difficulties of implementation raised by incentive, informational, and strategic issues (especially the differential information available to the government and its citizens). We then examine some alternative criteria (versions of fairness as a lack of envy) that do not rely on interpersonal utility comparisons but often do utilize markets for their implementation: This will highlight some of the profound difficulties in implementing utopian theories of justice.

The last sections focus on some issues that have arisen in the 1980s (in fact, most of them were raised in articles that I read for other purposes while preparing this review) that are important to any consideration of justice, be it utopian or realistic. I first look at some of the empirical data on incentives. Here, the data are certainly more encouraging to those who would minimize the relevance of disincentive effects than conventional wisdom had it at the beginning of the 1980s. We also look at revisionist views of inheritance and savings that should inform a theory of justice. The last section on the internal economy considers questions of aid, trade, and immigration that raise many disturbing problems for radical advocates of justice as well as for defenders of free markets.

THE WELFARE THEOREMS

Much of the debate on the relation of markets to justice revolves around a defense, attack, or modification of the fundamental theorems of welfare economics. It might first be useful to sketch the standard welfare theorems. The more widely known result, taught in all economic theory courses, is that markets are efficient because a perfectly competitive equilibrium is Pareto optimal (that is, that no person can be made better off without making someone else worse off). A second theorem, less well known, but one, as we shall see, central to the analysis of the relation of markets to justice, states that any Pareto-optimal allocation can be reached by a competitive market equilibrium after appropriate lump-sum taxes and transfers.

The assumptions required to prove these theorems are well known and their validity is controversial. The assumptions required for the first are usually viewed as minimal: a competitive equilibrium (fixed prices, supply equal to demand in all markets, and maximization of profits and utility), a full set of markets, and perfect information. Behind these assumptions lies some additional structure. The assumption of a full set of markets requires a market for property rights (the lack of which creates externalities). Also, to incorporate intertemporal choice and uncertainty there needs to be a competitive market for each commodity in each time period and for each outcome of the world, so that bread this year and next year is distinguished, and bread next year if the Republicans win is distinguished from bread next year if the Democrats win. The second theorem has similar requirements for its validity, but also requires additional assumptions about the concavity of preferences and production sets.

The argument between critics and defenders of the usefulness of the first theorem can best be described as a series of ritualized thrusts and counterthrusts. A standard argument is that the presence of government, externalities (without property rights), the absence of the necessary markets, and noncompetitive influences would greatly limit the applicability of the result. When these conditions obtain, second-best theory is used. Now the goal is to achieve an optimum given an additional constraint—so, for example, where there are governmental as well as private participants the government can choose the optimal level of expenditures to produce public goods and then raise taxes in the least distortionary manner.

A competitive equilibrium asumes that all markets clear. Where is macroeconomics with its inflation and depressions? Once again some recent theories try to demonstrate the optimality of cycles with theories about the voluntary nature of unemployment—so, for example, unemployment is higher in depressions because workers choose to work less when their wages are lower than in good times. The persistence of high unemployment rates in Europe as well as the recent crash in the stock market has raised serious questions about theories that assume market clearance.

Another objection, the focus of much recent work, is the possibility of asymmetric and incomplete information that leads to the problems of moral hazard and adverse selection. As will appear, these issues become even more important in any implementation of the second theorem, since that requires lump-sum taxes and transfers that differ among people.

The first theorem says nothing about end-state notions of fairness or justice of the competitive equilibrium—it simply gives us the minimal result that no further gains can be exploited by production or trade. The second theorem that any Pareto-optimal outcome can be achieved by the use of markets and lump-sum taxes and transfers is important to our understanding of justice and markets. Assume that the goals of justice can be expressed as maximizing a function that depends on each individual's utility, as would be the case with utilitarianism, (with each individual's utility function depending only on the goods received). At the maximum it must be Pareto optimal, for otherwise we could increase the value of the function by making someone better off without making someone else worse off. We know from the second theorem that with appropriate lump-sum transfers and competitive markets we can achieve this Pareto-optimal point and so maximize the function.[7]

These results have given comfort to economists from a variety

of schools. Conservative economists can argue for the separation of efficiency and equity considerations: We can rely on the
market to make the correct efficiency judgements, while in principle allowing someone else to make the distributional ones. In
addition, they contend that the assumptions of the competitive
model are approximated well enough in the real world so that
we can rely on the market.

This theorem has also been used to justify a form of market
socialism where the state distributes lump-sum amounts and
also sets the market prices. To do this the state has to know each
person's preferences and initial endowment as well as the production sets. Advocates of a command economy can also build
on this result, and ask why, given that all of this information is
available to it, the state does not bypass the market and just
redistribute the final optimal equilibrium quantities of goods to
each consumer.

Although much of the discussion of these theorems is highly
abstract with assumptions that are unlikely to be met, it has
served as the basis for many of the later developments to which
we now turn.

INCENTIVES, INFORMATIONAL AND STRATEGIC ISSUES

We have already mentioned strategic behavior as a problem in
achieving social goals, but in recent years in economic theory it
has moved from being a caveat to general results to being analyzed as a primary force in economic behavior.[8] Much of the
discussion was foreshadowed by J. de V. Graff thirty years ago:
"It is clear that truly lump-sum measures are extraordinarily
hard to devise. A poll-tax, of course, meets all the requirements;
but it is not very helpful in securing desired redistributions
unless we tax different men differently. But on what criteria
should we discriminate between different men? . . . If we tax
able men more than dunderheads, we open the door to all
forms of falsification: we make stupidity seem profitable—and
any able man can make himself seem stupid."[9] The trouble is
that the state does not have all of the information that it needs
to achieve its goals. In this section we will show that the disincentive to reveal relevant information can lead to differential information on the part of the state and its citizens and can then
have a profound effect on the rules that we choose.[10]

Although these issues have dominated all branches of economic theory as of late, it seems best to illustrate them in the context of redistributive taxation, since the problems of implementation here are akin to those of most end-state theories of justice. A perusal of the literature shows that the seminal paper is by Mirlees, who moved us away from just making comments on the need to worry about the impact of redistribution on incentives to creating a rigorous model.

To highlight these issues they are examined in the context of utilitarianism. We know that the assumptions of identical utility functions with decreasing marginal utility, a fixed quantity of goods to be distributed, and maximizing the sum of interpersonal utility yield an outcome that requires equality. Also well known is that when the total amount to be distributed depends on the amount of work done, then this result must be modified to take incentives into the account. More recent work highlights even more subtle issues when there is differential information.

Some of the issues can be illustrated in a fairly simple model with two workers whose diminishing marginal utility functions are identical and are positive functions of consumption and leisure, and who differ only in their productivity. While the state knows the common utility function, in each of these examples it has differing amounts of information about the worker's ability, ranging from knowing each person's ability, to only knowing the underlying distribution of abilities. Here it is important to include leisure (which cannot be traded), since its taxation has been the major source of problems in analyzing optimal taxation.

If each individual maximized her own utility, then the more productive would have a higher utility. If the government has complete information as to who is in which group and can tax and subsidize them in a way such that their labor supply does not affect the tax paid (that is, a lump-sum tax), then the outcome using the utilitarian criterion radically diverges from that based on the individualistic criterion. The more productive workers now get a lower level of utility than the less productive; they work harder to subsidize the less able.

Once we make the realistic assumption that before imposing the tax-transfer scheme the government does not know which of the workers is more productive and has only information on their income, then it can't tell if the low-income workers are less productive or are high-productivity workers who choose more leisure. Now the state cannot use differential lump-sum taxes based on ability, and the issues of self-selection and incentive compatibility also enter; high-productivity workers will have an incentive to become low-productivity workers to raise their utility. The goal then becomes to design schemes so that at the end both high- and low-productivity workers work appropriately hard. Now the results change and higher-productivity workers have a higher utility level than when the government had complete information, though lower, because they are subsidizing low-productivity workers, than before any government intervention.

If the government can monitor income and hours (giving it a measure of revealed skill), then the optimal solution changes again and becomes one of equal utility.

The analysis also alters if we allow for somewhat different models. For example, if we recognize that those on whom the tax is initially levied need not bear its full impact if pretax wages change, we can get the even more surprising result that the marginal tax on the highest-ability group (in this case, skilled labor) should be negative. The optimal tax also changes if in addition to assuming that workers have different productivities in working in the market we recognize that people may differ in their ability to generate utility when combining consumption goods with time not spent at market work (for example, listening to records). If those who are more productive at market work are also the more productive in their use of nonmarket time, then the utilitarian framework requires that they should be given more of the consumption good.

The optimal tax also changes if we allow for a different type of tax system—say, that we allow for random taxation. For example, if high-productivity workers are risk-averse then the random taxation of low-productivity workers will reduce the temptation for high-productivity workers to appear as low-productivity workers, since they then could fall quite far.

The conclusions that we are forced to draw from this analysis are highly pessimistic about the possibilities of developing rules for end-state theories of justice. We see that even if we are willing to accept an ethical goal, which might seem the most problematical part, the rules we choose will not only be a function of the model of the economy but will also be highly dependent on the amount of information and tools that the government has available.

Still another set of problems is typically ignored by utopian theorists as merely technical issues to be left to bureaucrats, yet their solution can in fact have radically different effects on the functioning of the system. Thus, whether we consider the welfare of the individual or the family, or a lifetime versus a single year of welfare, can make a great difference. People's behavior may well depend on the definition of *welfare*. Effort will go into activities that are more favored. So, for example, once a distinction is made between ordinary income and capital gains with the latter taxed at lower rates, then we find that much of the tax code is devoted to defining this distinction as lawyers and accountants try to convert ordinary income to capital gains. An even more striking outcome results when families split or unite depending on the detailed provisions of the tax and welfare system.

In general, it would make most sense to build our theories on the assumption that information that can be hidden will be hidden. Even if we begin with a society with a high sense of compliance to truth, one "chiseler," unless deterred by Draconian means, often leads others to do likewise. In this respect, one need only notice the erosion of compliance with the U.S. income tax as people began to expect others to behave in a similar manner.

Of course, we can continue to get more and more information about people, but not only does this use up resources, it might lead to the "Machlup result." Machlup used to play a game called exchange control with graduate students in his international trade seminar. One half of the class were businessmen who wished to get their money out of a country with exchange controls, while the other half were the government which tried to prevent it. The game always ended the same way—with a totalitarian state.

Envy, Equity, and Fairness

One of the most interesting attempts by economists to deal with these issues stems from the work on envy and fairness.[11] It lies in the mainstream of traditional economics: interpersonal utility comparisons are avoided and competitive markets continue to play a major role in finding the desired solutions. It has now become apparent that many of the goals of this research program are not likely to be achieved, but by appraising it we can see the kinds of difficulties that economists face when they analyze questions of justice.

Conceptually, the use of fairness comes from the classical solution of the problem of the fair division of a cake between two people—one person cuts and the other chooses. This notion was then generalized so that a lack of envy means that A did not prefer B's bundle of commodities (in this case, his slice of cake) to her own. Note that no interpersonal utility comparisons are made since each person compares her valuation of her bundle to the other's bundle, and not the other's utility. Although terminology has varied widely, absence of envy will be called an equitable outcome.[12] When a fixed bundle of goods is to be divided the simplest equitable solution is an equal distribution of each of the goods, but when tastes differ the division might not be Pareto optimal. Much of the work in this area has been a search for outcomes that are fair, that is, both equitable and Pareto optimal.

A simple way to find fair outcomes might appear at first to start with an equal distribution and then let people trade. This process need not achieve fairness. For example, if there are three people (A, B, and C) and two (A and B) have the same tastes and only one (A) can trade with (C), then the other (B) will envy (A).

How can we achieve fair outcomes? Once again, the competitive market and the first theorem of welfare economics come to the rescue. If we distribute the commodities equally and then have a competitive equilibrium, we know that the result will be Pareto optimal; we also know that there cannot be envy since each individual had the same initial amounts of every good and faced the same prices, so each person could have chosen the final bundle of any other. Of course, many other fair outcomes are possible, but this particular one of the initial equality and trade to a competitive equilibrium has been the focus of much of the attention. Thomson and Varian argue that not only are these outcomes fair but they have many other positive attributes, including minimal information requirements, which suggests its centrality for appraisals of economic justice.[13]

Just as with the development of optimal taxation, serious problems arose with implementing this concept when economies were analyzed that have production as well as exchange. The difficulty appears in many guises in the literature. It is due to people having differing productive abilities and differing tastes for leisure and commodities: then where there is only leisure (or work) and commodities, efficiency may require the more productive person to work harder and have more commodities, but if she has a preference for leisure and the less productive person has a preference for work and more commodities, the outcome may not be fair.[14]

To deal with this unwelcome prospect, a number of alternative criteria have been suggested that attempt to capture other notions of equity, within a framework that treats all of the participants symmetrically. After reviewing some of these criteria, including the work of Varian, Thomson and Varian somewhat sadly have recently concluded, "So as of this date there does not seem to be an entirely satisfactory concept of equity in the case of a production economy. Perhaps this reflects an inherent difficulty with notions of justice based on symmetry. They seem to work well when everyone is similar, but if there are too many things that differ across individuals the demands of equity *and* efficiency become difficult to reconcile."[15]

INCENTIVES AND THE SUPPLY OF LABOR AND CAPITAL

To this point the arguments we have examined arise in the context of various theories with differing assumptions. Many of the assumptions are of an ethical or parable nature and therefore not easily verified. Now I wish to take up some of the empirical data, in particular changing beliefs as to the importance of incentives. If incentive effects are small, then redistributive policies introduced to achieve some goals of a just society would have relatively little effect on total output and growth.[16]

Much of the opposition to large-scale redistributions of income is partially justified by pointing to the possible negative incentive effects on both those who are taxed as well as those who receive transfers. Until the 1970s economists were in fairly wide agreement that the effects of taxes on labor supply and on savings behavior were minimal. Then a great deal of new research found large incentive effects. This provided the intellectual basis for many policy decisions of the Reagan administration and has become the new conventional wisdom. Being of the older generation, I have always been skeptical of this work and while writing this, a group of papers appeared that are also increasingly skeptical of this new research. This is not the place to rehearse the whole debate, but I would like to focus on some of the revisionist thinking that I believe makes it easier to implement a more equitable income distribution.

I turn first to the labor supply.[17] Contrary to the current conventional wisdom, for many years it was believed that labor supply was quite unresponsive (or even negatively related) to changes in the wage rate. (Almost all of these analyses assumed that the worker is concerned only with the after-tax wage rate, so that lowering wages and raising taxes would have similar results.) It was pointed out that over a fairly long time period, as wages have risen, the work week has fallen, vacations have lengthened, and retirement is earlier. Some also question the discretion that workers have in controlling hours actually worked. In addition, the results from the standard theory of labor supply were not conclusive: an income effect from higher taxes (workers were now poorer) implied that they wanted less leisure and more market work; and a substitution effect (leisure was now relatively cheaper) that had them wish to work less. The two effects went in opposite directions and so the quantitative size of these two effects was needed to get a qualitative result for the effect of taxes on labor supply. It should be noted that this is in contrast to the theory of demand for a commodity where, as long as more of it is desired with a higher income, we can be sure that taxing it will reduce demand.

This view began to be challenged in the 1970s and 1980s: the negative income tax experiments showed fairly large labor-supply effects in the poverty populations, especially among youths and women; there were estimates of significant earnings falls from transfers to the poor; it was argued that social security and disability insurance encouraged early retirement; the welfare loss of taxes was found to be large as a proportion of the revenue gained; and a theoretical argument that only substitution effects of tax changes mattered (which implied that disincentive effects were likely) because the increased government transfers to others or the government expenditure on goods that taxpayers wanted would eliminate the income effect.

Burtless and Haveman examine these arguments and conclude, "our assessment of the recent literature on tax and transfer distortions leads us to be skeptical of the claim that these distortions have led to massive reductions in work effort."[18] They cite the overall growth in labor-force participation rates in recent years, with women entrants compensating for retired men.

They and others are especially concerned with relying on the econometric studies that found large incentive effects (that is, large labor-supply elasticities) because of the variability of the estimates. Two of the leading scholars of female labor supply, Killingsworth and Heckman, have surveyed the field and point out that while the female labor supply elasticities are large when compared with males, they do vary greatly and range from −.30 or less to +14.00 or more.[19] They also compared this survey to an earlier one: "Six years ago [we and Thomas E. Macurdy] commented that elasticity estimates obtained using recently developed econometric techniques had increased the mean of what might be called the 'reasonable guesstimate' of the wage-elasticity of female labor supply. Work since then seems to have reduced the mean and substantially increased the variance of this guesstimate."[20] Pencavel, after surveying studies of the labor supply of men, argues that the studies of the past twenty years show a small elasticity of the effect of wages on hours of work, but he finds that the model is contradicted in enough instances to warrant skepticism about its applicability.[21]

A similar outcome occurred in the study of savings. For many years we had no econometric evidence that changes in the return to capital influenced the savings rate; once again the theory only provided income and substitution effects that moved in opposite directions. Then along came Boskin's major paper,[22] which began to change the profession's view of the matter and greatly influenced Reagan's early tax proposals. This view has recently undergone an empirical test. During the early 1980s real after-tax rates of return to savers increased both because of rise in real interest rates (nominal interest rates did not fall as fast as the rate of inflation) and because marginal tax rates were cut, and yet savings rates decreased.[23]

This increasing skepticism about the strong effects of changing incentives on labor supply and savings behavior should encourage those who believe in the possibility of a more just distribution of income without greatly decreasing the potential for growth.

INHERITANCE

The role of inherited wealth has always been central to reflections on economic justice. Recently, Haslett[24] has argued for its abolition, while Stiglitz has made the point that on utilitarian grounds it's a "twofer," since it provides utility to both the giver and the receiver.[25] It is also very important in designing the tax system: For example, recently there has been a strong argument made to move away from an annual income tax toward a consumption tax system, but the equity of the tax crucially depends on the treatment of gifts and bequests. While we continue the debate, in my view one's reaction to the institution of inheritance should be based on a sense of its empirical importance.[26]

To noneconomists, it seems self-evident that all of the wealth is passed on by inheritance. Economists, however, have tended to downplay the importance of a bequest motive for explaining the level of wealth in society. The dominant theory of savings in economics has been the life-cycle hypothesis, which argues that most saving is an attempt to even out consumption over a lifetime. In its simplest version, with no bequest motive, people save during their working years and then dissave in retirement. During his lifetime each person consumes all of his wealth. The major determinants, then, of the growth of wealth is the growing number of workers or their growing productivity so that their accumulation is greater than the dissaving of the retired. Modigliani (whose Nobel Prize came largely from this work) did not question that a bequest motive existed, but claimed that it was small and could account for only about 15 to 20 percent of total wealth in the U.S. It should be made clear that not all inheritance is included; we are measuring intergenerational transfers, so that an estate left to a spouse would not be included in the measure of the transfer.

This view has recently been challenged by Kotlikoff and Summers.[27] They estimate the proportion of savings that derives from the need to even out life-cycle consumption and identify the residual as intergenerational transfers. These transfers are large and depending on definitions constitute between 46 and 80 percent of wealth, with 80 percent as their preferred value. They contend that we cannot reconcile the observed data on savings with the consumption behavior of workers and retirees required by the life-cycle hypothesis. The reason is that very little saving is done by the below-45 age group and so this large group can contribute relatively little to life-cycle saving.

Do not be misled by the specificity of these percentages. These estimates are subject to great controversy because they are derived from calculations that make use of very indirect methods; these are not values found in probate records.

At this stage the reasons for the differences between the estimates of Modigliani, and Kotlikoff and Summers have become clear enough so that we can choose between them in thinking about justice. Modigliani is primarily interested in a bequest motive that focuses on the passage of resources at the termination of one generation, but excludes transfers that are made while generations overlap. The Summers and Kotlikoff definition includes all payments to children over age 18 (all payments to children below the age of 18 are considered as consumption expenditures of the parents); notice that this includes parents' expenditure on their children's education. For our purposes, this definition is preferable. In fact, it may be an underestimate of the value relevant for a theory of justice, since that may well include all expenditures, and certainly gifts, to children. Another difference in the definition is that they quite properly include in intergenerational transfers not just the bequest but the interest earned on it over this generation. (That is, life-cycle saving is the difference between labor income and consumption.) These two effects account for the bulk of the difference between the two estimates.

The results need not imply that the motivation is altruistic — it is simply the amount of saving that cannot be accounted for by life-cycle needs. Many explanations other than altruism were given. For example, it may be due to precautionary saving that did not have to be called on or its function may be to guarantee that children behave properly toward their parents with the potential inheritance being the club—with the now-classic observation that children are more likely to visit parents the greater the amount of bequeathable wealth.[28]

If currently intergenerational transfers are such a major factor in the generation of savings and the passage of wealth, then isn't any discussion of justice incomplete without more attention to these issues? Once again, informational and incentive concerns come to the fore. If we imposed substantial taxes on inheritances people would have a strong incentive to buy annuities (after all, it is the absence of the wide use of annuities that would be expected for life-cycle reasons that forms a major part of the rationale for a bequest motive) and to invest in their children's human capital. If we wish to minimize inherited wealth and maintain savings, we will have to rely on monetary and fiscal policy to generate the savings.

THE INTERNATIONAL ECONOMY

It is of course a platitude to say that we are now part of an increasingly integrated world economy. This realization has had a profound impact on work in economics, so that many widely held beliefs about monetary and fiscal policy as well as about the relation of domestic savings and investment have had to be reformulated. Here I will examine a few of the issues that it poses for our understanding of the relation of markets and justice.

One would expect that any theory of consequential justice would argue for a radical redistribution of income between the inhabitants of rich and poor countries. Whatever may be said about the degree of inequality in any one country, the variance for the world as a whole is much greater and, one would think, the demands of justice greater. Historically, a major source of the demand for economic justice was not so much inequality as the fact that people were living in extreme poverty. In the developed world we are much richer now, so that our poverty level is well above the average income in the rest of the world, much of which does live in extreme want. As Tullock puts it in commenting on Rawls, "If you actually do not know who you are, and you think therefore the likelihood of your being a citizen of India or of Communist China is as great as the likelihood of your being an American citizen, you would be in favor of very drastic transfers of funds away from American citizens. The best policy would be removing at least two-thirds of the present after-tax income of American citizens and giving it to the poorer parts of the world, and very likely 80 percent would be a more reasonable figure. Swedes, even if members of the socialist party, or members of the British Labour Party, etc., all would find themselves impoverished."[29]

Tullock even goes further. Using a second-best argument he claims that it may well be counterproductive to aim for justice in one country. If we tax the high-income people in the high-income countries to obtain economic justice there, strong incentive effects will arise that will lower worldwide output and hence hurt the poor in the poor part of the world.

In terms of some of the incentive arguments we made earlier, international transfers at more modest levels might have fewer distortionary incentive effects than if carried out in one country. (A quick look at per capita income levels would be convincing that some modest transfers from the wealthy countries would materially improve the living standards of the poorer countries.) Consider the incentive model we discussed earlier. Suppose residents of high-income countries were taxed with a transfer to low-income countries; large incentive effects are unlikely since very few residents of countries like the United States would then choose to move to countries like Bangladesh. In addition, increases in productivity in the poorer countries might come from improvements in health and nutrition made possible by the transfers.

I could continue giving the arguments for the merits of international redistribution and the reader will surely know that whatever its merits, it has far less chance than movements toward justice in a single country. This does have an important lesson: Since our moral theories lead to implications so contrary to any likely behavior, they clearly omit important considerations and we should be skeptical about their cogency.[30]

This lesson can be further seen in examining two pressing issues that are more likely to have a direct policy impact, namely trade and immigration. While free trade and immigration are likely to increase the world's output and efficiency, they are also likely to have differential impacts on labor and capital in different countries.

As Bronfenbrenner[31] points out, for many years now we have been aware of Samuelson's factor-price equalization theorem that argues that competitive international trade markets will tend to equalize the rates of compensation of factors between countries, and that in particular, for a capital-intensive country like the United States, it will tend to raise the return to capital and lower it for labor. As tariff barriers have fallen and with the increased integration of the world economy, this change in factor returns becomes a more important issue. Today, many observers see international trade as a major force in restraining the wages of American workers. Labor is further squeezed when this is combined with international capital mobility, which tends to equalize after-tax rates of return to capital so that capital might well move if it is taxed or wages raised. Of course, during this same process wage rates are increased in the rest of the world. On the other hand, other groups, including those with national and not international market power, will be made worse off by the new competition. These are all the results of the international extension of markets. Once again, how notions of justice are to inform our judgments depends strongly on the degree to which we count the welfare of non-Americans.

The question of immigration raises similar problems. Borjas[32] makes the argument that the more inequality in the distribution of income in the U.S., the better quality of immigrants we will get. This is because high-ability people will prefer to move to a place where they can make the most use of their skills and ability, while low-income people will be afraid of falling too low. If we have a more equal distribution of income it will mean a lower quality of immigrants, though we will also be lessening the negative effects of the brain drain on the countries from which they emigrate.

Melvin Reder,[33] in a discussion of Chicago economics, points out that freedom of immigration should be defended by economists of that tradition on grounds of both efficiency and ethics. Yet here we find a great inconsistency. Even Henry Simons, who is widely regarded as the intellectual godfather of many of today's leading conservative economists, strongly opposed free immigration. (Reder considers his vehemence on this point as "astonishing.") Friedman argues against free entry to countries having welfare programs that provide a minimum level of income that does not depend on productivity, as most of the richer countries do. Reder recognizes that resistance to international income equality through levelling is not consistent with free-market principles. He concludes, "Both freedom of opportunity and world wide efficiency of economic organization require freedom of choice in location. Intellectual defense of resistance to the implied redistribution of income and (possibly) of political power requires a quite sharp reformulation of the normative principles of traditional liberalism and the associated goal of an open society."[34]

These examples illustrate that when we include global issues difficult questions arise both for those concerned with justice and for traditional defenders of free markets.

Concluding Comments

In this chapter I have tried to highlight some recent theoretical and empirical developments that should inform our discussion of justice and markets. This is not the place to continue the longstanding debate about the degree to which knowledge in the social sciences is independent of the politics and ethos of its times. I believe, however, that there is wide agreement that the issues focused on, though not necessarily the validity of the arguments, often reflect the social issues of the period. As we have seen, the theoretical developments based on incentives and information that have dominated much of the recent work in economic theory raised serious questions about the implementation of end-state theories of justice. While these problems have raised concern before, these theorists may well have picked up and emphasized the greed and lack of public concern that has been widely commented on as so common in our society.[35]

A striking example of this change of ethos is the changed attitude toward scholarship policy at academic institutions. Friends of mine, now in their 50s, were told by their parents not to accept fellowships to graduate school because others might have a greater need. Today, as schools have tried to focus on need — free admissions policies, a move to the more just society of their parents—these same friends hire consultants who tell them the best way to structure their assets and present their financial statements so as to minimize college costs. Since I strongly support these new policies I am quite disturbed by this new attitude. However, there may be another reason for the change in attitude: These redistributive policies have markedly increased the costs of sending non-financially aided students to college, which may make parents feel that they have been taken advantage of. Thus this behavior may not be caused by increased greed, but may merely be a reaction to what is perceived as too much redistribution.

In a broader context, this recent emphasis on the possible use of individual advantage even when it works against social norms has served to reinforce some long-held views. A just economy may require a substantial reduction in output and efficiency. An alternative to this pessimistic outcome is that people be willing to forgo some individual advantage to make the system work even in situations of moral hazard and adverse selection; this is most likely when the procedures, if not the outcomes, are widely acceptable. While we can assume that another generation of economists will focus on other perspectives, the cautionary results reported here should serve as a brake for those who will be overly sanguine about the ease of implementing a just society.

A number of new theories and developing anomalies in the standard theory are changing our notions of the functioning of markets. These alternatives attack the textbook version of the behavior of markets and so will have a major, albeit indirect, impact on this discussion. A few of the ideas that are likely to have this impact are: a clear recognition of path-dependence, that previous history strongly shapes our current institutions; the dependence of quality on price, with efficiency-wage theory as a prime example where employers pay above the market-clearing wage to keep, attract, and discipline workers; the analysis of anomalies in the theory of rational behavior, many of them introduced to economics by psychologists, that are beginning to be taken up by economists; and the further development of non-profit-maximizing theories of the firm.[36] Currently, there is a great deal of flux and no uniform new view has emerged, at least in the sense that it has become the new standard textbook version. All of these developments do, however, tend to cast doubt on the earlier arguments for the optimality of the market arrangement. This poses problems for political theorists who wish to discuss the market and its ethics, since they would like economic theory to stand still for a while.[37] As I see it, much of the work I have surveyed as well as new material that has not yet been integrated into the debate will lead us to a more realistic sense of the potential and pitfalls in the use of markets for implementing our vision of economic justice.

NOTES

1. Martin Bronfenbrenner, in "Income Distribution and 'Economic Justice,' " *The Journal of Economic Education* 17 (1986): 36, gives the view of the economists of the 1930s who made the strong case for a more equitable distribution of income and who argued that there would be only small incentive effects. (Needless to say, he now rejects these views and the point of the essay is to make clear why he was wrong.) This 1930s view might be contrasted with an anecdote told by Samuelson, who in the late 1950s asked another eminent economist about a paper he had writen advocating the abolition of rent control in Japan. "I inquired indelicately about the income redistribution thereby implied. 'Oh' he said, on the run, 'if that is an issue, all that needs to be done is to compensate all the losers out of the enhanced gains of the winners made possible by the efficiency of market-clearing rentals.' I tell the complete story as it happened." Paul A. Samuelson, "How Economics Has Changed," *The Journal of Economic Education* 18 (1987): 109.

2. J. A. Mirlees, "An Exploration in the Theory of Optimum Income Taxation," *Review of Economic Studies* 38 (1971): 175–208. For a more elementary presentation as well as later developments see Anthony B. Atkinson and Joseph E. Stiglitz, *Lectures on Public Finance* (Maidenhead: McGraw-Hill, 1980), 394–423.

3. In economics much of the work has been carried out in a highly mathematical context. This literature has been surveyed in Kenneth J. Arrow and Michael D. Intriligator, eds., *Handbook of Mathematical Economics*, vol. 3 (Amsterdam: North-Holland, Elsevier, 1986), which includes "Social Choice Theory," by Amartya Sen and "The Theory of Optimal Taxation," by J. A. Mirlees.

4. There is little doubt that when compared with the population as a

a whole, economists strongly defend markets as part of the decision-making process. See Bruno S. Frey, "Economists Favour the Price System —Who Else Does?" *Kyklos* 4 (1986): 537–63, for the results of surveys in which he shows that economists in both the United States and western Europe tend to prefer allocative arguments that depend on markets, though those employed by the government are somewhat less enamored than are academics.

5. William J. Baumol, *Superfairness* (Cambridge: MIT Press, 1986), 5.

6. For a strong, polemical attack on mainline views from an Austrian perspective see Deepak Lal, "Markets, Mandarins, and Mathematicians," *Cato Journal* 7 (1987): 43–70 (the entire issue is titled "Essays in Honor of Peter Bauer"). Another defense of the Austrian view is Israel M. Kirzner, "Economic Planning and the Knowledge Problem," *Cato Journal* 4 (1984): 407–18; for a dissent see Leonid Hurwicz's comment in the same issue. The most articulate critique of Hayek are two papers by Partha Dasgupta, "Decentralization and Rights," *Economica* 47 (1980): 107–24 and "Utilitarianism, Information and Rights" in *Utilitarianism and Beyond,* ed. Amartya Sen and Bernard Williams (Cambridge: Cambridge University Press, 1982), 199–218.

7. Thus Varian concludes "all welfare maxima are competitive equilibria, and all competitive equilibria are welfare maxima for some welfare function." See Hal R. Varian, *Intermediate Microeconomics,* (New York: Norton, 1987), 537. The important point is that welfare maxima can be obtained as competitive equilibria. I find no normative significance in a competitive equilibrium maximizing *some* welfare function.

8. For example, instead of emphasizing that banks prefer to lend to those more willing to pay higher rates, now the argument is that they might be more reluctant because firms that are more likely to become bankrupt will be those willing to pay the higher rates. A good introduction to the flavor of this literature is Joseph E. Stiglitz, "The Causes and Consequences of the Dependence of Quality on Price," *Journal of Economic Literature* 25 (1987): 1–48.

9. J. de V. Graff, *Theoretical Welfare Economics* (Cambridge: Cambridge University Press, 1967), 78.

10. The illustrations in this section are taken from Dasgupta, "Decentralization and Rights" and "Utilitarianism, Information and Rights," and Joseph E. Stiglitz, "Pareto Efficient and Optimal Taxation and the New New Welfare Economics," in *Handbook of Public Economics,* vol. 2, ed. Alan J. Auerbach and Martin Feldstein, 991–1042 (Amsterdam: North-Holland, Elsevier, 1987). In this survey Stiglitz is primarily interested in what he defines as the New New Welfare economics which, in the second-best tradition, tries to find Pareto-optimal outcomes when the government is constrained by the available information and tools.

11. See Baumol, *Superfairness* 71–74 for a history of fairness theory.

12. Varian, *Intermediate Microeconomics*, 537-40.

13. William Thomson and Hal R. Varian, "Theories of Justice Based on Symmetry," in *Social Goals and Social Organization: Essays in Memory of Elisha Panzer*, ed. Leonid Hurwicz, David Schmeidler, and Hugo Sonnenschein (Cambridge: Cambridge University Press, 1985), 125–26.

14. Robin W. Boadway and Neil Bruce, *Welfare Economics* (Oxford: Blackwell, 1984), 171–75 gives a clear illustration of this outcome.

15. Thomson and Varian, "Theories of Justice Based on Symmetry," 120.

16. Unlike the earlier sections, this one focuses on output and not on welfare. We focus on the potential output loss and not on the distortionary costs of taxation. For a good, simple introduction to these distinctions see Harvey S. Rosen, *Public Finance* (Homewood, Ill.: Irwin, 1988), 291–312. For a summary of some of the empirical issues see Jerry A. Hausman, "Taxes and Labor Supply," in *Handbook of Public Economics*, vol. 1, ed. Alan J. Auerbach and Martin Feldstein (Amsterdam: North-Holland, Elsevier, 1985), 243–46, and Gary T. Burtless and Robert H. Haveman, "Taxes and Transfers: How Much Economic Loss?" *Challenge* 30 (1987): 45–51.

17. Much of my general discussion is based on Burtless and Haveman, "Taxes and Transfers: How Much Economic Loss?"

18. Burtless and Haveman, "Taxes and Transfers," 51.

19. Mark R. Killingsworth and James J. Heckman, "Female Labor Supply: A Survey," in *Handbook of Labor Economics*, vol. 1, ed. Orley C. Ashenfelter and Richard Layard (Amsterdam: North-Holland, Elsevier, 1986), 185.

20. Killingsworth and Heckman, "Female Labor Supply: A Survey," 196.

21. John Pencavel, "Labor Supply of Men: A Survey" in Ashenfelter and Heckman, *Handbook of Labor Economics*, 94–95.

22. Michael J. Boskin, "Taxation, Saving and the Rate of Interest," *Journal of Political Economy* 86 (1978): S3–S28.

23. "In 1980, the average married man's real after-tax return to savings through a Treasury bill fund was -1.37 percent. In 1985, the after-tax real return was 3.66 percent if marginal saving was channeled into an IRA and 2.32 percent if through taxable channels." Even greater benefits were available to upper-income groups. Yet the National Income Accounts personal savings rate, which was 8.7 percent from 1971–75 and 7.1 percent from 1976–80, fell to 6.2 percent from 1981–85. Similar results occur if the stock market boom is included. See Jerry A. Hausman and James M. Poterba, "Household Behavior and the Tax Reform Act of 1986," *The Journal of Economic Perspectives* 1 (1987): 117–18.

24. D. W. Haslett, "Is Inheritance Justified," *Philosophy and Public Affairs* 15 (1986): 122–55.

25. Stiglitz, "Pareto Efficient and Optimal Taxation and the New New Welfare Economics," 1035.

26. Much of this section is based on a recent review on these issues. See Franco Modigliani, "The Role of Intergenerational Transfers and Life Cycle Saving in the Accumulation of Wealth" and Lawrence J. Kotlikoff, "Intergenerational Transfers and Savings," both forthcoming in *The Journal of Economic Perspectives*, May 1988.

27. Laurence Kotlikoff and Lawrence Summers, "The Role of Intergenerational Transfers in Aggregate Capital Accumulation," *Journal of Political Economy* 89 (1981): 706–32.

28. B. Douglas Bernheim, Andrei Shleifer, and Lawrence H. Summers, "The Strategic Bequest Motive," *Journal of Political Economy* 93 (1985): 1045–75.

29. Gordon Tullock, *The Economics of Wealth and Poverty* (Brighton: Wheatsheaf-Harvester Press, 1986), 19–20.

30. Of course, it is possible to oppose this redistribution on the grounds that it might impede development (that is, using arguments analogous to those that focus on the reduction of self-reliance on welfare recipients) or just be redistributed to the members of the upper and middle class of the recipient country. I do not believe that these arguments explain much of the opposition.

31. Bronfenbrenner, "Income Distribution and 'Economic Justice,' " 49–50.

32. George J. Borjas, "Self-Selection and the Earnings of Immigrants," *American Economic Review* 77 (1987): 531–53.

33. Melvin W. Reder, "Chicago Economics: Permanence and Change," *Journal of Economic Literature* 20 (1982): 1–38.

34. Ibid., 31.

35. These disturbing results can also be the unintended consequences of behavior. One year I was in Washington renting a house. I had never owned a house or mowed a lawn. I did not mow the lawn of my rented house either; one day one of my neighbors came and mowed it for me. Was it a signal? If I had ignored it, would they have found other ways to prevent my imposing costs on them?

36. For an interesting and entertaining article on path-dependent economics and the typewriter keyboard see Paul A. David, "CLIO and the Economics of QWERTY," *The American Economic Review* 75 (May 1985): 332–37. See Stiglitz, "The Causes and Consequences of the Dependence of Quality on Price" for efficiency wage. For the new work on psychological choice theory and anomalies see Richard Thaler, "Toward a Positive Theory of Consumer Choice," *Journal of Economic Behavior and*

Organization 1 (1980): 39–60 and Mark J. Machina, "Choice Under Uncertainty: Problems Solved and Unsolved," *The Journal of Economic Perspectives* 1 (1987): 121–54. For a major revision of the analysis of the firm see Richard R. Nelson and Sidney G. Winter, *An Evolutionary Theory of Economic Change* (Cambridge: Harvard University Press, 1982).

37. Economists have a similar problem with philosophers who work on methodology. There was a time when they gave economists important guidelines, and in fact some of the most important work of this century, including Samuelson's *Foundations of Economic Analysis*, were developed as a response to the positivist program. Problems arose as the field of methodology in philosophy developed a dynamic of its own and economists could not be sure of its prescriptions, so they simply ignored it.

EPILOGUE
J. ROLAND PENNOCK

Where do we stand? Only the naive would expect that a symposium on this topic would lead to general agreement, to the solution of a problem, or complex of problems as old as philosophizing itself. It will do no harm however, and possibly some good, to ask ourselves what issues stand out for the agenda for the future of such endeavors.

First of all, an important distinction, maintained more consistently and clearly in some of the chapters in this volume than in others, is that between comparing ideal systems and comparing second-best or best-achievable systems. It is not that one is the correct procedure and the other mistaken, or even that one is better than the other; both are important. But it is also important to avoid comparing the ideal results under socialism with the practical results of laissez-faire, or vice versa.

When we compare the probable practical results of systems, we find ourselves dealing largely with what may broadly be called technical issues. Few if any would deny the existence, the inevitable existence, of market failures in any society that makes use of markets. The same may be said of governmment failures in any polity, although the phrase is less commonly used. (The stock market crash of October 1987 may exemplify each.) All but anarchists recognize the necessity for some governmental intervention. But if governmental coercion is required to secure protection of one group of people against incursions by another, it soon develops that no substantial group is devoid of subgroups, that the subgroups may not be identical for all issues, and so on. Slippery slopes abound. Deciding where lines should be drawn is what I refer to as a technical question. But two qualifications must be entered at once. It seems unlikely that this is a problem that can be settled once and for all and for all societies in the same way. The contexts of time, place, and cultures are always relevant. In speaking of such problems as "technical," we have exaggerated. Once agreement has been reached (if ever) on the most likely results of a given set of boundaries, the philosophical problem of evaluation must be faced. It is only because facing this problem is so fruitless until some substantial agreement has been achieved on the practical issues that I have referred to this whole area as technical.

Similarly, few if any today would support pure laissez-faire. As has been suggested already, that position, in the literal sense, has been given up in accepting the need for government. Passing over that point and also avoiding for the moment questions of justice, externalities in any modern society are bound to have such divisive effects that violence and even civil war will eventuate unless some government intervention is permitted. The alternative of negotiated trade-offs becomes so complicated, so time-consuming, as to be unacceptably costly. Complete commodification would be intolerable. Of course, it would be intolerable for philosophical as well as for economic reasons, but again I am seeking to hold these two types of reasons separate for the moment, because it seems to me that until we reach a greater degree of consensus on the technical issues much of the philosophical argument, at least unless it is aware of the unresolved economic issues and keeps them in view, amounts to so much flailing in the air.

None of this is to belittle the philosophical issues; it is only to suggest the need for keeping them separately in mind. What is social justice? Quite apart from contextual issues, we still have consequentialists and deontologists, utilitarians and contractarians. If contractarians predominate in this field at the moment, that still leaves a large area of controversy within this school of thought. After paying obeisance to Rawls, members of the school, if that it can be called, tend to fall apart. What original position is to be presumed? Should it be populated by ideal persons, rational persons, or persons as we find them, and so on?

Beyond this point, we find ourselves involved in questions

such as whether social justice demands equal staring points, and if so, is that enough, or must they be kept equal, in some way, or to some degree thereof? Many discussions of equality as an aspect of justice emphasize it to the almost total exclusion of desert, suggesting a topic given little attention in this volume. We also have the question of talent pooling. Apart from family influences, what of our genetic endowments? Are they our property, are they something that belongs to society, or some sort of abstract given, the consequences of which present an as yet unresolved puzzle?

The problem of how far the principles of distributive justice appropriate for a nation can and should be extended to the international realm—and the implications this would entail for the market system—opens a vast area calling for more study and reflection than it has yet received. It too is hardly mentioned in this volume except for Saffran's brief discussion.

One could of course go on indefinitely enumerateing the philosophical issues, such as how we deal with the question of welfare versus well-being. Do we accept each person's own judgment as to when he is well off and whether he is satisfied, or do we presume to make that judgment for him? Immediately we are faced with questions of degree. Do we force the homeless to come in out of the cold? That one may be easy, at least where it is a question of life or death, but again we face a slippery slope. Slippery slopes are inevitable, at almost every turn. The more agreement we can arrive at as to the probable factual consequences of various policies, I believe, the less difficult it will be for us to arrive at fuller agreement on the philosophical issues than is now possible. That at least is the conviction that is borne in on me by reading the chapters in this volume.

INDEX